The WAC Journal

Writing Across the Curriculum
Volume 27
2016

© 2016 Clemson University
Printed on acid-free paper in the USA
ISSN: 1544-4929

Editor

Roy Andrews

Managing Editor

Giuliana Caranante, Clemson University

Associate Editors

David Blakesley, Clemson University
Michael LeMahieu, Clemson University

Editorial Board

Art Young, Clemson University
Neal Lerner, Northeastern University
Carol Rutz, Carleton College
Meg Petersen, Plymouth State University
Terry Myers Zawacki, George Mason Univ.

Copyeditor

Christina Baswell

Review Board

Jacob S. Blumner, Univ of Michigan, Flint
Patricia Donahue, Lafayette College
John Eliason, Gonzaga University
Michael LeMahieu, Clemson University
Neal Lerner, Northeastern University
Meg Petersen, Plymouth State University
Mya Poe, Northeastern University
Carol Rutz, Carleton College
Joanna Wolfe, University of Louisville
Terry Myers Zawacki, George Mason Univ.
David Zehr, Plymouth State University

Subscription Information

The WAC Journal
Parlor Press
3015 Brackenberry Drive
Anderson SC 29621
wacjournal@parlorpress.com
parlorpress.com/wacjournal
Rates: 1 year: $25; 3 years: $65; 5 years: $95.

Submissions

The editorial board of *The WAC Journal* seeks WAC-related articles from across the country. Our national review board welcomes inquiries, proposals, and 3,000 to 6,000 word articles on WAC-related topics, including the following: WAC Techniques and Applications; WAC Program Strategies; WAC and WID; WAC and Writing Centers; Interviews and Reviews. Proposals and articles outside these categories will also be considered. Any discipline-standard documentation style (MLA, APA, etc.) is acceptable, but please follow such guidelines carefully. Submissions are managed initially via Submittable (https://parlorpress.submittable.com/submit) and then via email. For general inquiries, contact Lea Anna Cardwell, the managing editor, via email (wacjournal@parlorpress.com). The WAC Journal is an open-access, blind, peer-viewed journal published annually by Clemson University, Parlor Press, and the WAC Clearinghouse. It is available in print through Parlor Press and online in open-access format at the WAC Clearinghouse. *The WAC Journal* is peer-reviewed. It is published annually by Clemson University, Parlor Press, and the WAC Clearinghouse.

Subscriptions

The WAC Journal is published annually in print by Parlor Press and Clemson University. Digital copies of the journal are simultaneously published at The WAC Clearinghouse in PDF format for free download. Print subscriptions support the ongoing publication of the journal and make it possible to offer digital copies as open access. Subscription rates: One year: $25; Three years: $65; Five years: $95. You can subscribe to The WAC Journal and pay securely by credit card or PayPal at the Parlor Press website: http://www.parlorpress.com/wacjournal. Or you can send your name, email address, and mailing address along with a check (payable to Parlor Press) to Parlor Press, 3015 Brackenberry Drive, Anderson SC 29621. Email: sales@parlorpress.com

Reproduction of material from this publication, with acknowledgement of the source, is hereby authorized for educational use in non-profit organizations.

The WAC Journal
Volume 27, 2016

Contents

Jill Gladstein: A Data-Driven Researcher 7
CAROL RUTZ

Engaging the Skeptics: Threshold Concepts, Metadisciplinary Writing, and the Aspirations of General Education 17
CHRISTOPHER BASGIER

Quantitative Genre Analysis of Undergraduate Theses: Uncovering Different Ways of Writing and Thinking in Science Disciplines 36
JASON E. DOWD, ROBERT J. THOMPSON, JR., AND JULIE A. REYNOLDS

Investigating the Ontology of WAC/WID Relationships: A Gender-Based Analysis of Cross-Disciplinary Collaboration among Faculty 52
SANDRA L. TARABOCHIA

Inviting Students to Determine for Themselves What It Means to Write Across the Disciplines 74
BRIAN HENDRICKSON AND GENEVIEVE GARCIA DE MUELLER

Stories and Explanations in the Introductory Calculus Classroom: A Study of WTL as a Teaching and Learning Intervention 94
SUE DOE, MARY E. PILGRIM, AND JESSICA GEHRTZ

Of Evolutions and Mutations: Assessment as Tactics for Action in WAC Partnerships 119
FERNANDO SÁNCHEZ AND DANIEL KENZIE

Community College STEM Faculty Views on the Value of Writing Assignments 142
KOSTAS D. STROUMBAKIS, NAMJONG MOH, AND DIMITRIOS KOKKINOS

Review of *Toward a New Rhetoric of Difference*   155
TRAVIS GRANDY

Review of *Working with Faculty Writers*   162
MARY HEDENGREN

Contributors   167

Jill Gladstein: A Data-Driven Researcher

CAROL RUTZ

Readers of *The WAC Journal* may be familiar with the *National Census of Writing*, a 2013 database compiled from survey responses, web sites, and personal contacts at 680 four-year colleges and universities and 220 two-year schools. Funded by a grant from the Andrew W. Mellon Foundation, the *Census* has been conducted, shepherded, presented, and interpreted by Jill Gladstein of Swarthmore College and Brandon Fralix of Bloomfield College. Recognizing the importance of the *Census*, the Council of Writing Program Administrators in Raleigh this past July presented Jill and Brandon with a special award for "extraordinary service" to the profession.

A significant section of the *Census* addresses WAC programs: graduation requirements, number and type of courses, capstones, administrative structures, and more. Some of the responding institutions have agreed to make their data public, allowing for direct comparisons among those institutions. Obviously, this resource is a gold mine for WAC folks in search of answers to questions about everything from curriculum to staffing. The following interview with Jill Gladstein addresses the *Census* as well as her other work on and views about WAC.

Jill is an Associate Professor of English and Director of the Writing Associates Program at Swarthmore College in Swarthmore, PA, just outside Philadelphia. Her background in education and TESOL, as she explains, led indirectly to work in WAC, an interest in writing programs at small liberal arts colleges, and eventually to the *Census* project. On a personal level, I have appreciated Jill and her work over the years, and as my own career draws to a close, I will point toward the *Census* and the book she co-authored with Dara Regaignon, *Writing Program Administration at Small Liberal Arts Colleges*, as resources for the search committee who will find my successor. Read on to learn more about a WAC person with a penchant for collecting and disseminating data.

Carol Rutz: Did your background in education influence your interest in WAC?

Jill Gladstein: This is a good question and at first I would have said no. I often tell students who experience uneasiness about not knowing their next steps that life will take you where you are meant to go. As I look back at my career trajectory, I agree with this simple perspective. I studied early childhood education in undergrad, and through experiences teaching at the Eagle Heights Nursery School at the University of Wisconsin I developed an interest in TESOL. The students were predominately the children of international graduate students, so they came to school knowing little to no English. I was fascinated by how quickly they picked up the language and culture around them.

CR: Sounds truly inspiring. What then?

JG: That interest led me to graduate school for a master's in TESOL. At that point, I was planning to get my degree in two years and then return to the elementary classroom; however, that was before I took my first course in reading, writing, and literacy at the University of Pennsylvania with Mort Botel. My plan was to be certified as a reading specialist while completing my master's, but my experiences in those courses coupled with my teaching experiences in an intensive English program for adults led to my PhD work. Mort had shared the philosophy with me that if you have a question worth exploring, then you should pursue it. Up to this point I had never considered myself an academic or even a good student, but Mort helped me to see how I could pursue a question that had emerged from my teaching. He also had a great approach to the PhD process that spoke to my learning style. He would say, "You can make your PhD your life's work, or you can use the PhD to secure a position where you can do your life's work." I chose the latter path. For my PhD work I developed a curriculum that I implemented in several of my own intensive English classes on how students learning language engaged with the concepts of identity, culture, and difference. It's a long story, how I became interested in this topic, but you asked about WAC.

CR: I did indeed, but have we arrived at WAC yet?

JG: I finished my PhD and was looking for an academic position in TESOL when a friend from graduate school mentioned a part-time teaching job at Swarthmore. I had never taught students whose first language was English, but I figured it would be for a year, and I should be able to adapt what I knew from teaching writing to English language learners. During this year, a colleague had just taken over the writing associates (WA) program and wasn't sure it was something she wanted to stick with for any amount of time. My job search in TESOL wasn't going too well, and I wanted to stay in the area in a full-time position, so I offered to take over as director of the writing associates program.

The WA program was my introduction to WAC. The foundation of the program was made up of what some in the field call writing fellows, or course-based peer tutors. Swarthmore had adopted this approach when it added an explicit writing requirement that was WAC-focused. I came to discover that this new position was for both a WAC and writing center director. In order to be successful in this position, I had to learn not just how to teach writing to non-English language learners, but I also needed to learn the disciplinary genres that the writing associates (WAs) would be required to work with, because I now would be teaching the required course for all new WAs. I had to learn how to build community within the WA program with the students, and I had to uncover the culture of writing across campus in order to figure out how to support it.

Looking back, I realize I partook in an ethnography of my own campus and program in which I functioned as a participant observer. My professional experiences dating back to my PhD days planted the seeds for my work in WAC. I have always had an interest in culture and how cultures communicate and understand each other. Reflecting on all of that, I have been fascinated by how discourse communities function and this interest transfers into WAC work as I learn more about different disciplinary discourse communities.

CR: Good for you! You have been both observant and flexible—and quite courageous. None of this is a huge surprise, given that you have shown in your publications and your current work on the *National Census of Writing* that you have solid research chops in both qualitative and quantitative methods. How do you use your research savvy in your teaching?

JG: Thank you for your kind words, because it has taken me a long time to assume an identity as a researcher. Actually, earlier in my career I considered myself a practitioner-researcher, but the focus of this work was my teaching. As I mentioned, my PhD work comes from my teaching at intensive English programs at two neighboring universities. I was fascinated with how students discussed the target culture, and I was interested in exploring questions around cultural acquisition. So, I think my teaching has influenced my research, and then over time the two in combination with my work as director have influenced each other; however, my current research, which evolves out of my experiences creating the SLAC-WPA consortium, takes place outside of the classroom. That consortium consists of writing professionals from small liberal arts colleges, also known as SLACs.

CR: Speaking of the SLAC-WPA consortium, you went to considerable trouble to gather a large group of SLAC writing people—first through a survey, and then through a conference that inaugurated a professional organization. What inspired you?

JG: Actually the idea of a meeting came before the survey. As I already mentioned, I came into the field without much book knowledge on what it meant to run a writing center/program or WAC program. In retrospect I realize I did know something from my studies in TESOL and reading, writing, and literacy, but early on in my career I felt there was more to learn in order to do what was needed and to do it well. The advice I received from several local folks was that the national organizations do not speak to the small liberal arts context; however, I don't always believe what people tell me, so I attended the Council of Writing Program Administrators (CWPA) and International

Writing Center Association (IWCA) summer workshops and conferences as well as the Ivy Plus Consortium annual meeting. Though I was able to make some connections with other institutions, I did feel a disconnect between what I was hearing in plenary addresses and break-out sessions and what I was experiencing on my own campus. I also heard some misperceptions of SLACs.

I vividly remember sitting at a meal at a CWPA conference, and the table was discussing a current problem in the field. Someone said, "We all have this problem, except those small elite schools," the implication being that SLACs don't have problems because of our perceived wealth. Don't get me wrong, I am fortunate to work at an institution with a large endowment, but this wealth does not always lead to the ideal writing program.

CR: I have had similar experiences at conferences, even though my institution is not nearly as well-endowed as Swarthmore. All of us are trained at large, doctorate-granting institutions, and that institutional context can result in the tendency to apply the large university's ethos to all of higher ed. I'd like to know more about how you decided to counter that narrative with the SLAC context.

JG: The idea of creating a space for writing folks at SLACs was rattling around in my head for some time when I met up with Lisa Lebduska and Dara Regaignon at the CWPA conference in Tempe. There we decided to pitch the idea of a meeting of SLAC writing directors to colleagues at peer institutions, and I offered to host at Swarthmore. The goal of the meeting was to find out our shared questions and to see if and how these questions differed from national conversations. Fifty-two schools were invited to that initial meeting and representatives from thirty-four attended. The response from that initial meeting was overwhelming as people began to see the overlap in what we each did on our own campuses. Bianca Falbo offered at the Swarthmore meeting to host the next meeting at Lafayette, and as they say, the rest is history.

CR: I remember that first meeting as narrative based. One after another, SLAC writing people told stories, many of them irritating or painful, about "the situation at *my* campus." It was clear that people felt isolated, yet as the meeting continued, common themes were undeniable.

JG: Yes, it was clear from these initial conversations that, as you say, people felt isolated and misunderstood both on and off of their own campuses. As we were preparing to meet for the first time, another director suggested we gather preliminary information on the different participants, so we created a registration survey. This suggestion lined up with our thinking that we could do more on our individual campuses if we began to share information across campuses. We shared the collected information in the meeting materials. After the meeting, we developed the survey into a membership tool for the SLAC-WPA consortium. In order to be a member in the consortium, someone from the institution needed to complete an extended version of the registration survey. This membership survey was adapted and used as a research tool for the book that Dara Regaignon and I wrote on writing program administration at SLACs: *Writing Program Administration at Small Liberal Arts Colleges*. Later, with Brandon Fralix, we adapted the survey to collect data for the *National Census of Writing*.

CR: How would you characterize the SLAC group after 10 years? Can you mark particular milestones? Has a cohort emerged with an identifiable professional profile?

JG: This January (2017) Swarthmore will host the tenth SLAC-WPA meeting. It is now an organization of over one hundred schools in the process of applying for 501c3 status. It's been both fun and interesting to create an organization from scratch. An executive board oversees the operations of the organization, which mainly involve a listserv and annual meeting. Though in its infancy, the executive board members have worked to turn our initial idea about meeting into a sustainable organization.

CR: It's been fun to watch the organization grow. How would you describe the major changes over the last decade?

JG: When we first began to meet I am pretty sure all we needed was a room, food, and plenty of time for conversation. We still maintain these three important pieces, but over the years we have explored shared questions and created a couple of traditions. There are parallels between the consortium and the SLAC context as a whole. In both cases, size does play a factor and there seems to be a shared mission and collaborative nature among its participants. The consortium's size allows us to hold such annual activities as the *Speedshare*, where participants have the opportunity to rotate every fifteen minutes among a group of presenters to learn about new initiatives at different campuses, and the *Artifacts from our Practices*, where participants are invited to bring a syllabus or some other featured artifact to share with the group.

In the WA program at Swarthmore, we share with students the mantra, "You're not alone," to let them know they are not the only ones who have challenges with the writing process and that they can come to us for assistance. I never thought about this before, but I think SLAC-WPA has adopted the same mantra. Many writing directors at SLACs are the only writing professionals on their campuses, so they can feel isolated and misunderstood; however, the listserv and annual meeting provide perspective for these folks that they can bring back to their individual campuses.

CR: You articulate beautifully what I have observed.

JG: Related to that idea of perspective, one of my favorite graphs from the current *Census* that I recently presented at CCCC illustrates how SLACs are different from most other institutions in their approach to first-year writing. They rely on tenured or tenure-track faculty from across the college to teach and develop students as writers. During the first SLAC meeting we heard a lot of "I found my people." We knew that our institutions were different from what we heard in national conversations but because of our separateness from each other, we weren't able to articulate what was behind that difference. Between the consortium, book, and now *Census*, people at SLACs have perspective on their own local cultures of writing because they can now put them in conversation with peer institutions.

CR: I hope you know how your work and your willingness to collaborate have influenced the SLAC writing professionals all over the US. In that connection, the book you co-authored with Dara Regaignon presents data about writing at SLACs as well as theorizing the SLAC environment as a context for writing, especially WAC. What would you say to tempt readers who are not employed at a SLAC to seek out the book?

JG: Besides the obvious about learning about SLACs, what I am most proud of in that text is the methodology for our research and the lens we used to analyze the data. Early on in our research process we agreed that we had to look at both what were the explicit and embedded sites of writing if we were going to fully understand the history and culture of writing at SLACs. I knew from my own experiences at Swarthmore that if we just asked about the explicit writing requirement and the writing center that the full picture of our culture of writing would be misrepresented. Just focusing on the explicit sites of writing would have made it easy for participants to argue that the survey doesn't speak to each of their particular contexts. In the book we make the argument that there are features of the SLAC culture that speak to WAC initiatives and what makes them sustainable, and it would be interesting to apply some of the questions we asked and analysis we did to other institutional contexts.

CR: Interesting indeed. Is that argument part of the foundational thinking for the *Census*?

JG: Absolutely. We hypothesized that SLACs were different from other institutional types, but comparable data were difficult to find at the time to fully support this conclusion. The book project had gathered data on SLACs, but now we thought it just as important to gather data on other institutional types in order to have a better understanding of the differences that might exist across types. We had seen the power of having a shared data set that people could utilize on their own campuses and thought it would be useful for the field to gather these data from all two- and four-year public and not-for-profit institutions and make them available on an open-access database.

At this same time, Brandon Fralix, who is at a minority-serving institution, and I were co-chairing the diversity task force of CWPA charged with the question of how to diversify the organization's membership. We saw the *Census* project as an opportunity to begin to define what diversity exists among and within different institutions.

CR: That data-gathering on diversity is certainly timely. Back to the book: what else about it would benefit the non-SLAC reader working in WAC?

JG: The other argument from our book I'd like people in other institutional contexts to consider refers to the tradeoffs that an institution makes in developing its approach to writing. For example, as mentioned, many SLACs have WAC faculty teach the first-year writing seminar. Some would argue these sections should be taught by composition/rhetoric specialists; however, because these sections are taught by tenured or tenure-track faculty, class sizes average around twelve to fifteen. The researcher in me wants to know the pros and cons of the different tradeoffs. People argue that the ideal first-year writing course should be taught by a rhetoric/composition specialist, in a small class setting, around the content of threshold concepts, writing about writing, and teaching for transfer. However, the reality remains that schools need to make tradeoffs based on their local contexts. When we completed the book, I was left wondering what it would look like to research the different combinations to document what changes. For example, I wonder if a first-year writing seminar taught by WAC faculty is more conducive to the concept of teaching for transfer than a first-year comp course taught by TAs in an English PhD program.

CR: I like that question a lot, and I can hear the chorus of research university WPAs screaming about the costs of such a program, even if the outcomes were measurably better.

JG: The work on the book and then the *Census* has helped me to better articulate the questions and decisions institutions make around how best to teach and support student writers. From looking at the administrative structures of hundreds of writing programs, I have learned what questions to ask faculty across the college to help inform their own teaching of writing.

Now when I am invited to another campus to lead a WAC workshop or for an external review, I often look for or ask about both the different explicit and embedded sites of writing in order to try to find out why some are explicit while others are embedded or diffused. In helping faculty look through this lens from an institutional perspective, it has also at times helped individuals use this same lens to think about what is explicit and embedded about the teaching of writing within their departments or courses.

CR: I'm sure *The WAC Journal* readers would be interested in one or two examples of questions that you have found to be productive.

JG: Sure, though I imagine they already know them. When I visit a campus or look at their structures around writing, I want to find out, "How are the different stakeholders defining writing and the rationale for having writing as part of the curriculum?" It's the collective responses at an institution or within a department that determine the culture of writing. I imagine this collective may be easier to gauge at a smaller institution, but I also imagine that when we unpack the different structures around writing on a given campus or in an individual department, we can see how definition(s) of writing informed decisions to create or change those structures. For example, does a department have a place in the curriculum where particular disciplinary genres are assigned or taught? How explicit is this teaching? This connects to the next question, "What does it mean to 'teach' writing?" This question trips up some WAC faculty. They don't see themselves as teachers of writing, and yet they value developing students as writers. This belief often leads me then to ask, "How do we (WAC faculty) both institutionally and individually foster and support the culture and goals of writing?" This third question circles back to the first. If as a faculty we believe that students need to learn how to effectively communicate their learned knowledge in order to be successful academic citizens or disciplinary members, then as WAC professionals we can help faculty think through what is needed to achieve this goal at an institutional or departmental level and within their own classroom. Sometimes what is needed is a shared vocabulary for how to discuss writing pedagogy across the disciplines. These questions were informed by what I've learned about the SLAC context, where, for the most part, there is shared responsibility for supporting all students as writers, but isn't this belief in a shared responsibility a necessary ingredient for most WAC programs or initiatives to be sustainable?

CR: Of course it is. Your challenge to faculty and administrators elsewhere inevitably produces useful local knowledge. We are all prisoners of our experience, and you are unlocking the cell, as it were, to help people recognize their own contexts more fully as well as think about positive changes. Do you have an example that speaks to that kind of insight at a place you have visited as a workshop leader or program reviewer?

JG: Wow, I never thought of it that way before. Recently I was invited to a peer institution to give a talk based on the book and *Census* and to lead a WAC workshop around assignment design. A faculty committee had spent the year reviewing the writing requirement and right before my visit had proposed changes to be discussed and voted on next fall. I was invited to campus to put their discussions into a broader context and to help address "a lack of coherence and consistency in terms of faculty understanding of writing pedagogy and the implementation of writing instruction practices." My goal for the visit was to pose questions and provide opportunities for the participants to better understand the culture of writing at their institution and how they each connected with this culture in their own courses. One concept that seemed to resonate with several of the participants was intentionality, which circles back to the idea of embedded and explicit practices.

During one exercise where I ask faculty to deconstruct an assignment into its tasks and challenge the faculty to think about where they expect students to learn how to do these tasks, a faculty member shared an insight that I have heard before from other WAC faculty: "In my department we discuss when the different content knowledge will be taught in the major, but we never talk about when the different aspects of writing should be introduced and taught." You know from your own experiences facilitating these workshops and witnessing these light bulb moments that you might never know what happens after you leave campus, but in that moment it feels like the individual participants will take these insights and use them to inform their own courses and perhaps their departments' approaches to writing.

CR: I agree that one hopes that the insight during the workshop or discussion will inspire additional discussion and action after the event is over and the invited facilitator has left, and one rarely finds out what, if anything, actually happened.

Finally, what do you particularly want *The WAC Journal* readers to know about you, your work, and your approach to WAC?

JG: I'm not sure how to answer this question. My work and approach to WAC has evolved and been informed by numerous experiences in and out of the classroom. I didn't realize how much until you asked me these questions. So as I mentioned before, my current research agenda evolved out of my work with the SLAC-WPA consortium. During my PhD work I had received training on different research methods and had learned about grounded theory. This background came in handy as my research interests stretched out of the classroom. Through both the work on the book and the *Census*, I have learned that I am a person who believes in a data-informed practice, and this connection with data has helped me with my work in WAC.

I hope people see that I didn't set out to create these national projects: questions that emerged from my practice led me to these projects. The same can be true about my approach to WAC. I don't go meet with a colleague or go into a particular institution with a plan; rather, I listen and observe and then together work out the best process moving forward. I also could not have done any of these projects or my work at Swarthmore without the help of others. I may be insane enough to take some risks and start out on one of these projects, but there have always been others there willing to take the risk with me or to support me along the way.

CR: You have no reason to apologize for the SLAC-WPA consortium or the *Census*! Are there other projects on the horizon that those of us reading *The WAC Journal* can look forward to?

JG: Brandon and I have begun to work on the next iteration of the *Census*. We're taking the year to revise the survey and update contact information before launching the *2017 Census* next June. Until then, we are launching a blog as a companion to the *Census* where folks can submit a five-hundred- to one-thousand-word post in response to a question or two from the *Census*. We will be writing the first few posts, but then we hope others will see this as a worthwhile publication opportunity.

My own research based on the *Census* data extends the work I began with the book, in which I'm interested in mapping the different administrative configurations across institutional types. In the book we defined six different configurations and the rationale and outcomes for a particular configuration. I imagine this mapping will uncover a whole host of questions around positioning of resources within and around writing programs and centers. Another idea rattling around in my head involves creating a data cooperative where people can share raw data from assessment and research projects in order to build large data sets. There are many obstacles to this idea, but who knows?

CR: Who knows, indeed? As you have demonstrated, curiosity and methodological imagination can lead a person into unexpected territory. Thank you for your work to date and for your willingness to discuss it with me.

Works Cited

Gladstein, Jill, and Brandon Fralix. *The National Census of Writing*. 2013, writingcensus.swarthmore.edu.

Gladstein, Jill, and Dara Rossman Regaignon. *Writing Program Administration at Small Liberal Arts Colleges*. Parlor Press, 2012.

Engaging the Skeptics: Threshold Concepts, Metadisciplinary Writing, and the Aspirations of General Education

CHRISTOPHER BASGIER

Scholars in writing across the curriculum (WAC) have long puzzled over the troublesome relationship between general education and disciplinary preparation. Summarizing the problem, Chris Thaiss (1992) writes, "The goals of general education courses tend to be idealistic—e.g. 'cultural literacy,' 'the ability to write in college,' 'appreciation of scientific method'—whereas goals of major courses tend to be specific and preprofessional" (p. 63). As a result, he suggests, students tend to view general education courses "as so many unrelated fragments" (p. 72). According to David Russell and Arturo Yañez (2003), this fragmentation alienates students: "On one hand, students and teachers are pulled toward one disciplinary specialization; on the other hand, they are pulled toward 'general' or broad education for civic life or other professional specializations—with alienation often resulting" (p. 332). These feelings of alienation can also stem from students' experiences writing in general education courses: often, students believe their instructors' writing advice is nothing more than individual whim, rather than part and parcel of disciplinary or professional expectations, leading them to see such experiences as irrelevant to their educational goals and career aspirations.

Such tensions appear in many types of general education programs. A broad spectrum exists, of course: Lauren Fitzgerald (2013) explains that general education can range from "a traditional distributive model in which students take a set number of courses from specific disciplines or disciplinary clusters" to "a newer integrative model that makes explicit connections among the disciplines" through any number of curricular arrangements (p. 94). In the former case, programs organized around distribution areas (such as arts and humanities, social sciences, and math/science/technology) may lend themselves to perceptions of curricular fragmentation and a "checklist" mentality—with first-year composition at the top of the list. In the latter case, integrative programs organized around liberal learning principles (such as critical thinking, information literacy, and civic engagement) are often difficult to define in a coherent way that is meaningful for faculty from diverse disciplinary backgrounds, which often leads to generic, catchall definitions, including supposedly universal expectations for "good writing."[1]

While scholars like Thaiss (1992) and Russell and Yañez (2003) locate these tensions squarely within institutional structures and the activities that constitute them, I argue that the tensions also exist because the kinds of transferrable knowledge and abilities that we hope students will gain in general education are often counterintuitive, alien, and troublesome, for instructors and students alike. In other words, they are *threshold concepts*.

Originally developed by educational researchers Jan H. F. Meyer and Ray Land (2006), the theory of threshold concepts holds that certain disciplinary concepts represent significant, challenging entry points into disciplinary ways of thinking. Generally speaking, threshold concepts are defined through four key features: according to Linda Adler-Kassner and Elizabeth Wardle (2015), they proffer an epistemological and ontological transformation for learners; they are not easily reversed once learned; they help learners perceive and create connections among seemingly disparate phenomena; and they are "troublesome," overturning learners' intuition (p. 2). In writing studies, for example, threshold concepts include the socio-rhetorical nature of writing (p. 17), its influence on identity and ideology (p. 48), and its cognitive dimensions (p. 71).

But not all threshold concepts need to be so strictly disciplinary. Indeed, I suggest in this article that the key features of threshold concepts described by Adler-Kassner and Wardle (2015) are at work in liberal learning principles such as critical thinking. Such principles should not be seen as unproblematic, catchall abilities, easily learned through simple exposure. Rather, in hallway conversations and faculty development workshops, we should encourage our colleagues across the curriculum to see these principles as grounded in often implicit, troublesome (but transformative), cross-curricular threshold concepts that can be taught and learned explicitly, especially through writing. In so doing, we may be in a good position to articulate shared, but often unspoken, ways of knowing, doing, and writing that cut across general education and the majors.

In fact, Linda Adler-Kassner, John Majewski, and Damian Koshnick (2012) claim that the theory of threshold concepts can be applied to general education reform efforts. To avoid curricular fragmentation, they argue, general education programs should take as their primary task the explication of common, cross-disciplinary threshold concepts:

> Working from this perspective enables us to consider, as we have done here, whether there are concepts that exist within specific disciplines, like composition and history, that then can also span *across* disciplines. This perspective positions these concepts not as all-purpose habits that exist within liberal learning, as in the distribution model, but as discipline-specific concepts that operate within some number (two, in our case) of different contexts. When

these areas of shared concepts can be identified, it might then be possible for instructors to explicitly articulate the concepts for themselves [...] and work them explicitly into their teaching. ("Conclusion," para. 10)

When put into practice in this way, Adler-Kassner, Majewski, and Koshnick (2012) suggest, the theory of threshold concepts capitalizes on faculty members' investment in disciplinary ways of knowing and communicating[2] and offers potential shared language across disciplines. In a best-case scenario, they claim, this curricular model can facilitate "more effective transfer" across disciplinary contexts ("Conclusion," para. 10).

However, in seeking this kind of curricular change, advocates of threshold concepts are likely to encounter several obstacles, not least of which are the difficulty of interdisciplinary teaching (see Nowacek, 2009), sub-disciplinary differences (see Schaefer 2015), and institutional inertia (see Dryer, 2008). Moreover, recent WAC research has shown that some general education instructors forgo strict disciplinary expectations for writing, instead assigning a range of academic and alternative genres to achieve personal enrichment, civic engagement, and other goals often associated with general education (Soliday, 2011; Thaiss & Zawacki, 2006). In this article, I focus specifically on engaging these skeptics: I demonstrate how WAC professionals can work with faculty members who, out of a commitment to liberal learning principles, may be reluctant to take on the disciplinary perspective entailed by threshold concepts when thinking about the learning goals that drive their general education courses and writing assignments.

In working with our skeptical colleagues, we can look for opportunities to highlight course objectives and writing assignments that tap into metadisciplinary, if not disciplinary, ways of knowing, doing, and writing, even as they promote liberal learning principles. Michael Carter (2007/2012) defines metadisciplines as "collections of disciplines that share an emphasis on certain metagenres" (p. 226), or collections of genres that entail similar ways of knowing, doing, and writing. He adds, "At the center of each metadiscipline is a way of doing shared by its constituent disciplines despite their differences in content knowledge," which "complicate[s] the assumption that disciplines are defined exclusively or even primarily by content knowledge" (p. 227). In other words, groups of similar disciplines tend to share common ways of building and communicating knowledge, despite differences in specific content. These metadisciplines can also indicate broad, metadisciplinary threshold concepts at work—ones we can use when working with instructors who are put off by too heavy an emphasis on disciplinary knowledge in general education courses.

To illustrate how an otherwise a-disciplinary course mobilized metadisciplinary threshold concepts, I discuss ethnographic data I collected in "Film and Folklore," a 200-level course taught by Professor Emeritus Rob Robertson at University of the

Midwest (UMW).[3] In designing and teaching this course, Professor Robertson was especially invested in a specific and unique vision of critical thinking, to the point that he disavowed any disciplinary function for his course at all. Nevertheless, I demonstrate how the ways of knowing, doing, and writing that Professor Robertson taught, while not strictly disciplinary, were nevertheless metadisciplinary; he emphasized ways of knowing and doing common to the humanistic metadiscipline, which suggests a pair of threshold concepts shared by those disciplines (despite their apparent differences): 1) that values and beliefs are open to critical scrutiny and 2) that one must produce logically sound arguments even while critiquing others' problematic beliefs. The students initially found these concepts troublesome and challenging to implement in their writing and in multimodal presentations, but eventually they were transformative. In other words, they demonstrate the key features of threshold concepts described by Adler-Kassner and Wardle (2015). In teaching these concepts, Professor Robertson laid the groundwork for transfer. As I will demonstrate, his students reported taking skeptical thinking beyond the classroom, and they also recognized similar concepts at work in their other classes, especially those in the humanities. Based on this analysis, I conclude by offering several questions WAC and general education professionals can ask of colleagues in faculty development workshops to generate discussion about the metadisciplinary threshold concepts undergirding their teaching and the kinds of writing assignments that can best support threshold learning. These strategies, I hope, can help us convince reluctant faculty members of the value of threshold concepts for transforming general education, building a grassroots movement reminiscent of WAC's early days of curricular reform (Farris and Smith, 1992; McLeod and Miraglia, 2001; Russell, 2002).

Methods

I studied "Film and Folklore" at UMW, a large research institution in the Midwest with over forty thousand students, during the Fall 2010 semester, as part of a bigger research project about writing in general education courses. Following the tradition of ethnographic and naturalistic research in writing studies (Beaufort, 2007; Carroll, 2002; Herrington, 1994; Nowacek, 2011; Soliday, 2011; Walvoord and McCarthy, 1990), I used a range of methods to triangulate my findings: Professor Robertson and I held four interviews, and we discussed the course's relationship to disciplinary preparation and general education, as well as his students' learning. I also held four focus groups, consisting of three students who agreed to discuss their experiences writing over the semester.

To analyze my observation, interview, and focus group notes, I adapted the principles of grounded theory, and particularly Barney Glaser and Anselm Strauss's (1967) constant comparative method, by coding notes and transcripts, developing analytical categories, comparing incidents within and across categories, and teasing out implications of conflicting explanations (p. 105–07). I also analyzed students' writing and course documents following Anis Bawarshi's (2003) process for genre analysis: I "collect[ed] samples of the genre, identif[ied] and describe[ed] the context of its use, describe[ed] its textual patterns, and analyz[ed] what these patterns revealed about the context in which the genre is used" (p. 158). I outlined the socio-rhetorical dimensions of each document based on close reading of textual details, as well as my assumptions, the professors' explanations, and students' reflections on rhetorical considerations such as audience, author, purpose, and textual strategies.

Course Background and Overview

Professor Robertson conceived of his course amid one general education initiative at UMW—a special topics seminar program—and continued to teach it during a second, more comprehensive, general education reform. As he recalled, the Dean of Arts and Sciences decided to institute the original topics seminars because he thought students had lost their ability to think critically. Ever since, Professor Robertson has maintained that his course is first and foremost a course in critical thinking. By the time I observed the class, he had had it changed from a special topics seminar to an elective in the department of folklore aimed at non-majors. He also had it approved for UMW's new (as of 2010) general education requirements, which promote critical thinking in foundational courses, including "arts and humanities" courses like "Film and Folklore."

Although Professor Robertson did design the course around his own disciplinary interests in supernatural phenomena, myths, and conspiracy theories, he distinguished sharply between his discipline and the practice of critical thinking. During our first interview, he told me:

> This is not a customary folklore class. The focus is on critical thinking, and the subject matter that we deal with is taken from folklore and popular culture. We don't do critical thinking in folkloristics. What we do is we collect what people believe and we find out why and how and when and where and the context and the function. [. . .] We don't do critical thinking. We don't question somebody's belief in Bigfoot. That's why this course is not a typical folklore course, because in here we do question their belief.

At base, "Film and Folklore" shared content with the discipline of folkloristics. However, as Professor Robertson saw it, a typical course in folkloristics would not teach students to criticize strange beliefs; rather, it would offer tools and concepts for analyzing the origins and social purposes of those beliefs, no matter how fantastical.

In contrast, he did in fact ask his "Film and Folklore" students to criticize beliefs in the pseudoscientific, the paranormal, and the conspiratorial.

This distinction derived largely from Professor Robertson's definition of critical thinking, which drove the ways of knowing, doing, and writing in the course (and not, as we might expect, disciplinary methodologies from folkloristics). Rather than define critical thinking through a disciplinary perspective,[4] an institutional mandate,[5] or a professional standard,[6] Professor Robertson equated critical thinking with skepticism. He drew his definition directly from the course textbooks: Carl Sagan's (1996) *The Demon-Haunted World: Science as a Candle in the Dark* and Michael Shermer's (2002) *Why People Believe Weird Things*, both of which criticize beliefs in conspiracies, myths, and the paranormal. In his avowedly a-disciplinary approach to critical thinking, Professor Robertson represents perhaps the most extreme example of the larger issue, that some instructors, in some general education courses, may not care to teach disciplinary threshold concepts to students (and indeed, he told me disciplinary initiation was not his goal in this class). Nevertheless, I hope to show how he still employed *metadisciplinary* perspectives that could offer valuable inroads to threshold thinking and pathways for transfer to other educational contexts.

Take, for instance, Professor Robertson's use of Sagan and Shermer, who describe skepticism as a strategic approach to evaluating the accuracy of arguments, rather than a dogmatic point of view.[7] Professor Robertson emphasized this distinction early in the semester when he shared with students the credo of the Skeptics Society, published in every *Skeptic* magazine. In part, this credo says:

> Some people believe that skepticism is the rejection of new ideas, or worse, they confuse "skeptic" with "cynic" and think that skeptics are a bunch of grumpy curmudgeons unwilling to accept any claim that challenges the status quo. This is wrong. Skepticism is a provisional approach to claims. It is the application of reason to any and all ideas—no sacred cows allowed. In other words, skepticism is a method, not a position. Ideally, skeptics do not go into an investigation closed to the possibility that a phenomenon might be real or that a claim might be true. When we say we are "skeptical," we mean that we must see compelling evidence before we believe. (Skeptics Society, n.d., para. 3; reproduced in the Detection Kit)

Professor Robertson used this credo to distinguish between the skeptic as an identity and skepticism as a critical thinking strategy. According to this formulation, the skeptic is often considered a fixed identity, at least when it is equated with the kind of curmudgeonly cynic who automatically gainsays any suspicious claim. Adopted as a critical thinking strategy, however, skepticism professes to treat belief as always open to investigation, criticism, and change—the first of two interlinked threshold concepts for the community of skeptics and for the course.

To help students learn this concept, Professor Robertson found particularly useful Sagan and Shermer's tools for practicing skepticism and recognizing flawed arguments. According to Sagan (1996), "What skeptical thinking boils down to is the means to construct, and to understand, a reasoned argument and—especially important—to recognize a fallacious or fraudulent argument" (p. 210). Here, Sagan emphasizes the recognition of logical or rhetorical fallacies as the central move of skepticism. To that end, he includes a chapter called a "Baloney Detection Kit," which he believes "helps us recognize the most common and perilous fallacies of logic and rhetoric" (p. 212). Similarly, Shermer's (2002) chapter, titled "How Thinking Goes Wrong: Twenty-Five Fallacies that Lead Us to Believe Weird Things," covers problems with scientific, pseudoscientific, and illogical thinking. Taken together, Sagan and Shermer's toolkits bespeak a second threshold concept for the course, this one shared by skepticism and rhetoric: that rhetorical commonplaces (and fallacies) can be resources for producing an argument as well as a means of argumentative critique. As Douglas Eyman (2015) puts it, "The power of rhetoric, as I see it, is that it can be employed as both analytic method and guide for production of persuasive discourse" (p. 16)—and the same can be said of Professor Robertson's version of critical thinking *qua* skepticism.

As a means for helping students practice critical thinking, and critique the lack thereof, Professor Robertson extracted Sagan and Shermer's toolkits from their books and combined them into his own list, which he titled "Critical Thinking Tool Kit: A Comparative List," or the "Detection Kit" for short, a nine-page handout including quotes from Sagan in black, quotes from Shermer in blue, and his own additions in red. Rhetoricians would recognize the Detection Kit (and Sagan and Shermer's prior versions) as one instance in a larger genre of rhetorical tool kits, including the sections on fallacies like *ad hominem*, begging the question, and slippery slope that often appear in argument textbooks (see for example textbooks by Lunsford and Ruszkiewicz, 2009; Ramage, Bean, and Johnson, 2011; or Williams and Colomb; Lanham's [1991] *A Handlist of Rhetorical Terms* would be a standalone analogue). One example from Professor Robertson's kit reads:

> Begging the question~Assuming the Answer~Tautology—{when the proposition to be proved is used as one of the assumptions.}
>
> *We must institute the death penalty to discourage violent crime.* But does the violent crime rate in fact fall when the death penalty is imposed? {I.E. We assume that the death penalty will discourage violent crime, but we actually have proof to the contrary.}

Or: *The stock market fell yesterday because of a technical adjustment and profit-taking by investors*—but is there any *independent* evidence for the causal role of "adjustment" and profit-taking; have we learned anything at all from this purported explanation? {I.E. The fall of the value of stocks is assumed to have been caused by a technical adjustment that is not explained.}

Like many rhetorical tool kits, the Detection Kit lists each fallacy, defines it, provides a short example (above, in italics), and briefly critiques the problem with the example. Professor Robertson took this example from Sagan's (1996) list (p. 213) but added his own explanations, which I have bracketed (those sentences are red in the Detection Kit). The students used the Detection Kit actively throughout the course. It became a springboard for metadisciplinary ways of knowing, doing, and writing characteristic of the humanities, as well as a tool for helping students "see" and "sell" connections (Nowacek, 2011) across courses, suggesting the value of metadisciplinary threshold concepts for facilitating transfer.

Threshold Learning and Metadisciplines

To reiterate, two primary threshold concepts drove students' learning in "Film and Folklore": first, that belief ought to be persistently open to critical investigation and second, that writers must produce logically sound arguments critiquing illogical ones. The bulk of students' practice with these concepts occurred during weekly panel presentations, which required students to apply the Detection Kit to videos, films, and popular books. During the first of two seventy-five-minute class periods, most groups showed a video, such as a Discovery Channel or History Channel program, and summarized a book for the class, which students gathered from Professor Robertson's personal library of materials on topics ranging from Atlantis and Bigfoot to JFK assassination theories and the alleged UFO crash at Roswell. On the second day, the student panelists used game shows, debates, and mock trials to get the class to critique the video and passages from the book with the Detection Kit in hand. Students supplemented these larger genres with handouts, notecards, PowerPoint presentations, video interviews via the application Skype, scripts, and images from the videos and books. In other words, students' threshold learning in this course was highly multimodal and interactive.

However, their threshold learning was not necessarily easy or automatic; the course's key concepts were often troublesome for students during these panels. Paraphrasing David Perkins (2006), Adler-Kassner, Majewski, and Koshnick (2012) explain that threshold concepts are troublesome "because they challenge existing beliefs, past practices or inert knowledge, or can be conceptually difficult" ("Transfer and Threshold Concepts," para. 1). Indeed, some student panels treated strange beliefs as "inert knowledge," as unproblematic facts to be recalled (during a "Jeopardy" game, for instance), rather than as opportunities for practice with the Detection Kit. To account for such oversights, Professor Robertson often found opportunities to challenge the class with more critical thinking by asking them to identify flaws in fact-based questions and answers. As with other threshold concepts, this one placed students in a liminal position. According to Adler-Kassner, Majewski, and Koshnick (2012), threshold learning "does not happen in a straight line but instead in iterative and recursive stages" ("Transfer and Threshold Concepts," para. 1), demonstrated in this case by the continual practice Professor Robertson felt students needed in avoiding flawed arguments.

Eventually, the course's skeptical threshold concepts became a "portal" (Adler-Kassner, Majewski, and Koshnik, 2012) for students to learn larger metadisciplinary ways of knowing, doing, and writing—and particularly ones associated with the metadiscipline that Carter (2007/2012) argues is "composed of disciplines that emphasize research from sources," especially "disciplines in the humanities" (p. 228). This may come as a surprise, considering that Sagan and Shermer explicitly link skepticism to the sciences, which generally fit in the metadiscipline involving empirical inquiry (Carter, 2007/2012, p. 228). However, the metadiscipline involving research from sources—the humanistic metadiscipline—more accurately describes skepticism as Professor Robertson taught it via the Detection Kit. According to Carter (2007/2012), genres within the humanistic metadiscipline have "two primary distinguishing characteristics":

> (1) the kind of research that is done, that is, not based on data gathered from independent observations but largely on sources that have their origins elsewhere; and (2) the goal of the research, which typically does not have extrinsic value, such as solving practical problems or investigating hypotheses, but value that is intrinsic to the discipline. (p. 222)

Despite the absence of a clear link to the disciplinary ways of knowing, doing, and writing in folkloristics, and although students were not conducting "research" in the strong (read: *disciplinary*) sense of the word, these two distinguishing characteristics—data from external sources and analysis with intrinsic value to the discipline—also characterize students' work in the course. For instance, the critique of videos and books points to the intrinsic value of working with sources that Carter (2007/2012) argues is characteristic of the humanistic metadiscipline, in that research is seen as "a means to an end defined by the individual discipline" (p. 223). In "Film and Folklore," the end derives not from a way of knowing defined by folkloristics, but rather from one defined by and valued in the "field" of skepticism and embodied in the Detection Kit. Maura put the matter succinctly in our first focus group: "I do want to know the truth, and I do want to expose and really look at things and see [whether it is] just manipulation, or what's the truth? Or what's accurate, I guess?" Truth versus manipulation: this is the key distinction defined intrinsically by, and valued within, the field of skepticism itself. To explore the relationship of truth and manipulation, students had to use the Detection Kit to critique a host of other genres, many with "their origins elsewhere," as Carter says of the humanistic metadiscipline's objects of inquiry. Students gained practice addressing this larger motivating question through a recursive process of threshold learning, enacted on the panel presentations and in their final papers for the course.

Metadisciplinary Writing in "Film and Folklore"

As on the panels, the students in "Film and Folklore" enacted metadisciplinary ways of writing in their final papers, which required a critique of a video and a book on a topic that had not been covered by one of the panels. According to the prompt, "Students *are not being asked to solve any of the problems* represented by the topics; the only task here is to critically assess the use of critical thinking in the video and the book chosen for analysis." In this prompt, Professor Robertson's proscription against problem solving distinguishes the assignment from the problem-solving metadiscipline, which would entail an extrinsic motivation.[8] Instead, the prompt effectively solidified the course's association with the humanistic metadiscipline, which involves research from sources (here again, a video and a book), and entails intrinsically defined motives.

Unsurprisingly, given the above prompt, the Detection Kit continued to dominate students' approach to writing. As with the panels, it drove their analyses of the videos and books, and it also shaped both the form and content of their papers. When talking to my focus group about their papers, I found that they all followed a similar process of invention: they always began by watching the film or video and reading the book (sometimes re-watching or re-reading them), Detection Kit in hand, in order to identify fallacious claims and flawed reasoning.

Because of its near omnipresence during their writing, the Detection Kit helped students articulate a rhetorical purpose, structure their papers, and execute their analyses. As Lane, one student in the focus group, explains in his introduction, he analyzes "fallacies of reasoning" in the book and video in order to "avoid falling into the trap of unreasonable thought." Both of these quoted phrases come directly from the Detection Kit; Lane's use of the phrases illustrates the intrinsic rhetorical purpose motivating his work, and, by extension, his peers'. Without another genre, like a game show or debate, in which to deploy the identification of fallacies, students wrote by reproducing the list-like structure of the Detection Kit, which defines a flaw, provides an example, and analyzes the example. For instance, early in his paper on the alleged predictions of Nostradamus, Michael writes:

After the terrorist attacks of 9/11, some supporters of Nostradamus claim the third antichrist is Osama Bin Laden. Lorie poses the question in reference to the third antichrist, "Is this Osama Bin Laden? It would be convenient to suppose so" (Lorie [2002] 36). In this case, this exhibits an example of special pleading or stacking the deck. Lorie is using an argument to support his point of view by asking a question that he can answer.

According to the Detection Kit, "A common technique in special pleading is to use unanswered questions as a way to suggest unproven assumptions or as a way to guide the reader/observer to a desired (albeit unproven) conclusion." Here, Michael follows the general statement-flaw-analysis pattern that was common in his peers' papers and in the Detection Kit. It seems, then, that the "Film and Folklore" students produced a "mutt genre," which Elizabeth Wardle (2009) defines as "genres that do not respond to rhetorical situations requiring communication in order to accomplish a purpose that is meaningful to the author" (p. 777)—often because students are caught up responding to a rhetorical situation that is meaningful to the instructor within the context of the learning environment set up in the course.

Within this classroom situation, not only did students use the Kit to structure their critiques, but also they were aware of its presence when writing sentences and choosing words. In part, this awareness stemmed from Professor Robertson's main writing advice, which was a warning about writing sentences that exhibited a lack of critical thinking—a warning that would fall under Janet Giltrow's (2002) definition of metagenre. According to Giltrow, metagenres are "talk about genres" (p. 187) or the "demonstrated precedents or sequestered expectations—atmospheres surrounding genres" (p. 196). In other words, metagenres (in her formulation) police generic boundaries, delineating appropriate and inappropriate forms and functions for individual instances of genres. Professor Robertson's metageneric language appears on the back of a writing handout, where he includes pairs of statements, a "poor sentence" and a "correction." For example, he first writes, "Exorcisms are rituals performed in order to relieve a person of a demon or evil spirit," and then corrects it by writing, "Exorcisms are rituals performed in order to relieve a person *believed to be possessed* by a demon or evil spirit." The qualifier in the second sentence, "*believed to be possessed*," eliminates a flaw in critical thinking.

In a focus group, Michael told me, "One thing I made note of is how I would word things in the paper. When I referred to [Nostradamus's] predictions, I would be sure to use words like 'alleged,' 'supposed,' 'claimed,' rather than just [. . .] making it sound like a true statement. I wouldn't even use 'true,' I would use 'accurate,' rather than making flaws in my own critical thinking." Michael clearly took Professor Robertson's admonishments to heart: he avoided writing his own flawed statements while analyzing others'. Without this kind of attention to the rhetorical effects of their word choices, students' writing itself might be subject to critiques using the Detection Kit, in much the same way that the doomsday panelists' flawed questions were. Professor Robertson's metageneric writing advice and Michael's concomitant rhetorical strategy (repeated by my entire focus group) were thus bound up with the course's metadisciplinary threshold concepts, particularly the one focused on production as well as critique.

Some students' critiques took on metadisciplinary qualities beyond the ones entailed in the Detection Kit, too. For example, Michael pushes his own critique further in ways that are characteristic of the disciplines that Carter (2007/2012) associates with the humanistic metadiscipline. After the above statement-flaw-analysis, Michael argues, "Many translations from the original texts have been altered in order to make connections between recent events that have already happened. Translations of the text can change from time period to time period as major world events occur." Before 9/11, Michael asserts, Nostradamus supposedly predicted "Ayatollah Khomeini, Saddam Hussein, and Slobodan Milosevic" as the anti-Christ, not Osama Bin Laden. In making this claim, Michael seems to be developing an argument about the influence of historical context on interpretations of Nostradamus' quatrains—a way of knowing that might be considered a metadisciplinary threshold concept characteristic of many disciplines in the humanities, including history, certain schools of literary criticism, and religious studies.

Moreover, during our focus groups, both Michael and Maura connected their work in "Film and Folklore" with other classes in the humanities. Both majored in the sciences, where they experienced a distinct emphasis on memorization in the service of exams. As Michael put it, in the sciences, "I know exactly what I have to write." In contrast, he compared "Film and Folklore" to a children's literature class, both of which required textual interpretation: "You reflect a little bit and you apply more than you would [with] just straight memorization. [. . .] It was taking something pretty simple [like a children's book or a single statement from a video] and applying something complex to it [like a theory or a skeptical perspective]." In fact, Michael told me in our final focus group that he wished he had had access to "actual, direct translations" of Nostradamus's text so that he could analyze the language himself, rather than relying on Lorie's (2002) book. In so doing, he demonstrates a humanistic way of doing—direct recourse to source texts—employed in the service of skeptical critique. Similarly, Maura compared "Film and Folklore" to a philosophy class in which, after reading articles about different ethical perspectives, she "would be assigned a point of view, and [she] would have to argue for it." Like Michael, Maura realized her humanities courses entailed ways of knowing similar to those in "Film and Folklore": in both courses she had to craft arguments using an assigned perspective (ethical, skeptical) that she had encountered in outside readings (an ethics article, the Detection Kit).

Broadly speaking, then, both students demonstrated an awareness of the larger metadisciplinary interpretive methods they were engaging in the course. With explicit curricular attention to the metadisciplinary threshold concepts undergirding these interpretive methods, students like these might be in an excellent position to explicate the similarities and differences among their courses and transfer ways of knowing, doing, and writing across them. After all, as Adler-Kassner, Majewski, and Koshnick (2012) explain, students' "knowledge [. . .] becomes less tacit and more explicit, discursive, and conscious" when learning new threshold concepts ("Transfer and Threshold Concepts," para. 2). Such conscious knowledge can serve as a resource for transfer even when an overtly disciplinary perspective is absent.

We can see this potential in some "Film and Folklore" students' experiences taking critical thinking beyond the classroom—a commonplace goal of most general education programs, including UMW's. Late in the semester, my focus group reported that they started thinking skeptically in their everyday lives. As Michael told me, "A lot of the things I'll see now, I can definitely see how things are a lot more slanted. [. . .] I am more aware of it, whereas before I would brush it off. I wouldn't give it any thought, but now I'm a lot more conscious of it, especially in the news." Here Michael points to the "unforgettable" nature of threshold concepts, which, "[o]nce understood, [. . .] are often irreversible" (Adler-Kassner and Wardle, 2015, p. 2). Maura added that she had tried to share the Detection Kit with a friend who believed the moon landing was a hoax: "I had a friend who happened to be watching the moon landing things right when we watched it. I told him, watch 'Mythbusters' [a Discovery Channel show that sometimes debunks hoax claims] [. . .] So I got [the Detection Kit] out to share with him. And I told him [. . .] about the fallacies. I've been able to share the fallacies with different people and point them out." Clearly these students saw the value of the Detection Kit for practicing and promoting critical thinking. In fact, their comments suggest that they were able to act as "agents of integration," or "individuals actively working to *perceive* as well as to *convey effectively to others* connections between previously distinct contexts" (Nowacek, 2011, p. 38). Michael and Maura's ability to "see" and "sell" connections across contexts, as Nowacek puts it (p. 39), indicates the potential value of metadisciplinary threshold concepts for facilitating transfer—after all, such concepts are "integrative, demonstrating how phenomena are related, and helping learners make connections" (Adler-Kassner and Wardle, 2015, p. 2), a potential that could be borne out in future longitudinal studies.

Metadisciplinary Learning in General Education

To be clear, although I found the course successful when I observed it, and although Professor Robertson reported that he was largely pleased with the outcome at the end of the semester, I am not arguing that the course is especially unique or that it ought to be taken as a model for all general education courses. Rather, I am suggesting that "Film and Folklore" is fairly representative of general education courses where successful learning, and successful writing, need not be strictly disciplinary. Although "Film and Folklore" was linked to the discipline of folkloristics through its content and its departmental location, those divisions of content and department can mask larger conceptual links among disciplines—precisely the kinds of links that many general education programs hope to promote. A metadisciplinary perspective can accomplish this goal. As Carter (2007/2012) argues, "[I]n de-emphasizing the knowledge base of the disciplines, metagenre and metadisciplines also highlight relationships among the disciplines that are often otherwise obscured, a concept of the disciplines that is much more fluid than the focus on specialized knowledge would promote" (p. 232). If we consider the implications of Carter's (2007/2012) analysis for general education, we can see that it is less important in such courses to introduce students to any single area of declarative knowledge, any one body of disciplinary discourse, and even any one set of disciplinary threshold concepts; it is more important to help students engage in larger, metadisciplinary ways of knowing, doing, and writing.

We might do well, then, to ask colleagues like Professor Robertson to reflect upon the potential metadisciplinary threshold concepts—texts and beliefs being open to critique rather than containers of truth, or the influence of context on textual interpretation—that underlie their general education courses and writing assignments, and to share those concepts with students explicitly.

In making this recommendation, I part ways with Carter (2007/2012), who suggests that the concept of metadisciplines is of more use to WAC professionals than to faculty in the disciplines because "[f]aculty focused on their own programs may not find that the concept resonates with their needs," whereas WAC professionals could benefit from "the ability to perceive broader disciplinary formations and to understand the way genres shape and are shaped by those formations" (p. 229). From my perspective, if skeptical instructors can appreciate the ways their courses and their writing assignments mobilize metadisciplinary threshold concepts, as I have done here, they may become allies with WAC in our efforts toward general education reform. To that end, in course and curriculum development workshops and consultations, we might ask them to articulate the following:

1. *How do you define liberal learning principles like critical thinking, civic awareness, or information literacy? What relationship, if any, do those principles have to learning and writing in your discipline?* In answering these questions, faculty members can make explicit their (perhaps tacit) assumptions about what students ought to be learning in general education, as well as the role disciplinary ways of knowing, doing, and writing play or do not play in liberal learning.

2. *What are your central pedagogical tools (i.e., toolkits, texts, writing assignments, and activities) for helping students accomplish these goals? How successful are these tools? In what ways to students struggle with them?* These questions are designed to get instructors to articulate the ways their pedagogical practices are designed to teach liberal learning principles. WAC professionals may want to pay special attention to the ways faculty align their writing assignments with liberal learning goals. In tandem with the last question, about students' struggles, these questions can turn instructors' attention toward threshold concepts, since those are defined as "troublesome" (Adler-Kassner, Majewski, and Koshnick, 2012) sites of struggle.

3. *What genres do you typically assign, and why are those genres especially useful for promoting liberal learning for your students?* In asking about genres, we can highlight the typified rhetorical actions (Miller, 1984) that instructors employ in their general education courses. As Carter (2007/2012) argues, such genres can be grouped in to collections, called metagenres, according to their shared ways of knowing and doing; we can then look to the larger metadisciplines that share metagenres to articulate their commonplace epistemological assumptions, actions, and rhetorical principles. By grouping genres in this way, faculty members can see the metadisciplinary assumptions underlying their writing assignments, even if they forgo disciplinary education in their classes. The process may also help them avoid teaching mutt genres (Wardle, 2009). Those metadisciplinary assumptions, in turn, can point to metadisciplinary threshold concepts that they might work with their students to explicate, especially in writing.

4. *Finally, and crucially, how do all these concepts, tools, and methods benefit students as they move beyond general education, into the disciplines and beyond?* This final question asks instructors to work with transfer in mind, to ask of each course objective, writing assignment, and lesson, how students might use their learning in subsequent situations, particularly when they write in other general education courses, in their majors, in the workplace, or in community or civic contexts.

In asking such questions, we need not default to a strictly disciplinary perspective on teaching and learning about writing where one is not needed or wanted. Through threshold concepts, we can instead take a metadisciplinary perspective on writing and promote general education's aspirations of integrated, expansive learning.

Acknowledgments

I would like to thank Professor Robertson, Michael, Maura, and Lane for their time during this study. I am also grateful to the two anonymous reviewers also offered valuable feedback that I believe helped me sharpen this argument. Finally, I want to thank my writing group at UND, along with Kim Donehower, for working with me on earlier drafts of the article.

Notes

1. Of course, these are not the only options for general education, nor are they mutually exclusive. Broadly speaking, according to the AAC&U (2015b), general education exposes students "to multiple disciplines and forms the basis of developing essential intellectual, civic, and practical capacities" (para. 2). Beyond this broad definition, though, general education looks very different both historically (see Russell, 2002) and across institutions.

2. WAC scholars have long known that faculty typically want their students to approximate the discourse conventions, authorial roles, knowledge-building purposes, and social activities associated with writing in their fields, even if they are not entirely aware of the disciplinary roots of those expectations (Beaufort, 2007; Carroll, 2002; Herrington, 1994; Nowacek, 2011; Walvoord and McCarthy, 1990; and Wilder, 2012), knowledge that threshold concepts could help support.

3. In accordance with IRB protocols, names of all participants have been changed, along with the institution. All students signed permission forms to release their writing.

4. William Condon and Diane Kelly-Riley (2004) argue, "The kind of critical thinking" that instructors typically expect "is driven by the values and the types of work required in the discipline" (pp. 63–64). In folkloristics, critical thinking might involve interrogating the structure and social function of folk beliefs and practices.

5. UMW's college of arts and sciences overview of liberal learning states, "The liberal arts teach students to think critically and creatively. As perceptive analysts of what they read, see, and hear, students must learn to reason carefully and correctly and to recognize the legitimacy of intuition when reason and evidence prove insufficient." However, Professor Robertson never referenced UMW's liberal learning principles when defining critical thinking for his class.

6. The AAC&U (2015a) defines critical thinking as "a habit of mind characterized by the comprehensive exploration of issues, ideas, artifacts, and events before accepting or formulating an opinion or conclusion" (para. 2), but again, Professor Robertson did not invoke a definition of critical thinking promoted by any professional academic organization.

7. Sagan and Shermer's brand of skepticism should be distinguished from the tradition of skeptical philosophy. According to Richard H. Popkin and Avrum Stroll (2002), skeptical philosophy invites "a general skepticism about all assertions, promises, and verbal commitments," thus "challeng[ing] the very existence of knowledge and certainty" (p. 31). They contrast this radical skepticism with "everyday, practical doubts, which are more local" and which "allow for the existence of knowledge and certainty in some cases, while denying it in others" (p. 31). Sagan and Shermer's skepticism is more akin to these everyday doubts than to radical skeptical philosophy.

8. Carter (2007/2012) outlines a constellation of disciplines that "generally call for students to define a problem, establish parameters for a solution to the problem, generate possible solutions, and identify and justify a recommended solution to the problem" (p. 220).

References

AAC&U (2015a). Critical thinking VALUE rubric. Retrieved from https://www.aacu.org/value/rubrics/critical-thinking

AAC&U (2015b). What is a 21st century liberal education? Retrieved from https://www.aacu.org/leap/what-is-a-liberal-education

Adler-Kassner, L., Majewski, J., & Koshnick, D. (2012). The value of troublesome knowledge: Transfer and threshold concepts in writing and history. *Composition Forum, 26*. Retrieved from http://www.compositionforum.com/issue/26/troublesome-knowledge-threshold.php

Adler-Kassner, L., & Wardle, E. (2015). *Naming what we know: Threshold concepts of writing studies*. Logan, UT: Utah State University Press.

Beaufort, A. (2007). *College writing and beyond: A new framework for university writing instruction*. Logan, UT: Utah State University Press.

Bawarshi, A. (2003). *Genre and the invention of the writer*. Logan, UT: Utah State University Press.

Carroll, L. A. (2002). *Rehearsing new roles: How college students develop as writers*. Carbondale, IL: Southern Illinois University Press.

Carter, M. (2012). Ways of knowing, doing, and writing in the disciplines. In T. M. Zawacki & P.M. Rogers (Eds.), *Writing across the curriculum: A critical sourcebook* (pp. 212–38). Boston: Bedford/St. Martins. (Reprinted from *College Composition and Communication, 58*(3), 385–418.)

Condon, W., & Kelly-Riley, D. (2004). Assessing and teaching what we value: The relationship between college-level writing and critical thinking abilities. *Assessing Writing, 9*, 56–75.

Dryer, D. B. (2008). The persistence of institutional memory: Genre uptake and program reform. *WPA: Writing Program Administration, 31*(3), 32–51.

Eyman, D. (2015). *Digital rhetoric: Theory, method, practice*. Ann Arbor, MI: University of Michigan Press.

Farris, C. R., & Smith, R. (1992). Writing intensive courses: Tools for curricular change. In S. H. McLeod & M. Soven (Eds.), *Writing across the curriculum: A guide to developing programs* (pp. 52–62). Newbury Park, CA: Sage.

Fitzgerald, L. (2013). What is general education? In R. Malenczyk (Ed.), *A rhetoric for writing program administrators* (pp. 93–104). Anderson, SC: Parlor Press.

Giltrow, J. Meta-genre. In R. Coe, L. Lingard, & T. Teslenko (Eds.), *The rhetoric and ideology of genre: Strategies for stability and change* (pp. 187–206). Cresskill, NJ: Hampton Press.

Glaser, B. G., & Strauss, A. L. (1967). *The discovery of grounded theory*. Chicago: Aldine Publishing.

Herrington, A. (1994). Writing in academic settings: A study of the contexts in two college chemical engineering courses. In C. Bazerman & D. R. Russell (Eds.), *Landmark essays on writing across the curriculum* (pp. 97–124). Davis, CA: Hermagoras Press.

Lanham, R. A. (1991). *A handlist of rhetorical terms*. Berkeley: University of California Press, 1991.

Lorie, P. (2002). *Nostradamus 2003–2025: A history of the future*. New York, NY: Pocket Books.

Lunsford, A., & Ruszkiewicz, J. (2009). *Everything's an argument*. Boston, MA: Bedford/St. Martin's.

McLeod, S. H., & Miraglia, E. (2001). Writing across the curriculum in a time of change. In S. H. McLeod, E. Miraglia, M. Soven, & C. Thaiss (Eds.), *WAC for the new millennium* (pp. 1–27). Urbana, IL: NCTE.

Meyer, J. H. F., & Land, R. (Eds.) (2006). *Overcoming barriers to student understanding*. London, UK: Routledge.

Miller, C. R. (1984). Genre as social action. *Quarterly Journal of Speech, 70*, 151–67.

Nowacek, R. (2009). Why is being interdisciplinary so very hard to do?: Thoughts on the perils and promise of interdisciplinary pedagogy. *College Composition and Communication, 60*(3), 493–516.

Nowacek, R. (2011). *Agents of integration: Understanding transfer as a rhetorical act*. Carbondale, IL: Southern Illinois University Press.

Perkins, D. (2006). Constructivism and troublesome knowledge. In Jan H. F. Meyer & Ray Land (Eds.), *Overcoming barriers to student understanding* (pp. 33–47). London, UK: Routledge.

Popkin, R., & Stroll, A. (2002). *Skeptical philosophy for everyone*. Amherst, NY: Prometheus Books.

Ramage, J., Bean, J., & Johnson, J. (2011). *Writing arguments*. Boston, MA: Pearson Longman.

Russell, D. R. (2002). *Writing in the academic disciplines: A curricular history* (2nd ed). Carbondale, IL: Southern Illinois University Press.

Russell, D. R., & Yañez, A. "Big picture people rarely become historians": Genre systems and the contradictions of general education. In C. Bazerman and D. R. Russell (Eds.), *Writing selves/writing societies* (pp. 331–62). Fort Collins, CO: The WAC Clearinghouse and Mind, Culture, and Activity.

Sagan, C. (1996). *The demon-haunted world: Science as a candle in the dark*. New York, NY: Ballantine.

Schaefer, K. L. (2015). "Emphasizing similarity" but not "eliding difference": Exploring sub-disciplinary differences as a way to teach Genre Flexibility. *The WAC Journal, 26*, 36–55.

Shermer, M. (2002). *Why people believe weird things*. New York, NY: St. Martin's Griffin.

Soliday, M. (2011). *Everyday genres: Writing assignments across the disciplines*. Carbondale, IL: Southern Illinois University Press.

Thaiss, C. (1992). WAC and general education courses. In S. H. McLeod & M. Soven (Eds.), *Writing across the curriculum: A guide to developing programs* (pp. 63–77). Newbury Park, CA: Sage.

Thaiss, C., & Zawacki, T. M. (2006). *Engaged writers and dynamic disciplines: Research on the academic writing life*. Portsmouth, NH: Boynton/Cook.

Skeptics society. (n.d.). A brief introduction. Retrieved from http://www.skeptic.com/about_us/

Walvoord, B. E., & McCarthy, L. P. (1990). *Thinking and writing in college: A naturalistic study of students in four disciplines*. Urbana, IL: NCTE.

Wardle, E. (2009). "Mutt genres" and the goal of FYC: Can we help students write the genres of the university? *College Composition and Communication, 60*(4), 765–89.

Wilder, L. (2012). *Rhetorical strategies and genre conventions in literary studies: Teaching and writing in the disciplines*. Carbondale, IL: Southern Illinois University Press.

Williams, J. M., & Colomb, G. G. (2007). *The craft of argument*. Boston, MA: Pearson Longman.

Quantitative Genre Analysis of Undergraduate Theses: Uncovering Different Ways of Writing and Thinking in Science Disciplines

JASON E. DOWD, ROBERT J. THOMPSON, JR., AND
JULIE A. REYNOLDS

Introduction

One of the challenges for writing in the disciplines (WID) programs and practitioners has been to replace the commonly held view in academia that disciplinary conceptual knowledge is a specialized skill but writing is a generalized skill. This view stems from the understanding of disciplines primarily as domains of specialized content knowledge. Disciplinary knowledge, however, includes both conceptual content knowledge (i.e., *knowing that*) and procedural knowledge (i.e., *knowing how*). Learning in a discipline is sometimes understood as acquiring content knowledge, whereas the focus of WID "tends to be on procedural knowledge, writing as a way of knowing in a discipline" (Carter, 2007, p. 387). More specifically, "WID developed as a response to the recognition that different disciplines are characterized by distinct ways of writing and knowing. Thus, a specialized conception of disciplinary knowledge is integrated with a specialized conception of writing" (Carter, 2007, p. 387). Carter has drawn on the idea of disciplinary ways of doing (Herrington, 1981; Russell, 1997) as "a link between ways of writing and ways of knowing in the disciplines" (2007, p. 387).

A second challenge for WID programs has been to characterize and teach salient differences in disciplinary ways of knowing, doing, and writing. Ways of knowing and doing include epistemic beliefs, methods of inquiry, and processes for making meaning of findings. Experts across disciplines utilize different paradigms, or "system[s] of beliefs and practices that guide a field" (Morgan, 2007, p. 49), by specifying the following: appropriate problems for study and research questions that are considered important and solvable; types of questions that are asked; methods that are employed and considered valid; and ways of making meaning (Kalman, 2009). More specifically, experts across disciplines differ in epistemic beliefs about the nature of knowledge and the truth criteria employed for the justification of claims, as well as the methods and cognitive processes involved in the construction of knowledge. At the broadest level, these disciplinary differences are evident in comparing the humanities and sciences (Phillips & Burbules, 2000). The humanities focus on human thought and action as text, employ metaphor and the cognitive processes of analogy and intuition, and rely on the method of hermeneutics (i.e., the interpretation of meaning). The sciences, in contrast, focus on the natural and social worlds, employ rationalism and empiricism and the cognitive processes of deductive and inductive reasoning, and rely on objective evidence that is publicly available for inspection and replicable by the relevant professional community (Phillips & Burbules, 2000).

While broad differences between the humanities and the sciences are most readily apparent, there are also differences in ways of knowing and writing between and within the physical/life and social/behavioral science disciplines that employ scientific methods. Some science disciplines pose "what" questions, while others pose "how" questions, to explain the mechanisms by which certain processes take place. For example, the concept of "mechanism" is particularly important for understanding the biological sciences (Machamer, Darden, & Craver, 2000). Explanation relies upon isolating causal factors, and science disciplines differ in their reliance on experimental or statistical control. Some disciplines rely more heavily on deductive reasoning and engage in "hypothetico-deductive" theory building (e.g., theoretical/mathematical physics), whereas other disciplines rely on inductive reasoning and model building (e.g., biochemistry or economics) (Thagard, 2006). Even within a particular science discipline, multiple approaches to reasoning may be appropriate in different contexts. This has led to the recognition that there is no single scientific epistemology (Rudolph, 2000; Russ, 2014). Students must learn and become enculturated into the ways of knowing, doing, and writing of specific scientific disciplinary communities of discourse.

One method for characterizing differences in disciplinary ways of knowing, doing, and writing is in terms of *genre*, which refers to patterns in social action of language in response to recurring rhetorical situations (Carter, 2007). Examples of genres of writing in science disciplines include laboratory reports, design/research application papers, and literature reviews of previous research. Kovac has argued that scientific research itself can be thought of as a set of rhetorical tasks: "What needs to be explained? What constitutes an explanation? How does an explanation constrain what counts as evidence" (2003, p. 237). Scientific writing, then, is a form of rhetoric in that scientists construct arguments—first to persuade themselves, and then others—that an interpretation of findings or an explanation is valid and interesting. Kovac also noted that the form that scientific writing takes reflects differences in approach: "Experimental articles are usually written so as to suggest that science is inductive, whereas theoretical articles are written to suggest that all theory is deductive" (2003, p. 236). Disciplines employ different rhetorical devices, such as metaphors. Chemistry, for example, may be considered a "metaphor-rich science" since chemists develop models or metaphors to describe the behavior of electrons, atoms, and molecules (Kovac, 2003).

Recently, Wolfe and colleagues (2015) developed a method, Comparative Genre Analysis (CGA), to illuminate both rhetorical differences among disciplines and the manner in which particular rhetorical conventions support disciplinary ways of knowing and core intellectual values. CGA can also serve as a pedagogical strategy by making visible to students the links between genre conventions and discipline-specific values and ways of knowing. In particular, Wolfe and colleagues (2015) describe three dimensions of rhetorical analyses of different academic genres that reflect these links. One dimension relates to the methods and conceptual lenses that are used in a discipline to identify patterns and formulate meaningful interpretations. In this context, lenses are concepts, theories, or hypotheses that are used to organize and interpret the phenomena being studied. Although goals may vary across disciplines, common elements include applying lenses to interpret primary material, evaluating the relationship between study results and pre-existing concepts or hypotheses, and reflecting on the original concept. A second dimension relates to macrostructures that are used to arrange arguments. A macrostructure is an organizational pattern that provides readers with a frame of reference that helps them recall information and make sense of the text. For example, within laboratory and experimental reports, the macrostructures of introduction, methods, results, and discussion are the common norms across disciplines that convey new information in a predictable format. Within literature reviews, multiple different macrostructures are evident. For example, Wolfe and colleagues (2015) found that the macrostructure of thesis-statement-first (i.e., beginning a section with one's thesis statement) is characteristic in psychology, whereas thesis-statement-last is more typical in biology. A third dimension relates to naming and citation conventions that differ across disciplines within the same genres, including the use/avoidance of passive voice, when and how to cite other authors, and whether to use direct quotations. These conventions reflect different disciplinary values and assumptions about research and authorship, such as whether to focus on ideas and findings or theorists and researchers. Disciplines differ in the extent to which they privilege individuality and particularity of knowledge, as well as how they handle controversy (i.e., whether to cite other authors by name to refute claims or focus on knowledge claims and alternative explanations) (Wolfe et al., 2015).

The use of genre analysis as a method of elucidating and teaching disciplinary-specific values, ways of knowing, and ways of writing is encouraging. The qualitative categories and descriptors discussed above provide a robust framework for discussion of differences. The aim of the current study is to contribute to this use of genre analysis, specifically though the use of quantitative methods for analyzing emergent differences across disciplines. Our work is focused on assessing and enhancing students' scientific reasoning and writing within the genre of the undergraduate thesis. In this study, we investigate disciplinary rhetorical differences and discuss our findings in relation to the three rhetorical dimensions of the CGA—conceptual lens, macrostructures to construct arguments, and naming and citation conventions—to further elucidate the general and discipline-specific nature of scientific reasoning and writing. We will discuss potential implications of our findings for educational practice, and we will highlight future studies.

Science Reasoning in Thesis Writing Across Disciplines

At Duke University, we have used the genre of the undergraduate honors thesis as the rhetorical context in which to study and improve students' scientific reasoning and writing. We view the process of writing an undergraduate honors thesis as a form of professional development in the sciences (i.e., a way of engaging students in the practices of a community of discourse). We have found that structured courses designed to scaffold the thesis-writing process and promote metacognition can improve writing and critical thinking skills in biology, chemistry, and economics (Dowd, Connolly, Thompson, Jr., & Reynolds, 2015; Dowd, Roy, Thompson, Jr., & Reynolds, 2015; Reynolds & Thompson, 2011). To enhance these structured courses, we developed the Thesis Assessment Protocol (TAP) as a tool for facilitating communication (the full text of the TAP, as implemented in Biology, is published in Reynolds & Thompson [2011] supplemental materials). The TAP systematically guides students and faculty through a "draft-feedback-revision" writing process, modeled after professional scientific peer review processes. The TAP includes activities and worksheets that allow students to engage in critical peer review, and provides detailed descriptions of the questions (i.e., dimensions) upon which such review should focus; these descriptions are presented as rubrics. Nine rubric dimensions focus on communication to the broader scientific community, and four rubric dimensions focus on evaluation by topic-specific experts (Table 1). These rubrics provide criteria by which the thesis may be assessed, and therefore allow the TAP to be used as an assessment tool as well as a teaching resource (Reynolds, Smith, Moskovitz, & Sayle, 2009).

Table 1. Theses assessment protocol dimensions.

Scientific community-focused	1	Is the writing appropriate for the target audience?
	2	Does the thesis make a compelling argument for the significance of the student's research within the context of the current literature?
	3	Does the thesis clearly articulate the student's research goals?
	4	Does the thesis skillfully interpret the results?
	5	Is there a compelling discussion of the implications of findings?
	6	Is the thesis clearly organized?
	7	Is the thesis free of writing errors?
	8	Are the citations presented consistently and professionally throughout the text and in the list of works cited?
	9	Are the tables and figures clear, effective, and informative?
Topic-specific	10	Does the thesis represent the student's significant scientific research?
	11	Is the literature review accurate and complete?
	12	Are the methods appropriate, given the student's research question?
	13	Is the data analysis appropriate, accurate, and unbiased?

In addition to facilitating communication and formative assessment during the writing of the thesis, the TAP functions as a method for assessment of the final product. In our work, we have used the TAP to quantitatively assess the relationship between thesis-writing courses (or specific interventions within the courses) and the strength of students' science reasoning in writing across different science disciplines: economics (Dowd, Connolly, et al., 2015); chemistry (Dowd, Roy, et al., 2015); and biology (Reynolds & Thompson, 2011). In our assessment of theses for research purposes (as opposed to assessment by instructors and thesis supervisors), we have focused exclusively on the nine dimensions related to reasoning and writing (Questions 1–9). The other four dimensions (Questions 10–13) are intended to be used by the student's thesis supervisor and are not included in our analyses of theses. In each case, we have found that the TAP is effective for facilitating instructors' feedback on thesis drafts and assessing students' scientific reasoning and writing within the thesis genre. Moreover, we have investigated whether meaningful constructs underlie thesis scores on the nine dimensions of the TAP that are of interest. We conducted exploratory factor analysis of students' theses in economics and chemistry and found one dominant underlying factor in each discipline; we termed the factor *scientific reasoning in writing* (Dowd, Connolly, et al., 2015; Dowd, Roy, et al., 2015) That is, each of the nine dimensions could be understood as reflecting, in different ways and to different degrees, the construct of *scientific reasoning in writing*, and this single underlying construct was evident in the theses in both chemistry and economics.

We are now well-positioned to expand prior studies *within* each discipline and make comparisons *across* disciplines. The purpose of the current study is to investigate whether the TAP reveals meaningful similarities and differences in disciplinary ways of thinking, doing, and writing across three disciplines that are representative of the life sciences (biology), the physical sciences (chemistry), and the social sciences (economics). More specifically, the aims are to investigate 1) whether the underlying single factor derived from the nine dimensions of the TAP in economics and chemistry theses is also evident in biology theses; and 2) whether the single underlying factor is measuring the same construct (i.e., the factors have the same meaning and implications) within each discipline. In other words, do the nine dimensions of the TAP have a similar pattern of relative contribution (emphasis) to the construct of scientific reasoning in writing in each discipline, or do the patterns suggest that the underlying factor of scientific reasoning in writing is constituted differently across these three disciplines?

Methods

Study Sample

The study sample data for this current work was comprised of the theses submitted by students at Duke University that were assessed using the TAP rubric and procedures described above and reported in previous studies: 190 theses submitted to the department of biology from 2005 to 2008 (Reynolds & Thompson, 2011); 93 theses submitted to the department of chemistry from 2000 to 2013 (Dowd, Roy, et al., 2015); and 244 theses submitted to the department of economics from 2001 to 2011 (Dowd, Connolly, et al., 2015).

Thesis Assessment

Each of the nine dimensions were scored on a scale from 1 to 5, where a rating of 1 indicates that the dimension under consideration is either missing, incomplete, or below the minimum acceptable standards for the department and a rating of 5 indicates that the dimension is excellent and the work exhibits mastery. Graduate students and postdoctoral fellows were hired to read and rate the majority of the theses, though some were also rated by faculty; theses were rated by raters with relevant disciplinary backgrounds (e.g., biology theses were rated by raters in biology-related disciplines). Each rater completed more than eight hours of training in the use of the TAP rubric, which included examination of sample writings and assessment and discussion of complete theses that were not part of the data set for calibration. Every thesis was read and independently assessed by two raters; raters then discussed their individual scores for a thesis with one another, explained their respective reasons for any differences, and formed a single *consensus* score for each dimension. The consensus is not an average, but rather the result of discussion; it may be one rater's score, the other's score, or an entirely different value. Raters generated a consensus score for each of the nine dimensions for each thesis; individual dimensions could be summed to yield a total score.

Interrater reliability statistics for the discipline-specific subsets of these data have been reported in prior studies.[1] For the current study, we determined interrater reliability for the pooled sample of 527 theses. The Pearson correlation coefficient between raters' pre-discussion scores is 0.88 for total scores, and range from 0.63 to 0.79 for the nine distinct dimensions. Raters' post-discussion consensus scores are 100% in agreement. We note that scores on each dimension are within one point of each other in 86% of cases. Taken as a whole, these results indicate moderate to strong pre-discussion agreement and very strong post-discussion agreement between raters using the TAP rubric. Consensus scores were used in all analyses.

Analyses

We generated summary descriptive statistics (means and standard deviations) for the ratings of the nine TAP dimensions of students' theses in each discipline. Then, two new factor analyses were conducted. First, to determine whether there were any meaningful constructs underlying the relationships among the nine TAP dimensions of theses in biology, we conducted an exploratory factor analysis just as we had previously done in chemistry (Dowd, Roy, et al., 2015) and economics (Dowd, Connolly, et al., 2015). Second, we subsequently carried out confirmatory factor analyses of the theses in all three disciplines to determine whether the derived factors measure the same construct (i.e., have the same meaning and implications) across disciplines. To make this determination, we used the test of factorial invariance (χ^2) to evaluate whether the factor loadings for the nine dimensions of the TAP (i.e., the weight with which each dimension contributes to the single underlying factor) are the same (i.e., invariant) across the theses in biology, chemistry, and economics.[2] We first compared factor loadings for all nine dimensions across all three disciplines simultaneously, and then between each pair of disciplines. Finally, we examined the proportion of variance accounted for by the nine dimensions in the underlying factors for each discipline.

Results

In Table 2, we highlight means and standard deviations for the ratings of the nine assessed dimensions of students' theses in each discipline.[3] These data reveal a range of performances across dimensions within each discipline. For example, students in chemistry demonstrated a relatively higher level of mastery on the dimension of *minimizing writing errors* than on *appropriate use of citations*. Regardless, relative level of performance on a specific dimension does not reflect the relative contribution of that dimension to the underlying construct of scientific reasoning in writing in that discipline.[4] Rather, underlying factors depend on the relationships among students' scores on different dimensions (stronger relationships correspond to stronger factor loadings).

Table 2. Summary statistics of the nine assessed dimensions of students' theses.[a]

Dimension	Biology n = 190	Chemistry n = 93	Economics n = 244
Appropriate for audience	4.0 (1.0)	4.3 (0.9)	4.5 (1.1)
Formulating compelling argument	4.3 (1.0)	4.0 (1.0)	3.9 (1.3)
Articulating goals	4.3 (1.0)	4.2 (0.9)	4.1 (1.3)
Interpretation of results	4.3 (1.0)	3.7 (1.1)	4.2 (1.3)
Implications of results	4.1 (1.1)	3.5 (1.1)	3.7 (1.3)
Organization of thesis	4.3 (1.0)	4.0 (1.2)	4.3 (1.2)
Minimizing writing errors	4.5 (0.9)	4.7 (0.6)	4.7 (1.0)
Appropriate citation	3.4 (1.8)	1.5 (1.1)	3.6 (1.6)
Effective tables and figures	3.7 (1.4)	3.2 (1.1)	3.6 (1.2)

[a] Mean values (and standard deviations, in parentheses) are shown.

Similar to previous findings in chemistry and economics, the exploratory factor analysis of TAP scores for biology theses yielded one dominant underlying factor that we have termed *scientific reasoning in writing* (Table 3). Thus, in each discipline, a single underlying factor has been identified. However, each of the factors is related to the nine dimensions of the TAP to varying degrees. When we compare across all three disciplines, we find that the factor loadings were significantly different across the disciplines ($p < 0.00001$). When we compare pairs of disciplines, we find no significant difference between the models for the factor loadings in biology and chemistry ($p = 0.68$); however, the comparisons between the models for biology and economics and between chemistry and economics were significantly different ($p < 0.00001$). Thus, the findings indicate that the underlying factors in biology and chemistry are not significantly different from one another, and the factor in economics is different from the other two factors.

To identify the nature of these differences in the constructs underlying the factors across the three disciplines, we examined the relationships reflected in the factor loadings of each of the nine dimensions of the TAP with the underlying factors (Table 3). Although we identify a single underlying factor in each discipline, the factors account for different amounts of the total variance, ranging from 22% in biology to 26% in chemistry to 52% in economics (Table 3). Additionally, the nine items load onto each factor to varying extents. Therefore, although a single dominant factor, *scientific reasoning in writing*, was identified for the theses in each discipline, the relative contribution of dimensions that make up each of the three factors varies. As shown in Table 3, the dimensions that load most strongly in biology are *formulating compelling argument* and *articulating goals*, whereas the strongest dimensions in chemistry involve the *interpretation* and *implication* of the results. The factor loadings across the nine dimensions in economics are more uniformly strong, except for the relative weakness of the loading for *citations*. Structural attributes of the writing, such as *organization* and *minimizing writing errors*, are more strongly related to the factor in economics than to the factors in biology and chemistry.

Table 3. Factor loadings of the nine assessed dimensions of students' theses.

Dimension	Biology	Chemistry	Economics
Appropriate for audience	0.48	0.46	0.69
Formulating compelling argument	0.67	0.50	0.75
Articulating goals	0.54	0.40	0.75
Interpretation of results	0.51	0.65	0.80
Implications of results	0.50	0.81	0.70
Organization of thesis	0.41	0.55	0.80
Minimizing writing errors	0.36	0.33	0.83
Appropriate citation	0.31	0.38	0.49
Effective tables and figures	0.20	0.25	0.63
Factor eigenvalue	1.9	2.3	4.7
Variance explained	22%	26%	52%

Note. Each discipline revealed a single underlying factor that we have termed *scientific reasoning in writing*. In biology, the dimension that loads most strongly onto the underlying factor is *structuring argument*. In chemistry, *implications of results* loads most strongly onto the underlying factor. In economics, factor loadings are uniformly strong across dimensions, except for the relative weakness of *appropriate citations*.

Discussion

The findings of this study provide support for the use of TAP as a method of quantitative thesis genre analysis that reveals disciplinary differences in thinking and writing across three science disciplines—biology, chemistry, and economics—that are of relevance for WID programs. The TAP scores of students' theses in these disciplines across nine dimensions yield single underlying factors in each discipline that we have termed *scientific reasoning in writing*. However, this factor of *scientific reasoning in writing* is not expressed in the same way across all three disciplines.

There are both disciplinary-specific and general components to scientific reasoning in writing, with the disciplinary-specific components perhaps relating to disciplinary-specific aspects of epistemic beliefs and paradigms. For example, epistemic beliefs have been linked to students' use of argumentation in science (Nussbaum, Sinatra, & Poliquin, 2008). It has been argued that disciplinary-specific aspects of the nature of science (and related epistemological beliefs) should emerge from content in the disciplines instead of being imposed as general features (Van Dijk, 2014).

With the findings of the current study, we can interpret the common single underlying factor in each discipline as reflecting a general element of scientific reasoning in writing; at the same time, we can interpret the differential loadings and the relative portion of variance accounted for by the nine contributing dimensions as indicating possible disciplinary-specific elements. The findings also indicate that the general underlying factors of scientific reasoning in writing in biology and chemistry are more similar to each other than they are to the underlying factor in economics. Even within biology and chemistry, meaningful differences occur in some of the factor loadings in these disciplines. Specifically, the contribution of *formulating a compelling argument* is stronger in biology, and the contribution of *implication of results* is stronger in chemistry.[5] We note that the variance explained by the underlying factors in biology and chemistry are relatively low (Table 3). Although there is clear evidence for one factor in each discipline, that factor does not account for a substantial amount of the variation in scores. In other words, the individual dimensions still convey substantial unique information about student exhibition of science reasoning in writing in these chemistry and biology theses.

These thesis genre analysis findings can be interpreted in light of Wolfe and colleagues' (2015) use of CGA to describe differences in disciplinary rhetorical conventions. The CGA rhetorical dimension of *conceptual lens* refers to concepts, theories, or hypotheses that are used to organize and interpret the phenomena being studied. This organizing and interpreting function is reflected in the TAP dimensions of formulating a compelling argument for significance of research, articulation of research goals, interpretation of results, implications of findings, and effective use of tables and figures. The TAP dimensions related to thesis structure (organization), effective use of tables and figures, and writing for an appropriate audience serve a similar function as the CGA dimension of macrostructure by providing a frame of reference to help readers recall information and make sense of the text. Similarly, both TAP and CGA assess the use of citations, though there are substantial differences in the assessment and related implications across both methods. Although TAP was not initially designed for genre analysis, the findings of this study indicate that it can function as a quantitative tool for comparative analysis across disciplines within the genre of the undergraduate thesis, and provide a view of disciplinary differences that complements qualitative analyses. Furthermore, interpreting TAP findings in terms of general and disciplinary-specific rhetorical dimensions enhances the utility of the TAP within WID contexts as a tool for facilitating communication and systematically guiding students and faculty through a "draft-feedback-revision" thesis writing process.

Building on this interpretation and the numerical values presented in Table 3, within the genre of the undergraduate honors thesis, scientific reasoning in economics writing appears to be characterized by emphasis on both the lens dimension of interpretation of results and the macrostructure dimension of thesis organization to convey new information, as well as the minimization of writing errors. We have no empirical evidence to make meaning of the seemingly critical role of minimizing writing errors, though we speculate that, in economics at Duke University, there is a relatively strong focus on learning to write alongside writing-to-learn. Scientific reasoning in biology writing is characterized by an emphasis on the lens dimension of formulating a compelling argument, and scientific reasoning in chemistry writing is characterized by an emphasis on the lens dimension of implications of results. Scientific reasoning in both biology and chemistry writing are less characterized by the macrostructure dimension of tables and figures than in economics.

These characterizations of writing, in turn, relate to disciplinary thinking. We argue that, in economics, students' research generally involves the proposition and development of a model, the analysis of data related to this model, and the interpretation of this analysis. The theoretical framework is self-contained in a way that is unique compared to natural sciences like biology and chemistry, and therefore scientific reasoning in writing leans more heavily on students' organization, attention to audience, and effective use of tables and figures. In biology, which is a field in which theoretical frameworks differ considerably across sub-disciplines, we suggest that students are usually employing a pre-existing model that nonetheless must be presented and justified. Thus, the argument is essential, and organization and effective use of tables and figures, while still important to a well-constructed thesis, are less discriminatory or informative with regard to underlying science reasoning and evaluative thinking. In chemistry, where theoretical frameworks are more consistent and coherent across sub-disciplines, students may not even consider the models employed as anything other than objective, coherent descriptions of the natural world. In other words, the argument may be treated as evident once the facts and principles are stated. Instead, we argue that the students' discussion of their own research, and particularly the implications of their results, is the primary component of the chemistry thesis requiring scientific reasoning and evaluativist thinking. While tables and figures are certainly important in the presentation of results, they may tend to be more or less effective in chemistry for idiosyncratic reasons (unrelated to science reasoning in writing) compared to economics. Interpretation of results is the primary goal of the discussion section and addresses "how" and "why" questions (Robinson, Stoller, Costanza-Robinson, & Jones, 2008). This could explain the relatively large differences in the contributions of the dimensions of *implications of results* and *formulating a compelling argument* in the factors characterizing students' scientific reasoning in chemistry and biology. Therefore, we see plausible explanations for both general and disciplinary-specific components when we consider thesis writing within these disciplines. If we are looking for evaluativist thinking, we would expect to find it in different places in different disciplines.

There are some limitations to the data that we must acknowledge as we make the arguments presented here. We've analyzed hundreds of theses collected over many years, but the representation from different years is not evenly distributed within our sample. Although we have no hypothesis to explain why there would be differences in how students exhibit scientific reasoning over time, such differences could manifest as disciplinary differences in this analysis. In comparing Tables 2 and 3, one can see that the relationships among the dimensions (Table 3) are not the same as students' performance in the dimensions (Table 2). We make no attempts here to interpret differences in performance across disciplines; such differences may reflect variation in students' preparation, variation in instructors' teaching, disciplinary differences, etc. However, we are attempting to interpret the differences in relationships among the dimensions. While these differences, like the differences in performance, may have underlying causes related to students' perspectives and instructors' points of emphasis, we argue that those perspectives and points of emphasis reflect the very disciplinary epistemic beliefs that we are interested in better understanding. We recognize, of course, that this analysis is limited to three specific departments at Duke University.[6] The arguments presented here resonate in conversations with instructors in these disciplines, but the perspectives and expectations of those instructors and the departments at this institution are not necessarily the same as those of the broader communities within each discipline. In short, more research is required to further test the ideas presented here.

While it may not seem groundbreaking to suggest that the social science of economics is more different from biology and chemistry than the two natural sciences are from one another, the fact that the same thesis assessment protocol is appropriate for three different disciplines implies that there is a shared orientation regarding the form of scholarly inquiry and communication. The protocol yields meaningful disciplinary rhetorical differences as well. Thus, we argue that the evidence increasingly suggests that one should not ask whether writing is generalized or discipline-specific but rather ask how to differentiate and teach that which is general and that which is discipline-specific.

This work carries implications and raises new questions that connect to both potential educational practice and future research. The implications for educational practices, particularly in WID programs, relate to the pedagogical strategy of making the links between genre conventions and discipline-specific values and ways of knowing visible to students. All of the dimensions that we discuss are valued across disciplines, but students may benefit from understanding how and why differences emerge. For example, it may be beneficial to make explicit to students why writing in biology involves a different kind of reasoning in the introduction than writing in chemistry, and how writing in chemistry builds that same kind of reasoning into the discussion. Instruction, whether occurring in writing studios or in writing courses to facilitate thesis preparation, may be more effective if it attends to disciplinary-specific as well as general elements of genre conventions, and the findings presented here lend empirical weight to conventional wisdom about how to discuss such genre conventions. We can only speculate about how effective these educational practices would be, but evidence suggests that they are worthy of investigation. Additionally, as our findings suggest that students' undergraduate honors theses reflect differences in disciplinary values and ways of knowing, the next step could be to conduct an analogous investigation of professional writing in these disciplines. Understanding if and how these patterns change as students become professionals (or, how professionals differ in their teaching of disciplinary writing and their practice of it) may shed further light on the development of scientists through writing.

The current study provides support for a quantitative method of genre analyses, TAP, that complements Wolfe et al.'s (2015) qualitative delineation of genre dimensions, particularly in terms of conceptual lens and macrostructures to construct arguments. This work provides evidence that within the genre of the honors thesis, *scientific reasoning in writing* is more strongly associated with *formulating a compelling argument for the significance of the research in the context of current literature* in biology, *making meaning regarding the implications of the findings* in chemistry, and *providing an organizational framework for interpreting the thesis* in economics.

Notes

1. Among biology theses, as reported by Reynolds and colleagues (2009), the Pearson correlation coefficient between raters' independent total scores, in which ratings on individual dimensions were combined, was 0.72. When scores were binned as either mastery (5) or non-mastery, the joint probability of agreement for individual dimensions ranged from 76% to 90%, with kappa values from 0.41 to 0.67 (all $p < 0.01$). Among economics theses, as reported by Dowd, Connolly, and colleagues (2015), the Pearson correlation coefficient between raters' independent scores was 0.94 for total thesis scores and ranged from 0.64 to 0.96 for the nine distinct dimensions. Among chemistry theses, as reported

by Dowd, Roy, and colleagues (2015), the Pearson correlation coefficient between raters' independent scores was 0.81 for total thesis scores and ranged from 0.53 to 0.78 for the nine distinct dimensions.

2. The test of factorial invariance (χ^2) compares two models in terms of criteria for best fit: the invariant model, in which factor loadings must be equal across all disciplines, and the variant model, in which factor loadings can vary freely in each discipline. The invariant model constrains the system because values that could be optimized independently of one another in the variant model now must be equal to one another. If the added constraint worsens the overall fit of the model, the χ^2 statistic will be statistically significantly greater and we can say that the factor loadings in the two disciplines differ. If the χ^2 statistic is not statistically significantly greater, we can say that the factor loadings in the two disciplines do not differ.

3. The shorthand names for TAP dimensions referenced in Tables 2 and 3 (and also referenced in the text) differ from shorthand names used in previous publications. We changed the names to better emphasize the nature of each dimension, but we emphasize that nothing about the actual dimensions or how they were assessed has changed.

4. In prior work, the differences between sub-groups within each discipline (students who participated in a specific intervention and students who did not) were investigated; those sub-groups are pooled together in both Table 2 and all of the analyses presented in this work.

5. Statistical analyses motivating the interpretation of some differences as being meaningful include both exploratory factor analyses of multiple bootstrapped samples from the data sets (which allows for comparison of confidence intervals for factor loadings) and confirmatory factor analyses in which only specific dimensions (as opposed to all dimensions) are constrained to be invariant. These analyses are not presented in this work, but they are available upon request.

6. We compared the underlying factor from biology theses at Duke University to that from biology theses collected at University of Minnesota between 2013 and 2015 to determine if the former was representative of biology as a discipline. Using the test of factorial invariance discussed in this work, we found that the factors are not statistically significantly different from one another. This supports our argument, although the support is certainly limited.

References

Carter, M. (2007). Ways of knowing, doing, and writing in the disciplines. *College Composition and Communication*, 58(3), 385–418.

Dowd, J. E., Connolly, M. P., Thompson, Jr., R. J., & Reynolds, J. A. (2015). Improved reasoning in undergraduate writing through structured workshops. *The Journal of Economic Education, 46*(1), 14–27. doi: 10.1080/00220485.2014.978924

Dowd, J. E., Roy, C. P., Thompson, Jr., R. J., & Reynolds, J. A. (2015). "On course" for supporting expanded participation and improving scientific reasoning in undergraduate thesis writing. *Journal of Chemical Education, 92*(1), 39–45. doi: 10.1021/ed500298r

Herrington, A. J. (1981). Writing to learn: Writing across the disciplines. *College English, 43*(4), 379–87. doi: 10.2307/377126

Kalman, C. (2009). The need to emphasize epistemology in teaching and research. *Science & Education, 18*(3–4), 325–47. doi: 10.1007/s11191-007-9135-1

Kovac, J. (2003). Writing as thinking. *Annals of the New York Academy of Sciences, 988*(1), 233–38. doi: 10.1111/j.1749-6632.2003.tb06103.x

Machamer, P., Darden, L., & Craver, C. F. (2000). Thinking about mechanisms. *Philosophy of Science, 67*(1), 1–25.

Morgan, D. L. (2007). Paradigms lost and pragmatism regained: Methodological implications of combining qualitative and quantitative methods. *Journal of Mixed Methods Research, 1*(1), 48–76. doi: 10.1177/2345678906292462

Nussbaum, E. M., Sinatra, G. M., & Poliquin, A. (2008). Role of epistemic beliefs and scientific argumentation in science learning. *International Journal of Science Education, 30*(15), 1977–99. doi:10.1080/09500690701545919

Phillips, D. C., & Burbules, N. C. (2000). *Postpositivism and educational research.* Lanham, MD: Rowman & Littlefield.

Reynolds, J. A., Smith, R., Moskovitz, C., & Sayle, A. (2009). BioTAP: A systematic approach to teaching scientific writing and evaluating undergraduate theses. *BioScience, 59*(10), 896–903. doi: 10.1525/bio.2009.59.10.11

Reynolds, J. A., & Thompson, R. J. (2011). Want to improve undergraduate thesis writing?: Engage students and their faculty readers in scientific peer review. *CBE-Life Sciences Education, 10*(2), 209–15. doi:10.1187/cbe.10-10-0127

Robinson, M., Stoller, F., Costanza-Robinson, M., & Jones, J. K. (2008). *Write like a chemist: A guide and resource* (1st edition). Oxford, UK ; New York, NY: Oxford University Press.

Rudolph, J. L. (2000). Reconsidering the "nature of science" as a curriculum component. *Journal of Curriculum Studies, 32*(3), 403–419. doi:10.1080/002202700182628

Russ, R. S. (2014). Epistemology of science vs. epistemology for science. *Science Education, 98*(3), 388–96. doi: 10.1002/sce.21106

Russell, D. R. (1997). Writing to learn to do: WAC, WAW, WAW—Wow! *Language and Learning Across the Disciplines, 2*(2), 3–8.

Thagard, P. (2006). Conceptual change. In *Encyclopedia of cognitive science.* John Wiley & Sons, Ltd. Retrieved from http://onlinelibrary.wiley.com/doi/10.1002/0470018860.s00500/abstract

Van Dijk, E. M. (2014). Understanding the heterogeneous nature of science: A comprehensive notion of PCK for scientific literacy. *Science Education, 98*(3), 397–411. doi: 10.1002/sce.21110

Wolfe, J., Olson, B., & Wilder, L. (2015). Knowing what we know about writing in the disciplines: A new approach to teaching for transfer in FYC. *The WAC Journal, 25,* 42–77.

Investigating the Ontology of WAC/WID Relationships: A Gender-Based Analysis of Cross-Disciplinary Collaboration among Faculty

SANDRA L. TARABOCHIA

Introduction

Cross-disciplinary relationships among faculty are the cornerstone of writing across the curriculum (WAC) / writing in the disciplines (WID) (Bazerman et al., 2005; Russell, 2002; Condon & Rutz, 2012). Yet relationship building across disciplines often remains difficult to do (Soliday, 2011; McConlogue, Mitchell, & Peake, 2012; Lillis & Rai, 2011; Paretti et al., 2009; Paretti & Powell, 2009). According to Marie Paretti (2011), to enhance relationship-building efforts in WAC/WID contexts, we need a better understanding of "the ontology" or "way of being" of collaborations among writing specialists and disciplinary content experts. While flexible theories are essential for "describing and enacting this work,"[1] Paretti (2011) reminds us that "larger macro structures—departmental, institutional, and cultural—impinge powerfully on" cross-disciplinary collaborations in ways that can "engage or destroy" any theoretical framework.

To shed light on the ontology of WAC/WID interactions, this article explores the effects of a particular macrostructure—gender—on interactions between a writing specialist and a political science professor.[2] Gender is an especially important dimension around which to study cross-curricular literacy (CCL)[3] work because gender dynamics, which impact all interpersonal exchanges, are further complicated in cross-disciplinary efforts wherein participants' professional identities are rooted in disciplinary gender regimes.[4] Complex gender dynamics affect the strategies disciplinary faculty can use to teach writing as well as enable and constrain cross-disciplinary relationships among faculty. Yet, gender has be systematically examined as a macrostructure shaping cross-disciplinary relational dynamics. As a result, writing specialists don't always take gender forces into account when deciding what and how to communicate with disciplinary faculty about (teaching) writing.

The gap is surprising given that composition and rhetoric has a rich history of gender-based research on (teaching and learning) writing (Flynn, 1988; Caywood & Overing, 1987; Phelps & Emig, 1995). In particular, technical communication research examines the role of gender in producing and consuming texts and teaching writing with technology (Hawisher & Sullivan, 1998, 1999; Hawisher & Selfe, 2003; Pagnucci & Mauriello, 1999; Rickly, 1999; Haas, Tulley, & Blair, 2002; LeCourt & Barnes, 1999). Although gender is not necessarily a focus of WAC/WID scholarship, scholars do acknowledge the implications of disciplinary discourse and professional identity for how we understand and teach writing (Dannels, 2000; Poe et al., 2010). In that vein, WAC/WID researchers have engaged issues of racial identity (Young & Condon, 2013), cultural and linguistic identity (Cox & Zawacki, 2011), and professional and disciplinary identities (Poe et al., 2010). While such rich identity-based research may seem to lead logically to the investigation of gender issues in WAC/WID contexts, by and large such has not been the case. Despite important critiques of the WAC enterprise based on feminist principles (LeCourt, 1996; Malinowitz, 1997) there is work to be done when it comes to bringing gender-critical lenses to bear on practice-based research in WAC/WID. Toward that end, this article presents a case study of cross-disciplinary interaction between Bill, a writing specialist, and Lena, a political science professor in order to investigate the following questions[5]:

- How do gender dynamics come to bear on WAC/WID relationships among writing specialists and faculty in other disciplines?
- How do disciplinary cultures inform faculty gender roles and identities in ways that enable or constrain cross-disciplinary conversations about teaching writing?
- How might awareness of how gender ideologies shape and are shaped through cross-disciplinary conversations improve faculty interactions in WAC/WID contexts?

Theoretical Framework: Gender and Disciplinary Culture

Navigating disciplinary differences is at the heart of WAC/WID work. Writing specialists recognize that academic disciplines produce particular "images of reality," providing a "cultural system" and a sense of professional identity for academics who associate with them (Klein, 1990, p. 104; Klein, qtd. in Strober, 2011, p. 13). We accept that disciplinary cultures profoundly impact the nature and potential of cross-disciplinary communication and collaboration (Klein, 1996; Lamont, 2009). We do our best to contend with "the power of disciplinary habits of mind and disciplinary cultures in impeding conversation across disciplines" (Strober, 2011, p. 49). Our professional literature offers strategies for scaffolding workshops and conversations about (teaching) writing that take disciplinary differences into account (for example, Jablonski, 2006; Anson, 2002; Soliday, 2011). However, we are often less attentive to how gender factors into disciplinary discourses and cultures to impact cross-disciplinary work.

Applying a gender-critical lens to theories of disciplinary difference foregrounds the importance of gender in WAC/WID contexts. Becher and Trowler (2001) argue that "gender plays a vital part" in "conditioning the shape" of "internal divisions of power, status, and labour" within disciplines (p. 54). That is, gender infuses the makeup of disciplinary discourse communities and relationships among community members. Moreover, gender does not "impinge on tribal cultures in an unalloyed way" (p. 55); disciplinary cultures also shape how gender operates. Tacit assumptions at the heart of disciplines "often involve taken-for-granted ideas about gender identities" (p. 55).[6] That is, individual disciplines tend to be perceived as masculine or feminine. The categorical lines depend on internal and external factors including local contexts, disciplines such as engineering, physics, chemistry, and math are often considered masculine, while English, biology, and psychology are often considered feminine (Abouchedid & Nasser, 2000; Archer & Freedman, 1989). These perceptions shape how faculty members experience their disciplinary cultures and how they understand their own professional identities in relation to their colleagues from other disciplinary areas. A growing body of literature reinforces the notion that disciplinary work is not only a matter of taking on a professional identity, but a gender identity as well.[7] This reality has important implications for WAC/WID practitioners and others seeking to foster cross-disciplinary collaboration.

Research Methodology

The case study I report on here is part of a larger research project in which I examined cross-disciplinary conversations about teaching writing to determine how faculty can engage more productively in such exchanges. For that project, I adapted Karen Tracy's (1997, 2005) Action Implicative Discourse Analysis (AIDA) as a theory and method for studying institutional talk in interaction, focusing on how talk among writing specialists and faculty in other disciplines constructs relationships among people, disciplines, and institutions (Black, 1998, p. 20). I collected data from five participant groups, each including at least one writing specialist and at least one disciplinary content expert, from four different post-secondary institutions. Each group submitted audio and video recordings of at least two face-to-face conversations about teaching writing over the course of a semester. In addition, I conducted at least two interviews with each participant, drawing on initial analysis of recordings to develop semi-structured interview questions. In this article, I focus on interview data collected from Bill and Lena, the only group consisting of a male writing specialist and a female faculty member.[8]

Data Analysis

Analysis of over 180 pages of transcripts from interviews with Bill and Lena took place iteratively over time. In the spirit of AIDA, I treat interview data as "metadiscourse about [Bill and Lena's] interactive occasion[s]." I do not take participants' comments "as straightforward descriptions of the 'way things [were],'" but rather interpret comments "in light of implicit evaluations conveyed" (Tracy, 1997, p. 16).[9] Adapting methods from constructivist grounded theory (Charmaz, 2006), I initially used line-by-line coding to analyze several transcripts. Using a recursive process of memoing and reading widely, I articulated patterns, processes, and points of interest. With Bill and Lena, questions about how disciplinary discourses shape and are shaped by gender and gender dynamics in cross-disciplinary conversations informed my interview questions and recursive data analysis from the beginning. I use a gender-informed theory of disciplinary difference to investigate how disciplinary culture(s) shaped their gender identities and how those identities enabled and constrained their cross-disciplinary collaboration.

The concept of dual identity is particularly useful in analyzing how Bill and Lena negotiate their gendered disciplinary identities in conversation. Rooted in social psychology, the concept of dual identity refers to a state in which a person associates (to varying degrees) with both majority communities and minority communities in a given context. I chose a dual identity frame, as opposed to multiple (see for example Jones & McEwen, 2000) or intersectional identity (Crenshaw, 1989) theories that examine identity across several dimensions (often including race, class, and sexuality) because it allows me to focus on a particular intersectional dynamic—gender and discipline. Moreover, while intersectional theories tend to frame various axes of identity as "reinforcing vectors" (Nash, 2008) and multiple identity models explain individual identity development, dual identity suggests conflict and division among identity dimensions within a particular context.[10] As Fleischmann and Verkuyten (2015) suggest, dual identity can be an asset as well as a potential liability; I examine both possibilities in Bill and Lena's case as a way to explore how the phenomenon can enable and constrain cross-disciplinary interactions in CCL contexts.

Context

Bill and Lena taught at Northeast State College, a small public, master's granting institution in the United States serving approximately nine thousand undergraduates, including many first generation and non-traditional students.[11] At the time of the study, Northeast State's unofficial WAC program featured an interdisciplinary writing board that sponsored faculty development around the teaching of writing. In addition, a summer seminar for teaching writing (SSTW) was offered each year through the faculty center for teaching and learning (FCTL). Although Bill and Lena had been acquaintances for years, they worked closely together for the first time during the 2012 summer seminar, which Bill co-facilitated. Traditionally, facilitators had little contact with participants after the seminar. However, Bill, a newly appointed FCTL "teaching fellow" planned to use a course release to follow-up more consistently with several seminar participants, including Lena. During their meetings, Bill and Lena discussed challenges Lena faced incorporating concepts from the workshop into her courses. As my analysis will show, Bill and Lena's gender identities and dynamic both enriched and constrained their cross-disciplinary conversations about (teaching) writing.

Participants

Bill described himself as a straight, white man. At the time of the study, he was thirty-nine years old, had been at Northeast State College for four years, and was preparing his tenure and promotion materials. Bill holds a master's of teaching degree in English education and a doctorate in composition and rhetoric. His research investigates how people learn to write and the bridge between academic and workplace writing. He teaches a range of undergraduate writing and rhetoric courses including one on gender and masculinity. Bill had significant practical experience working with faculty on (teaching) writing, though he admitted the field of writing across the curriculum was a fledgling scholarly interest for which he had no professional training. "[H]onestly, I'm shooting from the hip," he told me, "I'm making it up as a I go." Nevertheless, in the "small pond" of Northeast State, Bill was one of few with relevant background and expertise to support WAC/WID efforts; he embraced the role because he was committed to improving teaching and learning.

Lena described herself as a straight, white female. At the time of the study she was in her late 40s, had been at Northeast State College for 6 years, and been tenured there for about a year. Lena earned an undergraduate degree in political science and journalism and a PhD in political science. Lena's scholarship focused on the human dimension of politics, including the media's role in political debates and the material impact on human lives within particular demographics. Lena taught courses in American government, global perspectives on politics and popular culture, and contemporary political controversy. Inspired by the SSTW, Lena sought to incorporate more writing in all of her courses and looked forward to Bill's advice and support in the process. Lena and Bill believed they shared goals and expectations as they embarked on their collaboration; they both judged their efforts a success. My analysis usefully complicates their perceptions by showing how resonances and asymmetries between their gendered professional identities both enabled and constrained their work.

Findings

Findings from this case study reveal that disciplinary "gender regimes" significantly shaped how Bill and Lena were socialized into their disciplinary cultures and local disciplinary communities. The professional identities they developed as a result of disciplinary socialization impacted their perceptions of one another in both beneficial and potentially problematic ways. In what follows, I examine similarities and differences in how Bill and Lena experienced the "dual identity" problem in their disciplinary contexts and show how those experiences came to bear on their cross-disciplinary work (Becher & Trowler, 2001).

"It Really Is about Power": Political Science and Lena's Dual Identity

Lena's experience of the dual identity problem was rooted in a conflict between her "feminine" values as a teacher and researcher and the "masculine" values undergirding political science as a conservative discipline focused on power. Lena explained it this way:

> I think Political Science is a conservative discipline in its nature and by that I don't mean politically conservative.... But, to me there's not real interest in people [chuckle] and there's not real interest in the things that I find interesting anymore and so it's all about institutions and if I had to do it again I'd probably go into sociology or English, you know? Writing, I don't know. I guess that goes to the kinds of people[...] but you have a lot people who are really into power. I mean, a lot of people go into political science, students even, it's... it really is about power. It's still a very male discipline, I find... both with students and with faculty.

As with many disciplines, men are overrepresented in political science and "the discipline's categories and methods were developed by privileged men to consider those issues of concern to them" (Celis et. al., 2013, p. 7; Tolleson-Rinehart & Carroll, 2006). The rise of the rational choice model "amplified other divisions" (e.g., between qualitative and quantitative researchers and between problem- versus method-driven research) that separated political science professionals along gendered lines (Lamont, 2009, p. 95). These divisions contributed to Lena's dual identity as she felt a disconnect between the human-centered research questions and methods that inspired her and the disciplinary value placed on "institutions," "hypothesis testing," and "generalizability."

Lena confronted the gender regime of political science in the classroom as well when students dismissed her "feminized" teaching strategies (such as journaling) as inappropriate for the disciplinary context. Lena explained:

> Yeah, and that [male dominance in the discipline] affects writing. I think it can affect the writing that you have students do. I once tried to have students keep a journal in my American Government class and oh, the guys just couldn't stand it, you know? One sentence or they wouldn't do it. So you really have to think about the kinds of students you get . . . in your discipline. They're not creative types. Or they . . . don't see themselves that way and it's really hard to do that [teaching writing the way you want to], especially when you feel there's not a lot of room for creativity.

Lena's attempt to use writing to tap into students' "creativity" met resistance from male students who perhaps perceived journal writing as a "symbolically soft" form of expression that didn't fit with their "hard" views of political science (Miller, 1991, p. 50). The fact that Lena was a *woman* assigning a "feminine" form of writing in a masculine disciplinary context quite possibly compounded their reaction.[12]

Lena's relationships with her male colleagues in the department also contributed to her dual identity problem. She explained how senior male colleagues regularly diminished her disciplinary expertise during conversations about politics or current events:

> I have a colleague who really likes to, I feel, [chuckle] lord his knowledge of everything under the sun over . . . over not just me, but others, and especially over women, I feel. And so, that makes me not even want to open my mouth about anything that has to do with politics. And I think that also, I've known a lot of men like that in the political science discipline. [. . .] They just seem to thrive on being super knowledgeable about all these things that—current events or whatever. And that makes you really not want to talk to them. If you feel like they're judging you because you don't know what happened in Italy last week, that kind of stuff [chuckle].

Lena felt her disciplinary expertise was on trial in conversations with male political science colleagues who were fixated on power, status, and knowing. She seems to associate the problematic power dynamic with her disciplinary colleagues in terms of both gender and the (gendered) discipline. "A lot of men . . . in the political science discipline," she says "lord knowledge . . . over women." On the contrary, she told me she felt confident in her disciplinary knowledge when talking with Bill, perhaps because they were from "two different disciplines." The fact that Lena was reluctant to talk about politics with male colleagues and attributed her comfort with Bill, at least in part, to their disciplinary differences, suggests that her interactions with male peers was another factor contributing to Lena's dual identity experience in political science.

As Becher and Trowler (2001) point out, local environments significantly shape the interplay of gender and disciplinary culture. In this case, Lena's experience of local disciplinary culture was not only destructive to her professional sense of self, but it also thwarted her ability to change the culture of teaching writing in the department.[13] She explained:

> We've had a class, I guess for at least ten years, that one of the folks at our department, who I think really does care about the students, and he wants them to be prepared, he created, because he was concerned about their writing abilities. I feel like maybe it's time to change how we look at it, and I don't feel comfortable suggesting that ... I've taught this class twice ... and I've just taught it like he taught it. I'm trying to figure out if I can get up the nerve to say, well, maybe I don't think we need to have them do this, but we should have them do that instead. I'm struggling with that myself, because not feeling comfortable adjusting for other things we may want to do.

Lena's struggle to find the courage to change a course long taught by a male colleague exemplifies another effect of the dual identity problem on WAC/WID efforts. Ultimately, her discipline's "gender regime" impacted Lena's confidence and sense of self-efficacy, constraining her efforts to develop writing pedagogy and curriculum.

"Such a Schoolboy Exercise": Bill's Dual-Identity Experience

Just as Lena's professional identity and approach to CCL work was shaped by her experience as a woman in a masculine discipline, Bill was influenced by his position as a man in a "feminized" discipline. Feminization—the "process by which the field of composition has become associated with feminine attributes and populated by the female gender"—carries both pejorative and potentially radical connotations (Holbrook, 1991, p. 201). On the one hand, composition is characterized as "women's work" in the worst sense of the term (Schell, 1992)—it suffers "lower prestige [and] is taken less seriously"; it "is characterized by a disproportionate number of women workers"; "it is service oriented"; "it pays less than 'men's work'"; and "it is devalued" (Enos, 1997, p. 558). On the other hand, composition is feminized in a positive sense as the woman-dominated field has historically sought "gender-balance" in research and teaching (Miller, 1991, p. 39) and often embraces teaching strategies aligned with feminist philosophies of identity and voice that are cooperative, relational, interdependent, caring, and joyful (Lauer, 1995, p. 280).[14] That is, even as composition remains "the gendered 'woman' of English departments" the "frequently noted characteristics of composition equally define it as an already-designated place for counterhegemonic intellectual politics" (Swearingen, 2006, pp. 543-44; Miller, 1991, p. 52). Nevertheless, despite potentially positive dimensions, most professionals "are caught in the web of gendered experience that has led to the devaluation of the field.... Both male and female teachers of writing have had trouble getting tenure, with salary compression, and respect" (Enos, 1996, p. 2).

Bill weathered the consequences of marginal disciplinary status. He described a particular experience of belittlement he faced when delivering his annual report to the university curriculum committee as director of the writing board:

> It's such a schoolboy exercise. I have to hand my report to the chair and then I have to say a few words about what's in the report. There's like twenty or thirty people in the room, including vice presidents and deans. And then I'm done. I have to show up for ten minutes and do a little song and dance for everyone.

Bill's reference to the "schoolboy exercise" that required "a little song and dance" indicates his experience of marginalization and disrespect. In addition to going through the motions of reporting to a committee that didn't seem to care about his professional work, Bill had to shoulder demeaning exchanges with faculty colleagues. He described one moment in particular:

> So, this social work professor just launches in, you know. . . Wow! [. . .] [J]ust like the classic spiel about subjects and verbs and [students] can't put together a sentence, and I know this guy and he used to be on our writing board. [. . .] He either didn't come to meetings or he never said a single word. He was just dialing it in. So, now, after having had that experience with him, he launches in a very public way and is demanding a response of me in front of all these people. Many of whom know me and know, like, "Oh, God, poor [Bill]. He's in this position," you know? And so, he just goes on and on and on, and at the end, I'm thinking, "This is [. . .] not the venue for this right now. This is a meeting of the university curriculum committee. Why are you doing this?" And so I just said, "I hear you. I hear what you are saying. Your comments are not atypical . . . I don't think anybody else really wants to hear about all this right now in this setting. I'll be happy to talk with you. Why don't we meet?" No. He wanted an answer and I owed him at least that. [. . .] Shit like that happens.

As Bill's anecdote illustrates, he was treated poorly, perhaps even humiliated, because of his colleagues' assumptions about the work of teaching writing. Part of his professional identity resonated with disciplinary marginalization.

At the same time, Bill has created opportunities to reclaim power and authority in the face of marginalization. Bill found a way to make the uncomfortable, potentially demeaning interaction described above a platform for teaching his colleagues, sharing his expertise, and arguing for his cause. Here's how Bill describes his typical response to the common criticism publicly voiced by the social work professor:

> We have a social mission at our school. We serve first-generation college population. Everybody knows this. [. . .] This is not a mystery and so, I will say: "We're at the intersection of this decade's-long debate about access and standards. And, these are the decisions we ought to make about providing access to students of different backgrounds, but then also maintaining some level of rigor and the standards and whatnot. [. . .] And you know what? I hear what you're saying. I experienced it myself. I don't have the answer for you. I'm going through the same problems that you're going through."

In Bill's response, he commiserates with his critic without losing face; he admits he doesn't have all the answers and reclaims some ground by turning the question back on the denigrator. In contrast to Lena's experience of being silenced by her colleagues, Bill performed proactive discursive strategies that demonstrate confidence and rhetorical control in response to professional subordination.

As this example suggests, and research echoes, despite suffering some effects of their association with a feminized discipline, men do not experience the negative consequences of dual identity as women do (Enos, 1996). In 2001, Becher and Trowler proposed men in feminized disciplines maintained relative "immunity from the 'dual identity' problem" because they still tended to hold leadership roles (p. 56). According to more recent data from the National Census of Writing, more women than men report directing writing programs (including first-year writing, WAC, and writing centers). Nevertheless, Becher and Trowler's (2001) argument remains relevant; while men holding leadership positions in feminine disciplines are not immune from dual identity issues, they likely experience the problem very differently than do women in traditionally masculine disciplines. Bill's choice to employ confident discursive strategies in the meeting did not "challenge widely available ideas about gender roles" in the same way Lena would have had she refused to remain silent in conversations with her disciplinary colleagues (Becher & Trowler, 2001, p. 56). Still, Bill's experience as a male in a feminized discipline shaped his professional identity. As someone confronted with gender daily he considered himself cognizant of and sensitive to gender issues. In an email response to an early draft of this article, Bill explained:

> As a male in the field of composition, it's impossible not to think about gender—I've been outnumbered by women in almost all of my professional endeavors in the field (from grad school to my current position). [. . .] I like to think that I'm further along when it comes to gender awareness than most men.

While Bill suffered drawbacks of working in a feminized field with marginal status, he valued the gender awareness his discipline cultivated. Moreover, as a man in a leadership role, he was able to navigate complicated interdisciplinary relational dynamics and negotiate power. As I'll show, Bill and Lena's professional identities, shaped by the gender regimes of their disciplines, intersected in both beneficial and problematic ways.

Gendered Professional Identities: Resonances and Asymmetries

Lena identified with Bill as a kindred spirit, a teacher who cared about students in a way other colleagues across the university didn't always seem to despite the fact that Northeast State College is a teaching-focused institution. "Everybody seems to just want to do their own thing," Lena told me. "There's been some attempt to talk more about the students' needs and where they're at but it hasn't been as important here as at other institutions that I've taught at. It's a little discouraging in a way because if everybody is doing their own thing for themselves . . . ." In contrast, Lena found Bill's student-centeredness, rooted in his disciplinary training, relatively rare and "refreshing":

> [H]e comes across as someone who is good, and who cares, and who really wants the students to learn. [. . .] I've always thought about how you try to construct assignments, and how you talk to students, and how you get them to think. He really takes this approach that I find refreshing, that he really seems student-centered. I guess that's also part of why I think that he's a good teacher.

Lena also valued Bill's interactional style. "Bill listens," Lena told me:

> [He] asked me questions and helped me, at least that's how I feel. I worked with another person a little bit—a great person, but I felt I was being more talked to. I think in [Bill's] case he's really good at getting you to think about what it is you're doing, not doing and how you might do it differently.

Bill's interactional strategies, even though he took on the "expert" role of writing specialist in the context of their WAC/WID collaboration, were very different from what Lena experienced working with male colleagues in her department. In short, Lena found in Bill a professional identity that resonated with the part of her own dual identity that felt disparaged in her disciplinary/department context.

Bill, too, sensed resonances between his professional identity and values and Lena's. He chose to work with her because she seemed "receptive" to the ideas he offered in the summer seminar, a sensibility he associated with her gender and her approach to teaching:

> I find the women generally are more receptive, I think, than men. Most of the people who have participated [in the summer seminar] . . . I think that may be four men, twenty women. I think part of the receptivity issue has to do with their sense of their role as a teacher, whether these things we're advocating, like having students get into groups and share their work, whether—that would just be one example—whether those seem doable to them, whether they're open to those things, or whether they just seem . . . I guess I shouldn't suggest [. . .] that women are all open to those kinds of practices. I have found, at least so far, that women have tended to be more [open], among the people I have worked with.

A reflective practitioner, Bill struggled with his sense that gender had something to do with the connection he felt with Lena. His comments illustrate his desire to resist generalizing or stereotyping. At the same time, he maintains his felt sense that Lena's gender and teaching identity contributed to her receptivity and their camaraderie.

While resonances between Bill and Lena's (gendered) professional identities strengthened their relationship, interview data from this case study also suggest that hidden asymmetries in their gender dynamic might have unexpectedly hindered their work. While Lena consistently praised Bill and appreciated their time together, she was hesitant to raise or return to certain issues when she thought she knew Bill's stance. For example, Lena spoke at length during an interview about how she struggled to balance content coverage with a writing-based approach to teaching in her discipline:

> [I]n my department there's kind of an expectation that we're gonna cover X, Y, and Z in an intro to American government class, it's even kind of in the course description. [. . .] So if your colleagues kind of expect this and you're doing something quite different, that makes me feel a little bit . . . uncomfortable; even though I have tenure I don't really have to worry about those things in some ways.

Lena's concern about coverage surely influenced how she interpreted and tried to implement strategies Bill suggested for teaching writing. However, Lena told me she was reluctant to spend time discussing her concerns with Bill:

> [I]n thinking about my conversations with [Bill] I never felt . . . I didn't know how to broach that topic like, "Really, what do you do, [Bill], when you feel like you have to get this across?" [. . .] Like, "[Bill], I really need you to tell me what do I sacrifice? You know, how do I . . ." [. . .] "Do I just assume that they're gonna read all this stuff on their own and get it if I'm cutting out X-number of days of . . . material?"

Despite her concerns, Lena chose not to discuss the challenge of covering content and teaching writing because philosophically she agreed with Bill that teaching students to think and engage content was more important that coverage. She felt compelled to enact the mentality.

> [Bill] firmly believes and I think I do too, is that, it's not just about the content, it's about how students learn to think and how students learn to find content, to use content and I do, I do agree with this, and I took that mentality into the classroom. [...] I did that in part because I felt that's almost what I had to do given my earlier conversations with Bill about how it's not so much the content.

Lena's disciplinary culture created tension between a writing teacher mentality and the reality of teaching political science in her department, but she couldn't explore those tensions with Bill: "Knowing that he felt that way maybe I didn't really push it more." As a result, Bill and Lena weren't able to problem solve the challenges of teaching writing in political science honestly and strategically. It is difficult to know if Lena would have felt more comfortable raising the issue if she'd been working with a (white) woman.[15] However, complicated gender dynamic probably at least contributed to the disconnect. That is, the intersection of Bill and Lena's (gendered) professional identities, the same identities that resonated with one another and bolstered their relationship, potentially fueled a power imbalance that led to missed opportunities in conversations about teaching writing.

Bill would likely have been surprised to learn about Lena's reluctance to share her concerns. From his perspective, any disproportion in their power dynamic favored Lena as tenured faculty member:

> [O]ur relationship was somewhat asymmetrical in the sense that a) she was senior to me, [and] b) she had been at Northeast State College longer than me. While it may not have come up or shown, I always did feel that asymmetricality on some level.

Bill's comments show how relational forces, such as institutional position, can intersect with gender to shape perceptions of relational dynamics in WAC/WID contexts. The fact that Bill acknowledged Lena's position as a senior colleague shaped his performance of expertise. It might have led him to treat Lena respectfully in ways her senior disciplinary colleagues, who were invested in performing their power and superiority, did not. At the same time, Bill's perception of Lena as more powerful (based on tenure and time at the institution) might have obscured how the intersection of their gendered disciplines and their unique gender dynamic actually silenced Lena in certain instances.

Discussion

Findings from this case study suggest that disciplinary gender regimes shape the classrooms and departments in which content experts attempt to develop and enact writing curricula and pedagogy. Moreover, it shows how faculty members constantly resist, remix, and/or accept professional gender identities inflected by their disciplinary cultures. To help faculty reflect on their objectives for student writing and explore appropriate curricular and pedagogical options, writing specialists must deliberately strive to recognize and account for gender in WAC/WID contexts. I focused on gender-different/discipline-different relationships, but complex gender dynamics impact gender-same/discipline-different interactions as well, as my larger study indicated. Many different identity positions shape CCL relationships and I've offered one example here. My case study suggests, however, that the more writing specialists anticipate the role of gender (and identity more broadly) in cross-disciplinary conversations with faculty and in teaching writing in disciplinary contexts, the better we can work with colleagues to develop writing curricula and pedagogies that address the intersecting dynamics at play in a given situation and meet the needs of teachers and students.

For example, if Bill had realized what gender-inflected challenges Lena faced in assigning journal writing, he might have helped her frame the journal assignment for students likely to resist "creative" writing assigned by a female professor. In a similar vein, recognizing how gender dynamics affected Lena's ability, as a woman, to change and develop writing curricula in her department might have allowed Bill to respond more directly to the material realities constraining her efforts. Bill did not initially acknowledge how the qualities he admired in Lena—receptivity to learning, dedication to teaching, and care for students—were marginalized in her department's disciplinary gender regime. Had he been more attuned to those dynamics, Bill might have been able to explicitly address them, perhaps by validating Lena's concern about content coverage while maintaining a shared commitment to teaching writing. Together, they could have creatively considered tenable ways to enact the philosophy in Lena's context. Bill might have helped get Lena's colleagues involved in the project or urged her to develop pedagogies and curricula for her own classes first rather than in the department-designated writing-intensive course. In short, attunement to Lena's (gendered) reality would have helped Bill more effectively support Lena's efforts in her classrooms and department.

Bill admitted that his failure to acknowledge the impact of disciplinary gender regimes on Lena's lived reality might have led to "naïve" teaching advice:

> My goal was to try to offer Lena a new way of thinking about teaching, a more hopeful way and an empowering way. But what I've learned is that you

can't compartmentalize. If she was feeling beaten down by her department and colleagues and even by the "ways of knowing and doing" in her discipline, then me suggesting that she try peer-group workshops wasn't really all that helpful. It was, in fact, sort of naïve.

As Bill makes clear, while writing specialists would do well to recognize faculty colleagues holistically as multifaceted teacher-learner-scholars, the pull to compartmentalize is strong given the realities of CCL work. Bill explained:

It wasn't until I read your article that I learned or was reminded that there was more of a backstory to Lena's situation than just her unhappiness with teaching. . . . [. . .] Or, maybe I did have a sense of the larger backstory of her professional discontent, and I just tried to bracket it off as something that was outside of my control and so not worth trying to address. What I could address was pedagogy, so that's what I tried to do. [. . .] I don't think I understood or tried to understand the depths of her overall professional unhappiness. Or, perhaps I sensed it but "didn't want to go there" because as an untenured faculty member just trying to lead a seminar on writing, it seemed like a bigger problem than I could handle. [. . .] Also, I am friends with her direct supervisor/department chair, so how much I may have wanted to know about whatever pain he was causing her (and my sense is that he may be a part of the problems she was experiencing) is also an open question. Politics, politics!

As an untenured faculty member, Bill understandably sensed the depth of the problem and feared it was more than he could handle. He felt constrained by institutional forces such as tenure and campus politics. For his own professional survival he wanted to help Lena without digging too deep.

Ultimately, however, writing specialists *can* respond to complicated gender dynamics despite challenges. For example, Bill might have drawn on the institutional knowledge writing consultants acquire to put Lena in touch with writing-friendly faculty in other departments so she could build a community of teachers and scholars who welcomed all aspects of her professional identity. By putting Lena in touch with other women from "masculine" disciplines or departments invested in writing curriculum and pedagogy, Bill could have acknowledged and addressed her predicament without becoming embroiled in departmental politics or risking tenure. No matter the response, the first step in accepting gender as a critical axis of consideration for WAC is for writing specialists to recognize the gendered "backstory" shaping our own and our colleagues' professional realities. Doing so positions us to make informed decisions about how best to accomplish the rich and varied ends of CCL work.

Conclusion

Disciplinary gender regimes continue to limit the ability of female faculty to maneuver as writers, researchers, and teachers. Leslie, Cimpian, Meyer, and Freeland (2015) found that "field-specific ability beliefs"—beliefs about what is required for success in disciplinary activities—"can account for the distribution of gender gaps across the entire academic spectrum" (p. 262). Women "may be less represented in 'brilliance-required' fields" and those who make it "may find the academic fields that emphasize such [fixed, innate] talent to be inhospitable" (p. 262). These gendered conditions significantly impact how writing specialists build, maintain, and assess CCL relationships. Consideration of how gender forces operate in disciplinary contexts and in cross-disciplinary conversations should inform our communicative choices, our approach to community and ally-building, and the standards we use to measure the outcomes of our efforts. While writing specialists expect and regularly navigate disciplinary differences in WAC/WID contexts, we tend to be less attuned to gender dynamics, even when we focus on gender as part of our teaching and scholarship (Mullin et al., 2008). When we are not attuned to gender, we are less likely to make conscious decisions about how best to communicate with colleagues in conversations about (teaching) writing and less likely to suggest curricular or pedagogical options that are tenable for faculty within the constraints of disciplinary gender regimes and departmental contexts. As WAC/WID initiatives rapidly evolve in response to shifting educational climates, failing to make gender a "critical category" of consideration restricts writing specialists' understanding of the work we do and limits our ability to initiate and sustain cross-disciplinary relationships (Lutes, 2009, p. 247).

Case studies like this one mark an important step toward recognizing gender as a powerful force impacting CCL interactions. Findings suggest the need to make gender-based research more visible in the field. Future research might offer comparative case studies that consider asymmetrical power relations in CCL conversations between two women or two men. Researchers might trace discursive patterns across cases, noting similarities and differences in use and effect. Future research must also seek to build a more capacious view of gender that respects and explores the effects of non-binary gender diversity in WAC/WID contexts. As the National Census of Writing illustrates, writing specialists identify outside the man/woman binary and/or as LGBTQ. Pieces like Eric Anthony Grollman's (2016) in *Inside Higher Ed* attest to the unique challenges faced by queer faculty as well as how gender intersects with identity dimensions such as race and sexuality to negatively shape experiences of faculty from underrepresented groups. We need to study how the lived realities of faculty members can and should shape the nature and purpose of CCL work. More gender-critical WAC research is needed to highlight the "fault lines of gender that run unexamined beneath" day-to-day faculty interactions and to construct a more nuanced understanding of the ontology of these interactions (Lutes, 2002, p. 246). Only by cultivating a reflective awareness of how gender inflects WAC/WID discourse and practice, can writing specialists learn to recognize manifestations in our daily work and act purposefully to sponsor more meaningful cross-disciplinary interactions.

Notes

1. I've recently suggested pedagogy as a potential framework for faculty engaged in cross-disciplinary work around teaching writing (Tarabochia, 2013).

2. I employ a binary gender framework (man/woman, masculine/feminine) here because disciplines tend to demonstrate and enact this binary. However, I recognize the diversity of gender and hope this project is a first step toward highlighting non-binary gender diversity in the context of WAC/WID work.

3. Taking my cue from Jeffrey Jablonski (2006), who draws on David Russell, I use cross-curricular literacy work as an umbrella term that encompasses a range of initiatives geared toward literacy learning across the curriculum (including writing across the curriculum, writing in the disciplines, communication across the curriculum, etc.).

4. See Becher and Trowler (2001) for more about the role of gender regimes in disciplinary cultures (pp. 54–55).

5. Bill and Lena are pseudonyms.

6. Becher and Trowler draw on Kim Thomas's (1990) examination of the relationship between how students and instructors construct English and physics and social constructions of gender.

7. Becher and Trowler (2001) cite several telling accounts rendered in British educational journals. More recently, research sheds light on women's experiences negotiating professional and gender identities in American educational institutions particularly in the context of "masculine" disciplines such as science and engineering (see, for example, Jorgenson, 2002; Rhoton, 2011).

8. While my larger study included male/male and female/female participant groups as well, I chose to focus on one case study in order to capture the detail necessary for a nuanced gender-based analysis. Bill and Lena are cisgender individuals.

9. For example, when Lena tells me she appreciates Bill's interaction style, that she feels he really listens to her, I don't necessarily conclude that Bill is a good listener. I value Lena's description of her experience *and* consider her perception of Bill in relation to her experience (as she describes it) interacting with senior male colleagues in her department.

10. I associate the dual identity phenomenon with Pronin et al.'s (2004) notion of identity bifurcation wherein a victim of stereotype threat is able to selectively disidentify

with dimensions of the threatening domain and/or with aspects of her in-group that are criticized in the domain (p. 153).

11. The name of the institution has been changed to protect participants' privacy.

12. Papoulis (1990) situates the view—that narrative, personal types of writing are elementary and less intellectually challenging than expository, abstract forms of writing—within broader female-male binaries.

13. According to Laura Brady, "Personal experience is one interpretation of an event, shaped by a subject's positioning and type of agency; it should invite discussion and analysis of the conditions that construct both the event and the narrative" (qtd. in Lutes, 2009, p. 242). In that spirit, I treat Lena's description of her experience as one possible reality and a piece of data relevant for understanding the professional identity she carried in her interactions with Bill.

14. Lauer (1995) points out how the nature and value of "feminine" teaching strategies are complicated by feminist scholars who question the extent to which they support feminist values. For example, see Schell's (1998) argument that feminist teaching strategies contribute to the marginalization and exploitation of contingent writing teachers, who are most often women.

15. An exchange from my larger study between two middle-aged white women stands out in this regard. A speech pathology professor purposely raised the issue of passive voice, explaining that while she knew writing specialists favored active voice, she saw rhetorical and epistemological reasons to use passive voice in disciplinary genres. The point led to a rich discussion about disciplinary writing conventions. Again, I cannot claim that their gender-same dynamic allowed for the exchange, but the difference between this discussion among women and the lack of discussion between Lena and Bill seems telling.

References

Abouchedid, K., & Nasser, R. (2000). External and internal social barriers in stereotyping university majors. *Current Research in Social Psychology, 5*(9), n.pag. Retrieved from http://www.uiowa.edu/crisp/volume-5-issue-9-april-10-2000

Anson, C. M. (2002). *The WAC casebook: scenes for faculty reflection and program development*. New York, NY: Oxford University Press.

Archer, J., & Freedman, S. (1989). Gender-stereotypic perceptions of academic disciplines. *British Journal of Educational Psychology, 59*, 306–13.

Bazerman, C., Little, J., Bethel, L., Chavkin, T., Fouquette, D., & Garufis, J. (2005). *Reference guide to writing across the curriculum*. West Lafayette, IN: Parlor Press.

Becher, T., & Trowler, P. R. (2001). *Academic tribes and territories: Intellectual enquiry and the culture of disciplines* (2nd ed.). The society for research into higher education. Philadelphia, PA: SRHE and Open University Press.

Black, L. J. (1998). *Between talk and teaching: Reconsidering the writing conference.* Logan, Utah: Utah State University Press.

Caywood, C. L., & Overing, G. R. (1987). *Teaching writing: pedagogy, gender, and equity.* Albany, NY: State University of New York Press.

Celis, K., Kantola, J., Waylen, G., & Weldon, S. L. (2013). Gender and politics: A gendered world, a gendered discipline. In G. Waylen, K. Celis, J. Kantola, & S. L. Weldon (Eds.), *The Oxford handbook of gender and politics* (pp. 1–26). New York, NY: Oxford University Press.

Charmaz, K. (2006). *Constructing grounded theory: A practical guide through qualitative Analysis.* London, UK: SAGE.

Condon, W., & Rutz, C. (2012). A taxonomy of writing across the curriculum programs: Evolving to serve broader agendas. *College Composition and Communication, 64*(2), 357–82.

Cox, M., & Zawacki, T. M. (Eds.). (2011, December 21). WAC and second language writing: Cross-field research, theory, and program development [Special Issue]. *Across the Disciplines, 8*(4). Retrieved from http://wac.colostate.edu/atd/ell/index.cfm

Crenshaw, K. (1989). Demarginalizing the intersection of race and sex: A black feminist critique of antidiscrimination doctrine, feminist theory and antiracist politics. *University of Chicago Legal Forum, 1989*(1), 139–67.

Dannels, D. P. (2000). Learning to be professional: Technical classroom discourse, practice, and professional identity construction. *Journal of Business and Technical Communication, 14*(1), 5–37.

Enos, Theresa. (1996). *Gender roles and faculty lives in rhetoric and composition.* Carbondale, IL: Southern Illinois University Press.

Enos, Theresa. (1997). Gender and publishing scholarship in rhetoric and composition. In G. Olson & T. Taylor (Eds.), *Publishing in rhetoric and composition* (pp. 57–74). Albany, NY: State University of New York Press. (Reprinted in *Feminism and composition: A critical sourcebook,* pp. 558–72, Ed. by G. Kirsch, F. S.Maor, L. Massey, L. Nickoson-Massey, & M. Sheridan-Rabideau, 2003. New York, NY: Bedford/St. Martin's).

Fleischmann, F., & Verkuyten, M. (2015). Dual identity among immigrants: Comparing different conceptualizations, their measurements, and implications. *Cultural Diversity and Ethnic Minority Psychology.* Advance online publication. doi: 10.1037/cdp0000058

Fingerhut, Adam W., Peplau, L. A., & Ghavami, N. (2005). A dual-identity framework for understanding lesbian experience. *Psychology of Women Quarterly, 29,* 129–39.

Flynn, E. A. (1988). Composing as a woman. *College Composition and Communication, 39*(4), 423–35. doi: 10.2307/357697

Grollman, E. A. (2016). The importance of being authentic in academe. *Inside Higher Ed.* Retrieved from https://www.insidehighered.com/advice/2016/04/08/importance-being-authentic-academe-essay

Haas, A., Tulley, C., & Blair, K. (2002). Mentors versus masters: Women's and girls' narratives of (re)negotiation in web-based writing spaces. *Computers and Composition, 19*(3), 231–49. doi: 10.1016/S8755-4615(02)00128-7

Hawisher, G. E., & Selfe, C. L.. Teaching writing at a distance: What's gender got to go with it?" In P. Takayoshi & B. Huot (Eds.), *Teaching writing with computers: An introduction.* (pp. 128–49). Boston, MA: Houghton Mifflin.

Hawisher, G. E., & Sullivan, P.A. (1998). Women on the network: Searching for e-spaces of their own. In S. C. Jarratt & L. Worsham (Eds.), *Feminism and composition: In other words* (pp. 172–97). New York, NY: Modern Language Association.

Hawisher, G. E., & Sullivan, P. A. (1999). Fleeting images: Women visually writing the web. In G. E. Hawisher & C. L. Selfe (Eds.), *Passions, pedagogies, and 21st century technologies.* (pp. 268–91). Logan, UT: Utah State University Press.

Holbrook, S. E. (1991). Women's work: The feminizing of composition. *Rhetoric Review, 9*(2), 201–29.

Jablonski, Jeffrey. (2006). *Academic writing consulting and WAC: Methods and models for guiding cross-curricular literacy work.* Research and Teaching in Rhetoric and Composition. Cresskill, NJ: Hampton.

Jones, S. R., & McEwen, M. K. (2000). A conceptual model of multiple dimensions of identity. *Journal of College Student Development, 41*(4), 405–14.

Jorgenson, J. (2002). Engineering selves. *Management Communication Quarterly, 15*(3), 350–80.

Klein, J. T. (1990). *Interdisciplinarity: History, theory, and practice.* Detroit, MI: Wayne State University Press.

Klein, J. T. (1996). *Crossing boundaries: Knowledge, disciplinarities, and interdisciplinarities.* Charlottesville, VA: University Press of Virginia.

Lamont, Michele. (2009). *How professors think: Inside the curious world of academic judgment.* Cambridge, MA: Harvard University Press.

Lauer, Janice M. (1995). The feminization of rhetoric and composition studies. *Rhetoric Review, 13*(2), 276–86.

LeCourt, Donna. (1996). WAC as critical pedagogy: The third stage?" *Journal of Advanced Composition, 16*(3), 389–405. (Reprinted in *Writing across the curriculum: A critical sourcebook*, pp. 69–84, Ed. by T.M. Zawacki and P. M. Rogers, 2012, Boston, MA: Bedford/St. Martin's).

LeCourt, D., & Barnes, L. (1999). Writing multiplicity: Hypertext and feminist textual politics. *Computers and Composition, 16*(1), 55–71. doi: 10.1016/S8755-4615(99)80005-X

Leslie, S. J., Cimpian, A., Meyer, M., & Freeland, E. (2015). Expectations of brilliance underlie gender distributions across academic disciplines. *Science, 347*(6219), 262–65. doi: 10.1126/science.1261375

Lillis, T., & Rai, L. (2011, October 8). A case study of a research-based collaboration around writing in social work. *Across the Disciplines, 8*(3). Retrieved from http://wac.colostate.edu/atd/clil/lillis-rai.cfm

Lutes, J. M. (2009). Why feminists make better tutors: Gender and disciplinary expertise in a curriculum-based tutoring program. In P. Gillespie, A. Gillam, L. F. Brown, & B. Stay (Eds.), *Writing center research: Extending the conversation* (pp. 235–57). New York, NY: Routledge.

Malinowitz, H. (1998). A feminist critique of writing in the disciplines. In S. C. Jarratt & L. Worsham (Eds.), *Feminism and composition: In other words* (pp. 291–312). New York, NY: Modern Language Association.

McConlogue, T., Mitchell, S., & Peake, K. (2012). Thinking writing at Queen Mary, University of London. In C. Thaiss, G. Bräuer, P. Carlino, L. Ganobcsik-Williams, & A. Sinha (Eds.), *Writing programs worldwide: Profiles of academic writing in many places*. Perspectives on Writing. (pp. 203–11) Fort Collins, CO: The WAC Clearinghouse and Parlor Press. Available from http://wac.colostate.edu/books/wrab2011/

Miller, Susan. (1991). The feminization of composition. In R. Bullock and J. Trimbur (Eds.), *The politics of writing instruction: Postsecondary* (pp.39–53). Portsmouth, NH: Heinemann.

Mullin, J., Schorn, S., Turner, T., Hertz, R., Davidson, D., & Baca, A. (2008, March 29). Challenging our practices, supporting our theories: Writing mentors as change agents across discourse communities [Special issue on Writing Fellows]. *Across the Disciplines, 5*. Retrieved from http://wac.colostate.edu/atd/fellows/mullin.cfm

National Census of Writing. (2013–2014). *Data-based landscape of writing instruction at two- and four-year public and not-for-profit institutions of higher education in the United States*. Retrieved from http://writingcensus.swarthmore.edu

Pagnucci, G. S., & Mauriello, N. (1999). The masquerade: Gender, identity, and writing for the web. *Computers and Composition, 16*(1), 141–51. doi: 10.1016/S8755-4615(99)80010-3

Paretti, M. (2011). Interdisciplinarity as a lens for theorizing language/content partnerships. *Across the Disciplines, 8*(3). Retrieved from http://wac.colostate.edu/atd/clil/paretti.cfm

Paretti, M., McNair, L., Belanger, K., & George, D. (2009). Reformist possibilities? Exploring writing program cross-campus partnerships. *WPA: Writing Program Administration, 33*(1–2), 74–113.

Paretti, M. C., & Powell, K. (2009). *Bringing voices together: Partnerships for assessing writing across contexts*. In M. C. Paretti & K. Powell (Eds.), *Assessment in writing* (Assessment in the disciplines, Vol. 4, 1–9). Tallahassee, TN: Association of Institutional Researchers.

Papoulis, Irene. (1990). "Personal narrative," "academic writing," and feminist theory: Reflections of a freshman composition teacher. *Composition Studies: Freshman English News, 18* (2), 9–12.

Phelps, L. W., & Emig, J. A. (Eds.). (1995). *Feminine principles and women's experience in American composition and rhetoric.* Pittsburgh, PA: University of Pittsburgh Press.

Poe, M., Lerner, N., & Craig, J. (2010). *Learning to communicate in science and engineering: Case studies from MIT.* Cambridge, MA: MIT Press.

Pronin, E., Steele, C. M., & Ross, L. (2004). Identity bifurcation in response to stereotype threat: Women and mathematics. *Journal of Experimental Social Psychology, 40*(2), 152–68. doi: 10.1016/S0022-1031(03)00088-X

Rhoton, L. A. (2011). Distancing as a gendered barrier: Understanding women scientists' gender practices. *Gender and Society, 25*(6), 696–716.

Rickly, R. (1999). The gender gap in computers and composition research: Must boys be boys? *Computers and Composition, 16*(1), 121–40. doi:10.1016/S8755-4615(99)80009-7

Russell, David R. (2002). *Writing in the academic disciplines: A curricular history* (2nd ed.). Carbondale, IL: Southern Illinois University Press.

Soliday, Mary. (2011). *Everyday genres: Writing assignments across the disciplines.* Studies in Writing and Rhetoric. Carbondale, IL: Southern Illinois University Press.

Schell, Eileen E. (1992). The feminization of composition: Questioning the metaphors that bind women teachers. *Composition Studies, 20*(1), 55–61.

Schell, Eileen E. (1998). The costs of caring: "Feminism" and contingent women works in composition studies. In S. C. Jarratt & L. Worsham (Eds.), *Feminism in composition studies: In other words.* (pp.74–93). New York, NY: Modern Language Association.

Strober, M.H. (2011). *Interdisciplinary conversations: Challenging habits of thought.* Stanford, CA: Stanford University Press.

Swearingen, C. J. (2006). Review essay: Feminisms and composition. *College Composition and Communication, 57*(3), 543–51.

Tarabochia, Sandra L. (2013). Negotiating expertise: A pedagogical framework for cross-curricular literacy work. *WPA: Writing Program Administration, 36*(2), 117–41.

Tolleson-Rinehart, S., & Carroll, S. J. (2006). "Far from Ideal:" The gender politics of political science. *The American Political Science Review, 100*(4), 507–13.

Tracy, K. (1997). *Colloquium: Dilemmas of academic discourse.* Advances in discourse processes. Norwood, NJ: Ablex.

Tracy, K. (2005). Reconstructing communicative practices: Action-implicative discourse analysis. In K. Fitch and R. Sanders (Eds.), *Handbook of language and social interaction* (pp. 301–18). Mahwah, NJ: Lawrence Erlbaum.

Young, V. A., & Condon, F. (2013, August 7). Introduction: Why anti-racist activism? Why now? *Across the Disciplines, 10*(3). Retrieved from http://wac.colostate.edu/atd/race/intro.cfm

Inviting Students to Determine for Themselves What It Means to Write Across the Disciplines

BRIAN HENDRICKSON AND GENEVIEVE GARCIA DE MUELLER

Introduction

Situated in the literature on threshold concepts and transfer of prior knowledge in WAC/WID and composition studies, with particular emphasis on the scholarship of writing across difference, our article explores the possibility of re-envisioning the role of the composition classroom within the broader literacy ecology of colleges and universities largely comprised of students from socioeconomically and ethnolinguistically underrepresented communities. We recount the pilot of a composition course prompting students to examine their own prior and other literacy values and practices, then transfer that growing meta-awareness to the critical acquisition of academic discourse. Our analysis of students' self-assessment memos reveals that students apply certain threshold concepts to acquire critical agency as academic writers, and in a manner consistent with Guerra's concept of transcultural repositioning. We further consider the role collective rubric development plays as a critical incident facilitating transcultural repositioning.

Course Rationale

Although it could be said that composition courses are designed to prepare students "to meet the demands of academic writing across the disciplines"—the description for our writing program's second-year, intermediate composition course—scholars in composition studies, and writing across the curriculum and in the disciplines (WAC/WID) more particularly, have questioned the capacity of composition courses to do just that.[1] Whereas J. Paul Johnson and Ethan Krase find that the first-year composition (FYC) classroom can help students transfer general argumentative skills to upper-division writing tasks, Natasha Artemeva and David R. Russell separately argue that the traditional FYC classroom cannot adequately simulate writing and learning contexts within particular academic disciplines. To better prepare students, scholars such as Linda S. Bergmann and Janet Zepernick, Amy Devitt, and Elizabeth Wardle ("Understanding") recommend a shift in composition pedagogy from teaching generalizable skill sets or particular genre conventions to sets of metacognitive strategies.

How specific those strategies are to particular disciplinary contexts is a matter of debate. Anne Beaufort argues that students develop general types of writing knowledge, but only over time and in particular disciplinary contexts. Likewise, Chris Thaiss and Terry Myers Zawacki suggest that students develop as writers in accordance with the idiosyncrasies of particular disciplines, but in generalizable developmental phases leading to metadisciplinary awareness. Linda Adler-Kassner and Elizabeth Wardle also contend that learning to write involves the acquisition and application of a cross-disciplinary set of threshold concepts, and Kathleen Blake Yancey, Lianne Robertson, and Kara Taczak observe that FYC courses foregrounding reflection and explicit instruction in threshold concepts from composition studies support students' transfer of writing knowledge and practices more effectively than those grounded in expressivism or cultural studies. Although they don't set out to study the role prior knowledge plays in transfer, Yancey, Robertson, and Taczak find that the role it does play is equally if not more important, as Mary Jo Reiff and Anis Bawarshi have previously demonstrated.

This recognition of the value of students' prior literacies aligns well with scholarship in WAC/WID that Juan C. Guerra refers to as "writing across difference," or work that urges WAC/WID scholars and practitioners to "acknowledge the value inherent in the full repertoire of linguistic, cultural, and semiotic resources students use in all their communities of belonging"; "encourage them to call on these as they best see fit"; and institute campus-wide initiatives like the "Writing Across Communities initiative that attempts to integrate the individual college classroom, the campus and our students' other communities of belonging" (x–xii). "Writing Across Communities" is the term Michelle Hall Kells coined for her grassroots approach to creating a WAC/WID initiative that operates as "a mechanism for transdisciplinary dialogue to demystify the ways we make and use knowledge across communities of practice" (94). Kells elaborates, "It is a process that must directly involve students themselves. Moreover, it is a process that should include consideration of the range of rhetorical resources influencing students' lives in and beyond the academy" (90).

Writing across difference seemed to us a particularly relevant and necessary concept for re-envisioning the function of our writing program's second-year, intermediate composition course within the larger literacy ecology of our flagship, land-grant, Hispanic-serving institution. We were concerned that our writing program had not adequately addressed how this course would help our particular student population, largely comprised of students from socioeconomically and ethnolinguistically underrepresented communities, "improve their writing skills to meet the demands of academic writing across the disciplines." The lack of any explicit attention in the course description to where our students were coming from, where they were going, and what literacies they were bringing with them, raised concerns for us similar to those expressed in Donna LeCourt's critique that WAC/WID has "forgotten the concern for alternative literacies and voices Other to the academy" (390). Drawing upon LeCourt's vision for a critical "third stage" in WAC/WID, Victor Villanueva suggests addressing the field's assimilationist tendencies through an antiracist critical pedagogy developed in partnership with scholars in other disciplines.

Twelve years after Villanueva, and seventeen after LeCourt, Mya Poe continues to call attention to "WAC's limited engagement with race," which Chris M. Anson contends is partly due to its focus on faculty development, and partly to a habit in composition studies writ large of treating "students as a generalized construct, not as individuals who bring specific histories, experiences, and 'vernacular literacies' to their learning" (23). For these reasons, and out of recognition of the local demographic context of our institution, we wanted our own course pilot to be more responsive to individual students' racial and linguistic identities. Our state consistently ranks at or near bottom in terms of overall youth well-being and chances at success (*2014 Kids Count* 21; "State Report Cards"). According to the US Census Bureau, 19.5% of the state's population lives below the poverty level. A minority-majority state, 47.3% of the population are Hispanic or Latino, 10.4% are American Indian or Alaska Native (39.4% are white alone), and 36% speak a language other than English at home. During the semester in which we piloted our course, our university's official enrollment report stated that 84% of the student body claimed original residence in state, so it is no surprise that the demographics of the undergraduate student body of 21,008 closely reflected those of the state as a whole: 43% Hispanic and 6.4% American Indian (38.3% white).[2] That the average undergraduate student age was 23.7 years old further suggests a large nontraditional undergraduate student population.

If one reason for designing our course pilot was to better attend to where our students came from and what they brought with them, the other was to better attend to where they were going. It's difficult, though, to define what it means "to meet the demands of academic writing across the disciplines" without the assistance of a WAC/WID program capable of more systematically documenting the ways that faculty assign writing across the disciplines. At the time of our study, the university benefited from a strong grassroots network of students, faculty, and administrators advocating for a WAC/WID program with an emphasis on writing across difference, but it operated largely outside official channels, including reporting lines and budgets. The university's college for undergraduate student success did partner with the English department's core writing program to offer linked courses, or learning communities (see Nowaceck; Wardle, "Can"; Zawacki and Williams), but those offerings didn't extend beyond the first year. And though several academic units required writing-intensive courses in their majors in response to the requirements of their own disciplinary accrediting bodies, the university offered no formal oversight or support in the form of a mandate for writing-intensive upper-division courses (see Townsend). The writing program therefore offered no upper-division courses in writing in the disciplines beyond those particular to its professional writing degree concentration.

It did, however, offer two second-year writing courses as part of the university's core curriculum. Our course pilot took place in a section of one of them, English 202: Expository Writing, with the following full description: "an intermediate writing course designed for students who have passed 101 and 102, and who wish to improve their writing skills to meet the demands of academic writing across the disciplines." 202 was one of four options students could choose from to fulfill the second-year, university-wide core writing and speaking requirement, the others being professional and technical writing (201), public speaking, and reasoning and critical thinking. Though several colleges within the university, including business and engineering, required 201, only the college of fine arts required 202.

202 was billed to prospective instructors, mostly graduate students in the English department, as focusing "on one content subject, selected by the instructor, for the length of the semester." Despite the breadth of possible themes implied here, the course titles rarely reflected disciplinary interests beyond literary or cultural studies, even though at the time of our study, more than two-thirds of our university's undergraduate students had declared majors outside the college of arts and sciences, in which humanities-related disciplines were housed. As Carol Severino and Mary Traschel point out, generalist versus discipline-specific notions of academic writing are often shaped by the disciplinary or institutional context in which a course or initiative takes shape, and within the context of our English department, 202 seemed to operate under the assumption that humanities-related notions of academic writing were generalizable across the disciplines. What's more, a student planning to pursue a major complementary to the focus of a particular section would not likely know to look for the section-specific description on the writing program's website; only the general course description was included on the registration site, further suggesting that the course should be beneficial to the student regardless of its focus or their choice of major.

But was that what we were saying, and if so, were we really offering a course that could fulfill that promise? Beneath the surface of this question were other questions central to WAC/WID: "What does it mean to learn to write and teach writing within and across particular disciplines?"; "What role should core writing courses play in preparing students for the writing challenges they will face in their upper-division coursework?"; and "How can writing programs and WAC/WID initiatives best account for a particular student body's learning goals and learning incomes?"

Course Design

Our pilot course section, "Reading and Writing Our Communities," sought to productively engage with questions of disciplinarity, transfer, and identity—and in ways that honored the WAC/WID language in the course description—by prompting students to examine how their own prior and other literacy values and practices shape and are shaped by the communities to which they already belonged, then encouraging them to transfer their growing meta-awareness of that dynamic to the critical acquisition of academic discourse, i.e., the task of answering for themselves what it means "to meet the demands of academic writing across the disciplines."

In distinguishing between the kinds of literacy outcomes programs/courses privilege, Thomas Deans identifies "writing about the community" courses as emphasizing "personal reflection, social analysis, and/or cultural critique . . . [and] tend[ing] to advance academic and critical literacy goals" (18). With a writing-about-the-community pedagogy in mind, our course description read as follows: "In this course, students will develop their own academic writing identities by considering how language, power, and identity influence how we read (are shaped by) and write (shape) our communities." Similarly, our outcomes emphasize academic and critical literacy goals met through personal reflection and cultural critique:

> By actively, collaboratively, and critically engaging with course readings, community-based research, and the writing process itself, students in this course will:
>
> - Gain a greater understanding of the complexity of issues related to language, power, and identity within their own communities;
> - Explore the strategies of community writing centers and other community literacy initiatives for acting as responsible agents of change;
> - Reflect on their own academic literacy practices by:
>   - o Analyzing and evaluating the moves made by academic writers in relevant selected readings and further scholarly research;
>   - o Collectively developing assessment criteria derived from that analysis and evaluation;
>   - o Applying criteria in peer and self assessment and in composing drafts of major writing assignments;
>   - o Assembling a portfolio including revised drafts of major writing assignments and an outcomes-based self-assessment memo.

Our sequence of assignments moved from a focus on the cultural, ethnic, linguistic, professional, religious, and/or other communities to which students already belonged to the academic community to which they wished to gain entry. In each assignment, we asked students to analyze how various aspects of literacy shape and are shaped by specific communities, then apply that same analytical framework to consider how they were working in the course to acquire academic literacies. For each assignment prompt, we provided students with a rhetorical situation. Their audience was always their peers, and their context an undergraduate academic journal; as an example, we provided our own institution's publication featuring the best essays written by students in courses across the curriculum.

For the first assignment, students were asked to choose as their subject "an artifact—textual, audio, image-based, or a combination thereof—that exemplifies a particular valuable, idiosyncratic, or even undesirable literacy practice in [their] own community." In this assignment, as with the latter two, students were required to collect analyzable data from the community in question in the form of field notes, interviews, recorded images, and other texts. The purpose of the first assignment was "to demonstrate that [the] artifact is an interestingly representative example of a particular literacy practice in [their] own community." This assignment aimed to give students the opportunity to develop an understanding of literacy as shaping and shaped by a community's attempts at self-representation and to prepare students for the next two assignments, which asked them to analyze "a literacy education practice in [their] own community" and the "values and beliefs about what 'good' academic writing is (and isn't)," respectively.

Our assignment prompts allowed students a wide berth to explore what literacy means to them and their own communities. Whereas for the first assignment some students looked at textual and digital literacy practices, such as Facebook and Twitter usage among their friends, others described local street art and billboard advertisements as literacy practices reflecting the values, discursive conventions, and power dynamics within the local community. One student even analyzed how her brother's Grateful Dead shirt functioned as a literacy practice signaling his status within the touring community.

Whereas the first assignment emphasized text collection as the primary research method, the second assignment asked students to conduct actual observations and interviews. We and our students were surprised to discover that most of them were often already involved in some kind of literacy education practice beyond the university, prompting assignments about crisis center training, online home brewing forums, tour guide services, youth ministries, and even rugby practice, where a student analyzed how the rules of the game shaped how he coached and the values players were expected to learn.

If the first two assignments were intended to be more analytical than critical, the third assignment invited students to apply what they had learned throughout the semester in a more evaluative fashion. One student made an argument for greater awareness of the instructional needs of second-language writers, and another for those of students with disabilities, with a special focus on mental illness. Yet another evaluated digital literacy practices like Twitter as tools for teaching and learning that challenge traditional notions of "good" academic writing.

For each assignment, students relied on readings in composition studies and related disciplines to formulate research questions and protocols that analyzed how language and literacy practices determined membership in particular communities and how community members determined their language and literacy practices. Keeping in mind the work of Thaiss and Zawacki on differences and overlaps between academic and alternative discourses, we chose readings that modeled a range of moves that academic and nonacademic writers make, including breaks with writing conventions, whereas readings often interrogated the relationship between language, power, identity, and status in a particular community. In that respect, our course design borrowed from Douglas Downs and Elizabeth Wardle's "Writing about Writing" (WAW) pedagogy, which urges compositionists to act "as if writing studies is a discipline with content knowledge to which students should be introduced, thereby changing their understandings about writing and thus changing the ways they write" (553). As Nancy Benson et al. note regarding their WAC/WID-influenced "Guide to Writing in the Majors" course revision, WAW doesn't just teach students to write like writing studies majors; it provides them with tools for learning about writing in other disciplines. In our own course pilot, WAW also provided tools for students to study nonacademic literacies, comparing them with the conventions found in course readings, and with the writing they were doing in their other coursework. In many respects, we used WAW in the same way that Joanna Wolfe, Barrie Olson, and Laura Wilder use what they term "Comparative Genre Analysis": with the hope that what transfers is not so much proficiency in conforming to particular writing conventions but awareness of how those conventions shape communities, and vice versa (45).

To encourage students to exercise agency in the acquisition of academic discourse, we integrated collective rubric development into our pilot course via Asao B. Inoue's community-based assessment pedagogy. Inoue provides a systematic account of collective rubric development as shifting the culminating emphasis from instructor evaluation to peer and self-assessment. The basic concept behind community-based assessment pedagogy is that students collectively develop rubrics that describe holistically what a proficient/adequate (not excellent) paragraph—and eventually position paper—should look like. The rubric evolves over time from a list of traits to categories of traits, and the language of the rubric evolves in complexity and explicitness as students apply it in peer assessment and collectively revise it during class discussion. Inoue stresses the difference between critique and assessment, coaching students to focus on potential, and focusing class time on discussing strategies for assessing peers and interpreting peer assessment, and he makes reflection on assessment an integral component of the process as well. To maintain the emphasis on peer assessment and not instructor evaluation, Inoue does not grade students on their assignments. Instead, he negotiates their grades with them during one-on-one end-of-semester portfolio conferences.

In our application of community-based assessment pedagogy, we asked students to summarize and reflect on course readings in which the authors examine literacy artifacts, then draw inferences regarding how the community "reads" and "writes" the artifact, i.e., shapes and is shaped by the literacy practices associated with the artifact, and class discussion consisted of comparing and contrasting a range of popular and academic readings and analyzing how and why different readings with similar purposes were written in different ways for different audiences. These exercises paved the way for students to work in teams on what Barbara Walvoord and Virginia Anderson call primary trait analysis, in which lists of traits evolve into categories of traits that eventually form the dimensions of a rubric (67). In our version of primary trait analysis, students identified key traits from the readings that they considered relevant to the assignment's genre and rhetorical situation, then grouped those traits into rubric categories. In performing this exercise, students were instructed not to employ superlatives but to use qualitative language to describe traits that perform the function expected of a document given its genre and rhetorical situation. Each team then posted their rubric drafts to a discussion forum on our online course site, then assessed other teams' rubrics, noting what traits and categories they would like to see included in the final rubric to be used collectively by the class. Based on commonalities across rubrics as well as students' assessment of rubrics, the teams' rubric drafts were compiled into a single course rubric to be refined during class discussion before and after the peer assessment process, in which students used the rubric to describe in memo format what they saw in at least two of their peers' first drafts. We then evaluated as a class the effectiveness of the rubric as a resource and guide for peer assessment, and we revised it accordingly before students used it again to write self-assessment memos addressed to the instructor as accompaniments to their revised second drafts. We repeated this process through the following two sequences, during which we adapted the previous rubric based on new and increasingly longer and more complex readings and writing assignments.

Some of the benefits of giving students greater agency over rubric creation and revision are apparent in the evolution of the rubric itself. The first combined rubric draft evidenced the complicated nature of accounting for seven different teams' interpretations of the genre and rhetorical situation, and the students objected to it as too wordy, impersonal, abstract, and stuffy. Take for example this trait from the rubric's "Introduction" section: "Establishes the document's rhetorical situation as described in the assignment guidelines, introducing the document's topic and purpose and the relevance between them and the document's audience." After being led through a class activity in which teams revised the rubric, then advocated for their revisions to the rest of the class, students decided on the following language: "Introduces your paper's subject, a literacy artifact, as well as your paper's purpose, and the relevance between your paper's literacy artifact, purpose, and audience."

Although the style in which the rubric was written grew simpler over time, its descriptions of genre conventions and the requisite rhetorical awareness grew in complexity. The first assignment's rubric ended up with four categories of traits: introduction, body, conclusion, and style. In the final version of its "Introduction" section, another trait read: "Explains terms and methods of analysis by referring to sources so that a general audience of your academic peers could understand." By the final draft of the third assignment's rubric, the students had decided to give that trait its own category labeled "Terms, Methods, and Literature Review" and revised it as follows: "Explains terms, methods, and scholarly context of research by referring to sources so that a general audience of your academic peers can identify what/whose conversation you're entering and what you plan to contribute to it." The changes in the second example evidence students' growing awareness of the rhetorically situated purpose of genre conventions specific to academic writing. By negotiating the terms of the rubrics that served to concretize these conventions, students gain a sense of academic discourse as evolving, malleable, and questionable.

This approach aligns with one of our underlying assumptions in designing "Reading and Writing Our Communities": that instructors cannot coach students in the critical acquisition of academic discourse while presenting them with unquestionable guidelines and rubrics, then grading them on how well or poorly their writing conforms. Our students did not therefore receive evaluations of their writing. Borrowing one of Kathleen Blake Yancey's reflective writing practices, instructor feedback took the form of a response memo that reinforced students' insights in their self-assessment memos and directed their attention to other aspects of their writing that they might not have considered in their self-assessments. Though students did receive occasional prescriptive feedback when struggling with more foundational problems, most feedback took the form of a request that the student explore in her next memo how she was attending to a particular problem. Often that request was more prescriptive of the memo itself than of the assignment to which it referred, pressing students to further develop their reflections, explaining in greater detail how and why they made particular choices. So although students did not receive evaluations of their writing, they did receive feedback that directed them in revising their drafts for inclusion in their final portfolios. The goal in withholding evaluation and directing prescriptive feedback only at the students' self-assessments and not at the primary writing assignments was to highlight the course's emphasis on developing students' awareness of how they made their choices and not necessarily the choices themselves, thereby carving out a space for students to critically reflect on their acquisition of academic discourse. This emphasis on assessing students' reflective writing also aligns with the first of what Susan H. McLeod and Eric Miraglia identify as WAC/WID's "two different but complementary pedagogical approaches . . . 'writing to learn' and 'writing to communicate,'" which they claim is a key feature of WAC/WID's success as a pedagogical change agent (5).

Because our writing program required a more thorough record than afforded by Inoue's approach to deferring grades until the end of the semester, we adapted Jane Danielewicz and Peter Elbow's contract model to fit programmatic constraints. We assigned full credit for all assignments submitted on time and meeting minimum requirements. If students met these two conditions on all assignments leading up to the final portfolio, they earned an 85% in the course, or a solid B. The remaining 15% was determined by the extent to which students demonstrated in their portfolio self-assessment memos critical engagement with their own writing in terms of the course outcomes, and we collectively developed as a class the final portfolio rubric that distinguished qualitatively between an excellent (15%), proficient (10%), sufficient (5%), and unacceptable (0%) portfolio memo.

Coding Portfolio Self-Assessment Memos

In coding students' portfolio self-assessment memos, we hoped to identify if, when, and how students articulated any threshold concepts that may have aided them in their learning. In their portfolio self-assessment memos, students were asked to first provide a brief, general assessment of their experience in the course, explaining how if at all the course influenced their own writing; their understanding of writing and/or literacy in general; and their understanding of academic writing and/or literacy in particular. For the remaining majority of each memo, students were asked to describe decisions they made while writing and/or revising each assignment, citing as evidence specific pages in drafts whenever possible, and explaining how and why they made those decisions in terms of whatever aspects of the course they deemed relevant.

Data analysis took place over eighteen hours and ten meetings, during which the two of us coded fourteen students' end-of-semester self-assessment memos. We approached our data analysis inductively, a process described by Catherine Marshall and Gretchen B. Rossman as one in which the researcher "identifies the salient, grounded categories of meaning" that "then become buckets or baskets into which segments of text are placed" (159). Throughout the process, we refined all categories and subcategories with an eye for internal convergence and external divergence, ensuring that in adding, revising, and dividing categories all remained "internally consistent but distinct from one another" (Marshall and Rossman 159).

At the first level of coding, we identified any passages in students' self-assessment memos where they explicitly discussed any element of the course that played a role in their learning. At the second level, we placed those passages into three major categories that emerged during rereading. The first major category was comprised of potential threshold concepts. Then we had to create a second major category just for references to rubrics, and a third for references to both concepts and rubrics. Although we were initially looking only for threshold concepts, the prevalence of rubric references led us to also pay attention in our analysis to the role that rubrics played in student learning.

At the third level of coding, we further divided the major categories, creating five concepts categories of academic research, academic writing, literacy, rhetorical situation, and reflection. These category labels were fairly superficial in that they didn't describe how students used each respective concept. But the level-three rubrics categories did go into greater detail regarding how students found rubrics useful: for defining terms, developing ideas, focusing inquiry, integrating sources, structuring an assignment, reflecting in general, and revising in general. We also came up with a level-three rubric utility category of collective development that we had to refine further in our level-four coding to identify how students described the utility of collective rubric development: as clarifying concepts, cultivating individual agency, and/or establishing collective investment and accountability.

Level-four coding likewise consisted of identifying five further subcategories through which we differentiated students' references to concepts categories. The subcategories noted instances wherein students discuss the utility of a particular major concept as *self-empowerment* as an end in and of itself; *hermeneutic*, or a process of inquiry and/or interpretation; *sociocultural*, or a way of understanding the socially constituted nature of language, identity, and agency, but without a demonstrated recognition of how that understanding gains the student access and/or agency; *access*, or a means of gaining access via greater agency, but without a demonstrated recognition of how that access and/or agency operates within a sociocultural understanding of the concept; and *transcultural*, or the need and/or ability to apply a sociocultural understanding to transition between discourse communities, i.e. the *access* and *sociocultural* subcategories combined.

In all cases, we strived to construct what Michael Quinn Patton calls "indigenous typologies," or categories and subcategories that evidence an explicit relationship between a concept or rubric reference and a claim about how it contributed to a student's learning (457). At times, however, we did have to discern implicit references to the rubric from the way a student might describe a class conversation that influenced her writing, which we knew was a conversation that emerged during and necessarily in relation to the collective development of a rubric. In other, murkier cases, a student might demonstrate an understanding of literacy as sociocultural in the way she explains decisions she made while writing, but without explicitly describing the concept, in which case we would discuss at length whether the student makes any reference elsewhere in the memo that demonstrates the influence of a course concept on that decision, or if the student's language and reasoning adequately reflects the way a concept was discussed and applied in the course.

Once we had refined all of our coding, we tabulated the number of students who referenced a concept/subcategory pairing as well as the number of instances of references within each concept/subcategory pairing, making sure to document the student's identifying number in each case so that we could maintain correspondence between our tabulations and other tables containing students' passages. We also tabulated the number of instances a concept/subcategory pairing was mentioned in conjunction with the rubric; the number of students who referenced each category of rubric utility, and the number of instances of those references; and the number of students who referenced a rubric utility category in conjunction with a concept/subcategory pairing. These tabulations provided us a clearer picture of which concept/subcategory pairings and rubric utility categories were referenced most frequently and by the most students, separately and together.

Of all the concept/subcategory pairings, students in "Reading and Writing Our Communities" most often demonstrated an understanding and application of the category of literacy, and within it the subcategories of literacy as hermeneutic, sociocultural, and transcultural, in that order. These pairings align with Beaufort's writing process and discourse community knowledge categories, as well as Adler-Kassner and Wardle's threshold concepts of writing as a continuous learning process, as a social and rhetorical activity, and as enactment and creation of identities and ideologies. In terms of categories and subcategories of rubric utility, students most often referred to the category of collective rubric development, and within it the subcategories of collective rubric development as clarifying concepts, establishing a sense of collective investment and accountability, and cultivating individual agency, in that order. Furthermore, of all the concept category/subcategory pairings, students most frequently referenced the rubric in relation to their understanding and application of literacy as sociocultural.

Students' Theories of Writing Knowledge

Identifying these concept category/subcategory pairings allowed us to further analyze the relationships students articulated between them, so that the pairings existed no longer as isolated coding categories but as what Yancey, Robertson, and Tacsak describe as the theories of writing knowledge students develop through reflective practice. One major trend we noticed in students' theories was an appreciation for the dialectical nature of literacy and learning. Take for instance Student Nine's explanation of collective rubric development as hermeneutic; in her case, this development involved an interpretation of and inquiry into not only an area of scholarship with which she was previously unfamiliar but also her own extant understanding of literacy as sociocultural, and in that respect the process of collective rubric development serves for Student Nine as one of "self-discovery":

> For major writing assignment one, I chose the petroglyphs as my literacy artifact, and I explained the conflict of the local Native Americans and suburban population fighting for the petroglyph land to illustrate the power struggle that may arise when different groups understand varying forms of literacy. At first, the prompt for this writing assignment was confusing because I didn't understand the connection between literacy, a community, and language. However . . . the discussions held in class were very open-ended, and this allowed my peers and I to ask questions to sort out our thoughts. . . . By listening to the in-class discussions, I became aware of other concerns that had arisen and thought more critically about the major writing assignment. Before the class discussions, I received the prompt and was confused because the wording of the rubric was lengthy. However, during class we discussed how to change the rubric in groups, and thinking about how I wanted to change the rubric was a form of self-discovery. For instance, when thinking about standards for the assignment, I discovered more about my own understanding of the topic, and what I needed to learn more about, and this helped me focus my attention on certain aspects to better my understanding.

Student Nine explores the ways in which collective rubric development helped her further develop the knowledge she already possessed about her topic, and in a way that helped her rethink how she was writing about it, which in turn helped her learn that much more about her topic.

The dialectical relationship Student Nine describes between collective rubric development, conceptual knowledge acquisition, and the writing process involves a movement from confusion to greater clarity, and in a manner increasing individual agency while simultaneously emphasizing the sociocultural nature of literacy. That movement appears to play an important role in students' accounts of how a sociocultural understanding of literacy enables them to transculturally reposition as academic writers. Although the theory of transcultural repositioning had informed our course design from the start, we didn't explicitly recognize it as an outcome or look for evidence of it in students' self-assessment memos, but in coding students' self-assessment memos, we recognized that the more striking examples conformed to Guerra's definition of the term. Guerra derives the term from Min-Zhan Lu's description of learning in basic writing as repositioning, or boundary crossing catalyzed by an encounter with conflict. For Guerra, transcultural repositioning describes how all students, but especially the socioeconomically and ethnolinguistically underrepresented, overcome cultural and linguistic obstacles by transferring their prior and other literacies to the critical acquisition of new literacies.

Lu's original emphasis on the function of conflict in repositioning aligns with our own findings, as we discovered that students described their own critical acquisition of academic discourse less in terms of an explicit transfer of prior and other rhetorical knowledge and practices and more as a gradual movement from an encounter with conflict through collective rubric development to an insight into the dialectical nature of literacy understood as sociocultural; and in that respect, the notion of transcultural repositioning provided us a framework through which to examine students' individual accounts of this more longitudinal, collective process. For example, Student Seven connects her emergent understanding of literacy as sociocultural with her ability to transculturally reposition:

> Overall this class was personally challenging and rewarding. I learned about what it means to be literate, as well as the power that being extensively literate holds, and pushed [sic] me to improve my own writing.
>
> Regarding literacy and academic writing, my understanding has changed in a profound way. I now understand that literacy is based on community discourse and that the discourse of a community affects the community discourse, somewhat like evolution. This realization has changed my views on my own writing as well; my writing affects those who read it, and my writing is affected by what I read. As time goes on, I see that my writing has the power to change the discourse of its subject, and that this power comes from credibility.

Again, Student Seven acknowledges that the class was "personally challenging," and without first developing an appreciation for discourse communities as sites of contention and flux, she admits that she wouldn't see her own writing as carrying any consequence. Her understanding and application of literacy as sociocultural allows her to claim ethos and agency in the discourse communities to which she wishes to belong. Although Student Seven doesn't mention collective rubric development in the above passage, she does mention elsewhere that the "group assignments"—i.e., collective rubric development—helped her and her group members better understand course concepts in general, suggesting that the activity likely did play an important role in her development of an understanding of literacy as sociocultural. The following passage from Student Five more explicitly connects collective rubric development with transcultural repositioning:

> I chose to analyze written communication in the workplace as a means of exploring what is defined within this certain community as "good" writing. Focusing on this form of writing allowed me to consider how determinations of "good" or "bad" writing are made and how there is a more complex dynamic that prohibits a universal definition of "good" writing.
>
> The overall activities of constructing and revising rubrics for this class seemed to be most applicable to thinking about this assignment because it made me realize that determining what qualifies as "good" writing can differ depending on the class and teacher. Working together to compose rubrics seemed to counteract this disparity and allowed us to be able to more critically engage in the writing process.

Student Five describes how collective rubric development enabled her to better appreciate academic writing as sociocultural and to exercise agency within the academic discourse community of the classroom, and she suggests that this academic literacy knowledge and practice contributed to her evolving understanding of workplace literacy knowledge and practice. Again, her description of this relationship is more dialectical than linear, offering a glimpse into how prior and other literacies, academic literacy, threshold concepts such as the sociocultural nature of literacy, and collective rubric development are synthesized for her into an understanding and performance of academic writing as neither immutable nor inaccessible. Interestingly, this knowledge and practice again appears to arise out of an encounter with conflict, in the case of Student Five, due to the ability to "counteract [the] disparity" she observes between what different teachers value as "good" writing across the disciplines.

Discussion

At the time of our study, both the writing program and university in question were undergoing significant changes, but as we write this, those changes have yet to lead to a new course description or set of outcomes for the second-year "Expository Writing" course, or an administratively supported campus-wide WAC/WID initiative. We originally set out to develop an approach that our writing program might use to better align the composition classroom with the demands of writing across the disciplines, and in a manner that empowered our students to take agency in determining what that means. However, our research offers implications of relevance beyond the successful revision of a single course at one particular institution, and beyond the composition classroom in general, for scholars and practitioners interested in exploring the possibilities of a writing across difference approach to WAC/WID.

Our analysis of students' self-assessment memos adds dimension to the definition of transcultural repositioning that we inherited from WAC/WID scholars Guerra and Kells in that we were able to observe students applying their understanding of literacy as sociocultural to the task of accessing critical agency as academic writers, suggesting that for our students, a sociocultural concept of literacy operated as a threshold concept in transcultural repositioning. This finding led us to reflect on how explicitly foregrounding the concept of literacy as sociocultural in the composition classroom might help us reframe that work as the facilitation of transcultural repositioning. It's possible that doing so might be more beneficial to certain student populations, and further research might observe the effects of explicitly foregrounding the concept of literacy as sociocultural across multiple course sections and with a larger sample population of students who self-identify as belonging to a socioeconomically and ethnolinguistically underrepresented community. Alternatively, researchers might provide a more longitudinal description of how the concept of literacy as sociocultural operates as a threshold concept facilitating transcultural repositioning throughout students' upper-division coursework.

Our research suggests that transcultural repositioning may be a valuable guiding principle for curriculum design at the course and programmatic level, and we hope that our efforts will encourage others to afford this concept the extensive scholarly attention it deserves. At the same time, not all students' self-assessment memos evidenced transcultural repositioning. More often, they evidenced students' emergent and preliminary recognition of literacy as sociocultural, or the related recognition of literacy as hermeneutic, i.e., an ongoing process of inquiry and interpretation. That an understanding of literacy as sociocultural was a necessary but not sufficient attribute of transcultural repositioning suggests that the latter may be a difficult though nevertheless rewarding outcome to aim for, if not an objective that every student should be expected to achieve.

As indicated by Lu's definition of repositioning, transcultural repositioning did not occur for our students without conflict, but the occurrence of conflict appears to indicate an intersection at which students' prior and other literacies, academic literacies, and the conceptual knowledge students gained from the course all collided, interacted, and were synthesized in a manner consistent with Yancey, Robertson, and Tacsak's description of the critical incident model of prior knowledge use, in which "students encounter an obstacle that helps them retheorize writing in general and their own agency as writers in particular" (5). The indeterminacy and deliberation involved in collective rubric development presented obstacles that ultimately appeared to help our students retheorize academic literacy and claim agency in the process of determining for themselves what it means "to meet the demands of academic writing across the disciplines." In other words, what we imagined would function as a simple form of empowerment also seemed to play an important role in students' acquisition of conceptual knowledge of writing and literacy.

Further research might look more explicitly at how collective rubric development functions as a critical incident in students' attempts at transcultural repositioning. But we might also consider the utility of collective rubric development in curriculum design at the course and programmatic level. What if, for instance, we had more explicitly invited our students into the collective activity of revising our course description and outcomes in accordance with students' actual learning outcomes (and incomes)? To do so would be to place Inoue's community-based assessment pedagogy into conversation with Bob Broad's organic assessment protocol, so that actual courses take the place of focus groups in the collective process of curriculum design. Resituated within the context of WAC/WID, such an approach harkens back to Kells's insistence on "a reconceptualization of WAC through a deliberative process that engages diversity and the discursive possibilities of representation" (90). In that respect, our pilot course design also adds dimension to what such a reconceptualization of WAC/WID might look like.

Acknowledgments

We'd like to thank Jill Jeffery and Todd Ruecker for mentoring us through the course design and IRB application process; Kyle Fiore and Chuck Paine for encouraging us to experiment with our course pilot; and *The WAC Journal* editor, Roy Andrews, and our anonymous reviewers for their generous and encouraging feedback.

Notes

1. We have withheld identifying information in accordance with our research protocol, using pseudonyms where appropriate.

2. We use these racial/ethnic labels to remain consistent with the sources of our demographic data.

References

The 2014 Kids Count Data Book. Annie E. Casey Foundation, 22 July 2014, http://www.aecf.org/m/resourcedoc/aecf-2014kidscountdatabook-2014.pdf.

Adler-Kassner, Linda, and Elizabeth Wardle, editors. *Naming What We Know: Threshold Concepts of Writing Studies.* Utah State UP, 2015.

Anson, Chris M. "Black Holes: Writing Across the Curriculum, Assessment, and the Gravitational Invisibility of Race." *Race and Writing Assessment*, edited by Asao B. Inoue and Mya Poe. Peter Lang, 2012, pp. 15–28.

Artemeva, Natasha. "A Time to Speak, a Time to Act: A Rhetorical Genre Analysis of a Novice Engineer's Calculated Risk Taking." *Journal of Business and Technical Communication*, vol. 19, no. 4, 2005, pp. 389–421. *SAGE*, doi: 10.1177/1050651905278309.

Beaufort, Anne. *College Writing and Beyond: A New Framework for University Writing Instruction*. Utah State UP, 2007.

Benson, Nancy, et al. "Rethinking First Year English as First Year Writing Across the Curriculum." *Double Helix: A Journal of Critical Thinking and Writing*, vol. 1, 2013, pp. 1–16. *Double Helix*, http://www.qudoublehelixjournal.org/index.php/dh/article/view/3/78.

Bergmann, Linda S., and Janet Zepernick. "Disciplinarity and Transfer: Students' Perceptions of Learning to Write." *WPA: Journal of the Council of Writing Program Administrators*, vol. 31, no. 1–2, 2007, pp. 124–49. *CWPA*, http://wpacouncil.org/archives/31n1-2/31n1-2bergmann-zepernick.pdf.

Broad, Bob. "Organic Matters: In Praise of Locally Grown Writing Assessment." *Organic Writing Assessment: Dynamic Criteria Mapping in Action*. Bob Broad, et al. Utah State UP, 2009, pp. 1–13.

Danielewicz, Jane, and Peter Elbow. "A Unilateral Grading Contract to Improve Learning and Teaching." *College Composition and Communication*, vol. 61, no. 2, 2009, pp. 244–68. *JSTOR*, http://www.jstor.org/stable/40593442.

Deans, Thomas. *Writing Partnerships: Service-Learning in Composition*. National Council of Teachers of English, 2000.

Devitt, Amy J. *Writing Genres*. Southern Illinois UP, 2004.

Downs, Douglas, and Elizabeth Wardle. "Teaching about Writing, Righting Misconceptions: (Re)envisioning 'First-Year Composition' as 'Introduction to Writing Studies.'" *College Composition and Communication*, vol. 58, no. 4, 2007, pp. 552–84. *JSTOR*, http://www.jstor.org/stable/20456966.

Guerra, Juan C. *Language, Culture, Identity, and Citizenship in College Classrooms and Communities*. Routledge / NCTE, 2016.

Inoue, Asao B. "Community-Based Assessment Pedagogy." *Assessing Writing*, vol. 9, 2005, pp. 208–38. *ScienceDirect*, doi:10.1016/j.asw.2004.12.001.

Johnson, J. Paul, and Ethan Krase. "Articulating Claims and Presenting Evidence: A Study of Twelve Student Writers, From First-Year Composition to Writing Across the Curriculum." *The WAC Journal*, vol. 23, 2012, pp. 31–48. *The WAC Journal*, http://wac.colostate.edu/journal/vol23/johnson.pdf.

Kells, Michelle Hall. "Writing Across Communities: Deliberation and the Discursive Possibilities of WAC." *Reflections: A Journal of Writing, Service-Learning, and Community Literacy*, vol. 6, no. 1, 2007, pp. 87–109.

LeCourt, Donna. "WAC as Critical Pedagogy: The Third Stage?" *JAC*, vol. 16, no. 3, 1996, pp. 389–405. *JSTOR*, https://www.jstor.org/stable/20866089.

Lu, Min-Zhan. "Writing as Repositioning." *Journal of Education*, vol. 172, no. 1, 1990, pp. 18–21.

---. "Conflict and Struggle: The Enemies or Preconditions of Basic Writing?" *College English*, vol. 54, no. 8, 1992, pp. 887–913. *JSTOR*, https://www.jstor.org/stable/378444.

Marshall, Catherine, and Gretchen B. Rossman. *Designing Qualitative Research*. 4th ed., Sage, 2006.

McLeod, Susan H., and Eric Miraglia. "Writing Across the Curriculum in a Time of Change." *WAC for the New Millennium: Strategies for Continuing Writing-Across-the-Curriculum Programs*, edited by Susan H. McLeod, Eric Miraglia, Margot Soven, and Christopher Thaiss. National Council of Teachers of English, 2001, pp. 1–27. *WAC Clearinghouse*, http://wac.colostate.edu/books/millennium/chapter1.pdf.

Nowacek, Rebecca S. *Agents of Integration: Understanding Transfer As a Rhetorical Act*. Southern Illinois UP/Conference on College Composition and Communication of the National Council of Teachers of English, 2011.

Patton, Michael Quinn. *Qualitative Research and Evaluation Methods*. 2nd ed., Sage, 1990.

Poe, Mya. "Re-framing Race in Teaching Writing Across the Curriculum." *Across the Disciplines*, vol. 10, no. 3, 2013. *WAC Clearinghouse*, http://wac.colostate.edu/atd/race/poe.cfm.

Reiff, Mary Jo, and Anis Bawarshi. "Tracing Discursive Resources: How Students Use Prior Genre Knowledge to Negotiate New Writing Contexts in First-Year Composition." *Written Communication*, vol. 28, no. 3, 2011, pp. 312–37. *SAGE*, doi: 10.1177/0741088311410183.

Russell, David R. "Activity Theory and Its Implications for Writing Instruction." *Reconceiving Writing, Rethinking Writing Instruction*. Edited by Joseph Petraglia. Erlbaum, 1995, pp. 51–77.

Severino, Carol, and Mary Trachsel. "Theories of Specialized Discourses and Writing Fellows Programs." *Across the Disciplines*, vol. 5, 2008. *WAC Clearinghouse*, http://wac.colostate.edu/atd/fellows/severino.cfm.

"State Report Cards." *Quality Counts 2014*. Education Research Center, 3 January 2014, http://www.edweek.org/ew/qc/2014/state_report_cards.html.

Thaiss, Chris, and Terry Myers Zawacki. *Engaged Writers: Dynamic Disciplines*. Boynton-Cook, 2006.

Townsend, Martha, A. "Writing Intensive Courses and WAC." *WAC for the New Millennium: Strategies for Continuing Writing-Across-the-Curriculum Programs*. Edited by Susan H. McLeod, Eric Miraglia, Margot Soven, and Christopher Thaiss. Urbana, IL: National Council of Teachers of English, 2001, pp. 233–58. *WAC Clearinghouse*, http://wac.colostate.edu/books/millennium/chapter10.pdf.

United States, Department of Commerce, Census Bureau. *State and County QuickFacts*. 8 July 2014, https://www.census.gov/quickfacts/.

Villanueva, Victor. "The Politics of Literacy Across the Curriculum." *WAC for the New Millennium: Strategies for Continuing Writing-Across-the-Curriculum Programs*, edited by Susan H. McLeod, Eric Miraglia, Margot Soven, and Christopher Thaiss. National Council of Teachers of English, 2001, pp. 165–78. *WAC Clearinghouse*, http://wac.colostate.edu/books/millennium/chapter7.pdf.

Walvoord, Barbara E., and Virginia Johnson Anderson. *Effective Grading: A Tool for Learning and Assessment*. Jossey-Bass / Wiley, 1998.

Wardle, Elizabeth A. "Can Cross-Disciplinary Links Help Us Teach 'Academic Discourse' in FYC?" *Across the Disciplines*, vol. 1, 2004. *WAC Clearinghouse*, http://wac.colostate.edu/atd/articles/wardle2004/Index.cfm.

—. "Understanding 'Transfer' from FYC: Preliminary Results of a Longitudinal Study." *WPA: Journal of the Council of Writing Program Administrators*, vol. 31, no. 1–2, 2007, pp. 65–85. *CWPA*, http://wpacouncil.org/archives/31n1-2/31n1-2wardle.pdf.

Wolfe, Joanna, Barrie Olson, and Laura Wilder. "Knowing What We Know about Writing in the Disciplines: A New Approach to Teaching for Transfer in FYC." *The WAC Journal*, vol. 25, 2014, pp. 42–77. *The WAC Journal*, http://wac.colostate.edu/journal/vol25/wolfeetal.pdf.

Yancey, Kathleen Blake. *Reflection in the Writing Classroom*. Utah State UP, 1998.

—, Liane Robertson, Liane, and Kara Tacsak. *Writing across Contexts: Transfer, Composition, and Cultures of Writing*. UP of Colorado, 2014.

Zawacki, Terry Myers, and Ashley Taliaferro Williams. "Is It Still WAC? Writing within Interdisciplinary Learning Communities." *WAC for the New Millennium: Strategies for Continuing Writing-Across-the-Curriculum Programs*, edited by Susan H. McLeod, Eric Miraglia, Margot Soven, and Christopher Thaiss. National Council of Teachers of English, 2001, pp. 109–40. *WAC Clearinghouse*, http://wac.colostate.edu/books/millennium/chapter5.pdf.

Stories and Explanations in the Introductory Calculus Classroom: A Study of WTL as a Teaching and Learning Intervention

SUE DOE, MARY E. PILGRIM, AND JESSICA GEHRTZ

Writing can play an important role in the teaching and learning of mathematics; the field itself comprises vocabulary, concepts, and symbols, the understanding of which provide a foundation for grasping the thinking processes involved in mathematics. Student understanding of math can be probed through writing, not just so that students can successfully solve problems but so that they can also understand underlying theorems, definitions, and proofs. Kittleson and Southerland have argued that constructing sound arguments and justifying reasoning in mathematics is a key to providing well-articulated solutions (verbal or written) and that communication, whether in writing or verbal, shapes understanding and plays a role in knowledge construction. The building of mathematical understanding has stretched to K-12 levels, as suggested by the Michigan Department of Education's endorsement of low-stakes write-to-learn (henceforth WTL) approaches such as journaling, imagery and visualization techniques, concept mapping, and vocabulary documentation ("WAC"). Similarly, Kelly McCormick, of the University of Southern Maine, reports that Maine pre-service mathematics teachers are urged to explore the instructional value of writing mathematical explanations. The organization Mid-Continent Research for Education Learning (Urquhart) has indicated that writing can be an essential aid in meeting a key objective of the National Council of Teachers of Mathematics—the deepening of students' mathematical understanding.

At the post-secondary level, Reynolds, Thaiss, and others, in an article published in 2011, reviewed the research on writing as a pedagogical tool in STEM disciplines. They posit that the relevance of writing to STEM education has been under-studied perhaps due to other priorities but also due to the reluctance of STEM disciplines to stake a claim in writing, an area they view as outside their expertise. Despite this disciplinary reluctance, Reynolds, Thaiss et al. were able to construct a database of over two hundred articles pertaining specifically to WTL pedagogy in STEM disciplines at the university level; they report that writing provides pedagogical opportunities that extend beyond communicating or performing knowledge in polished term papers. Among the studies they reviewed was work by Fleron and Hotchkiss, who argue for seminars involving writing at both the introductory and capstone level of mathematics instruction; such courses, they claim, help students conceptualize and unify mathematical knowledge, making them better contributors to the mathematics community. Another study, by Ganguli, examined twenty-five remedial mathematics students who made substantial strides in their mathematical thinking as a result of doing short in-class writing about mathematical concepts. Reynolds and Thaiss argue especially for the value of experimental studies of WTL in STEM, such as that provided by Cummings et al., who found that introductory physics students, regardless of writing ability, showed greater gains in understanding physics concepts than did peers from a comparison classroom where WTL was not used. In psychology, which in the local setting is considered more STEM than social science, Gingerich et al. (2014) found that performance on examinations was not only improved but retained six weeks after the course was over in classrooms where short writing was done. As these examples suggest, both descriptive accounts and experimental studies point to the value of writing in STEM disciplines.

The use of narrative, as a subset of writing integration in disciplinary contexts, has been a subject of particular interest to STEM scholars. However, narrative has often been positioned less as tool for learning than as a functionally useful way of expanding practitioner knowledge in applied settings. Sorrell, for instance, examined instruction in narrative in a healthcare context as a means for developing nurse empathy for patients. Others have undertaken rhetorical analysis in order to describe the types of narrative employed by STEM disciplines. For instance, Stockton examined the genre conventions and tacit expectations for narrative approaches in biology, and Heckelman and Dunn analyzed the "grammar" of mathematical narrative, saying that "algebraic notation is a form of argumentation. It is not just a representational but a persuasive exercise" (76). Dieteker perhaps comes closer to the aims of our study when she argues that mathematics instruction, as seen in textbooks, involves a layering of stories, which "allows new questions to be pursued, such as, What propels this mathematical story forward? How does this mathematical story build curiosity and desire to learn what will happen? What different (and new) types of mathematical stories can we find or design?" (19).

Our study extends this discussion by suggesting the use of narrative and expository approaches in the mathematics classroom as a means for building conceptual understanding. We align with Urquhart, who describes writing about math this way:

> Until I read what I have written, I don't see the holes in my logic, the missing steps, or the rambling thoughts. Writing informs me that I only have a cursory knowledge of the content when I need a deep one. Simply put, it doesn't let me cut corners. (4)

Similarly, Meier and Rishel describe the importance of writing in the teaching and learning of mathematics in this way:

> ... to get students to absorb mathematics, or any other subject, better, you need to have them think about, then write about, that subject. Let students tell you their thoughts, their confusions, their half-formed ideas, their frustrations and triumphs. From this, they will understand better, and we instructor[s] will, too, what the process of learning is all about. (5)

Meier and Rishel further state that "Our experience has shown that, when using short writing assignments, what we learn about the students and their understanding of the topic at hand is extremely useful in the day-to-day structuring of lectures, homework, and worksheets" (7). They argue especially for the value of narrative, distinguishing it from exposition, because narrative works "... in the interstices of papers, between the theorems and examples [that] tell us a *story* of the paper, of the proof" (89). They go on to say that when

> ... students write about mathematics, they are placing the subject in a context [that] makes sense to them. If they are going into the field, the narrative they learn is the story they will carry into their subsequent courses to inform them as to why they need to know the definition, the theorems, the proof techniques. If they are not going to continue in mathematics, they will probably forget the body of material they have studied; but, if they have written about the course they will be much more likely to hold that narrative in their memory as their record of what that area of mathematics is about. (90)

A Bridge to Our Study

For our purposes, working in the context of a large Research I institution in the Rocky Mountain West, we focus primarily on the narration of mathematical knowledge as a rational, problem-solving use of discourse that may be helpful to a broad range of students coming from varied levels of mathematics preparation. In this context we focus on student writing of conceptual understanding as might be obtained through narrations of knowledge. In particular, we look at narrative explanations, in which students write brief stories demonstrating that they understand a mathematical concept, and then we provide additional, sometimes expository, opportunities for students to demonstrate insight into the ways that they understand math concepts. With Manouchehri and St. John, as well as the National Council of Teachers of Mathematics, we argue that storytelling, as a form of discourse around mathematics, can be said to foster knowledge building and can play a key role in what students learn about mathematics as a field of study.

Our project acknowledges and draws upon the long pedagogical project associated with writing across the curriculum and distinguishing WTL from writing to communicate (WTC) (Thaiss and McLeod). WTL has been yoked with various kinds of thinking skills, going back to Janet Emig in 1977, who defined writing as a unique mode of learning, and forward to John Bean in 2011, who defined WTL as generative, exploratory, and contributory to critical thinking. Our work with WTL draws as well upon the classroom assessment work of D'Angelo and Cross as a mechanism for informing instruction. WTL, we argue for STEM program leaders, fosters the development of metacognition and the enhancement of problem-solving skills (Bangert-Drowns, Hurley, & Wilkinson; Bicer, Capraro & Capraro; Flores and Brittain; Pugalee) and deepens understanding and retention of information (Cavdar & Doe; Gingerich et al.). Writing acts as a method for internalization of and reflection upon ideas and is "self-rhythmed," thus allowing for learning to take place at the pace of the student (Emig 96), while also providing a durable, visible record (Emig 91; Urquhart 4) that is "epigenetic" or demonstrative of the evolution of thought (Emig 96).

As this short history suggests, it has long been held that students can develop, reflect upon, and revise their ideas about a subject through writing. For math instruction at the college level, however, there is increasing awareness that writing may also provide a mechanism for constructing and deepening the knowledge of undergraduates who arrive with varying levels of readiness but aspire to STEM disciplines as majors. Writing can provide valuable formative assessment information prior to graded (summative) assessment and as such allows for a more fully pedagogical, or interventionist, approach to mathematics instruction than has been the norm in university settings where, historically, students have mostly had to sink or swim on their own.

Indeed in the context of introductory calculus, where we situate our work, students are often greeted by unapologetically rigorous university courses focused on exam-based problem-solving that some might describe as unforgiving. In such courses, it is often the case that more students "wash out" than is necessary. Our study therefore sought to address the needs of students for whom such courses do not come naturally but for whom learning is possible through hard work, engaged instruction, and student narrations of understanding. Such narrations can influence instruction by helping faculty tailor teaching to more completely meet student needs. Such efforts, when accompanied by substantial feedback and coaching from college math teachers, may help to prevent many students from becoming D, F, or W (Withdrawal) statistics.

To this end, our study involved not only the discursive processes of students but also the conversations among mathematics faculty in a faculty development setting in which writing was the trigger but faculty discussion of curricular goals and classroom approaches was the target. This effort involved a half dozen mathematics and STEM faculty (notably physics), an assistant dean of undergraduate programs, and two faculty from the writing program who had extensive WAC experience. We undertook this collaborative effort with the hope of having positive effects upon student performance and with the aim that instruction might also be improved. This meant that not only did we envision that writing might become a persistent feature of mathematics instruction at the introductory calculus level but also that faculty, in their collaborative efforts around determining the best, most salient writing prompts, would identify their central instructional objectives and align their instruction accordingly, including the use of substantial feedback on student performance. We had the distinct advantage in this project of working toward a shared, unified purpose; as a group, we were dedicated to seeing more (and more diverse) students succeed.

Our efforts from the writing consultant side of the house involved a WAC approach that aspired to what Dr. Pamela Flash, director of the WAC program at the University of Minnesota, has described as anthropological. By this she means an approach that engages in ethnographic approaches such as listening to members of the community, observing teaching practices, and analyzing documents such as assignments and exams, rather than swooping in as writing "experts." The type of approach Flash recommends involves digging into the curricular and cultural dimensions of the learning context, which in our case meant engaging in an effort to understand a mathematics department and its calculus program. This involved talking extensively with the faculty and administrators in order to understand program objectives, internal pressures and constraints, motivations for integrating writing, and the politics around doing so. In this view of WAC, the writing consultants for this project served as, in Flash's terms, "external interlocutors," whom she describes as being "academic anthropologists engaged as participant observers in the study of a field and its pedagogical objectives."

The WAC faculty, both rhetoric and composition faculty, teamed with three math faculty, one physics faculty member, a program chair from math, an assistant dean of undergraduate programs, and an assessment expert. The group met once a week in the fall and every other week in the spring. The project was funded by a course redesign grant from the university's Institute for Teaching and Learning. As an interdisciplinary effort, our study suggests the value of this kind of prolonged study as one mechanism for achieving extended discussions among faculty; given our expansive timeline, we were able to talk at length across disciplines about instructional objectives and how writing might be put to work for achieving those goals. Since it was possible to have ideas discussed on a generous timeline, we were able to develop writing prompts that were tried, revised, and retried. Even then, the project could have used another year because we were unable to study the next and arguably more difficult phase, which would involve inexperienced graduate teaching assistants (henceforth GTAs) as the designated instructors of record for introductory calculus and hence as the key integrators of the initiative.

In this paper, we report not only on the findings of our writing integration in terms of student outcomes but also on the nature of our processes and their potential long-term value to participating faculty. We also discuss, although only in an introductory way, the second phase of the project where the needs of GTA preparation are addressed. While we know that our introductory efforts with lead faculty were essential, we acknowledge that all other factors being equal, the "problem" of GTA implementation of the writing-enhanced curriculum remains a crucial and difficult facet of this effort as it moves forward; we hope to offer reflection on emerging discoveries relating to the GTA factor in a future paper. For now, we offer only the slightest of insights into the importance of GTA preparation and ongoing support in mathematics instruction.

The Context and the Goal: To Get Students to Think More Deeply About Mathematics

While it is often the case that academic departments at colleges and universities are siloed from each other so that meaningful collaboration is hindered, perhaps particularly at large Research 1 institutions like our own, in our setting an energy had developed in recent years around efforts to have more conversations across academic units—conversations and activities tied specifically to the scholarship of teaching and learning. These conversations, under the rubric of High Impact Practices, had begun to partner disciplines in ways familiar to WAC scholars, linking, for instance, writing to psychology, mathematics, and physics and focusing on faculty development. To support such efforts, the provost's office had funded an institutional summer workshop organized by the university's Institute for Learning and Teaching. Specific faculty from across the university who shared a strong interest in pedagogy were invited to participate. The emphasis was on engaging students in active pedagogy in foundational courses with particular focus on courses with high D, F, and W rates.

Upon seeing presentations from various departments, faculty from the college of natural sciences (CNS) began to think about what they might derive from a cross-pollination of ideas with the university writing program, which was located within the English department. Facilitated by an associate dean for instruction, these participants began to have conversations, which resulted in a white paper, written jointly by STEM and writing faculty. This white paper evolved into an internal grant proposal, the purpose of which was to develop a WAC initiative focusing on WTL processes in natural science courses (mathematics, physics, chemistry, etc.) and teaming natural sciences and writing faculty. The ultimate goal of the project was to address the student experience in gateway courses across the CNS. The WTL Proposal, as it came to be known, eventually landed on a two-pronged approach focused on developing 1) WTL activities for students and 2) faculty understanding of WTL. It was hoped that WTL would enhance student learning by:

- Deepening learning and challenging misconceptions
- Fostering critical thinking, synthesis of ideas, and transfer of knowledge
- Shifting student focus from a short-term problem-solution orientation towards a long-term grasp of concepts, including grappling with complexity and counter-example
- Developing learning skills that transcend subject areas including the development of metacognitive abilities and self-regulation of learning

Beyond this, it was hoped that the project would support a similarly motivated learning community of STEM faculty as they worked to adopt robust teaching techniques and build teaching capacity. They would:

1. Learn how to implement writing assignments in science courses
2. Better their understanding of student comprehension in gateway courses
3. Balance their expectations of student maturity and the reality of the student experience
4. Build a sustainable course redesign initiative that could be implemented across departments within the college (CNS)

To this end, faculty from the department of mathematics and, in particular, the core introductory course in calculus took the lead. This group worked with writing program faculty who were known to the math faculty because of their successful implementation of a WTL initiative in the university's introductory psychology class, which was also part of the CNS and was a high-enrollment core curriculum course much like the introductory calculus course. The psychology initiative had shown not only that the design of writing prompts was crucial (Gingerich et al.) but also that the quality of feedback to students was essential to effective teaching through writing; the findings on feedback, in particular, provided a strong case for the professional development of faculty and GTAs (Doe et al.). The objective for the math project was similar to that of the psychology project: to develop writing prompts that would probe and deepen student knowledge on carefully scaffolded learning objectives and to develop feedback/response capabilities that would focus and prioritize teaching efforts. It was different in that writing in psychology had focused on discreet learning modules, such as student understanding of the differences between positive and negative reinforcement. For the math curriculum the goal was to deepen student understanding of foundational mathematics concepts, such as the notion of limits, so that as students matriculated they would have a solid foundation in essential areas of math knowledge.

From the beginning, the involved mathematics faculty understood that there was much work to be done to unpack long-term "baggage" about the course and legacies regarding instruction and students. There were assumptions about the readiness and work ethic of calculus students and there were also assumptions about the readiness and time constraints of GTAs. While these were challenges that had to be admitted, there were also distinct assets associated with the project: a math program leader and assistant dean for instruction, who were deeply committed to the project and were involved in high impact teaching and learning discussions at the highest levels of the university, and a pair of dedicated calculus faculty, who led the calculus program and identified as teaching and learning teacher-scholars. Along with the WAC consultants they asked, "What do we want to accomplish in Introductory Calculus?" and "Can writing help?"

Early on, Math faculty acknowledged student weaknesses as well as the challenge that a first semester calculus course poses for students. Students frequently arrive with gaps or shallow understanding of prerequisite knowledge, which makes the task of learning calculus difficult, as it relies heavily on the use of both algebra and trigonometry. In addition, poor experiences in a foundational STEM course, such as Introductory Calculus, play a significant role in the retention of STEM majors (Seymour and Hewitt). These challenges were further compounded by high D, F, and W rates. But circumstances had changed locally, and where once it might have been a sign of rigor to have many students failing the course or dropping out, now such outcomes were seen as a sign of weak teaching. Therefore, the key was to develop writing prompts in conjunction with a feedback loop that would address these teaching and learning shortfalls, a task much easier said than done.

In time it also became clear that changes were needed in terms of the preparation and supervision of the GTA instructors, for whom the course director for introductory calculus was also responsible. In the past the GTAs had received little to no training in the use of evidence-based pedagogy, such as WTL, nor did they have much experience in giving feedback on assessments or activities beyond counting things right or wrong. Faculty mentors of the GTAs saw their role as protecting GTA time so that they might pursue their graduate work to greatest effect. As a practical and creative solution to these competing demands, the course director connected the WTL initiative with an established and respected mechanism in the program, a notion called "DARTs" where GTA course instructors describe student answers on math homework problems as either 1) a bullseye (completely correct), 2) on the board (partially correct), or 3) off the board (completely wrong). This mechanism became a way for her to demonstrate to internal audiences that there was a meaningful range of student responses that could be discerned through writing. Furthermore, by using a method that was already understood by GTAs and faculty mentors, the potential problem of demanding too much GTA time was also averted.

Key Math Concepts in Introductory Calculus

The faculty engaged in this WAC conversation wanted students to derive definitions for mathematical concepts, rather than start with definitions and "solve problems." For example, the notion of "continuity" involves a definition that students can develop on their own if given appropriate prompts and opportunity to explore. Other key concepts, such as limits, differentiability, and rates of change, were identified as topics that beginning calculus students struggle to understand. Therefore, math faculty felt students would benefit from exploring through writing rather than through the more typical mimicking of procedures, copying of definitions, and routine testing (i.e., learning methods that address topics more superficially).

Having settled on some key concepts, almost immediately the faculty began to see how teaching might be done more effectively. In part, this willingness to make improvements to instruction was reflective of initiatives already sponsored by the university and getting wide attention. The notion of the "flipped classroom," for instance, had become an established idea where faculty were being provided with incentives for abandoning lecture in favor of creating engaged, active classrooms of hundreds of students. In the flipped classroom, lecture notes and slides were assigned for student review before class while class time was spent on applications, facilitation of student inquiry, small group projects, and elaboration into new terrain or novel problems. In this context, the long-established pedagogies of writing instruction not only fit favorably but offered variation and substance. Writing pedagogy was able to offer more than simple checking in and could be used to probe student understanding by asking them to write; in turn, the evidence deriving from such efforts became assessment information demonstrating students' level of understanding long before the time of examination.

In this context, the CNS faculty discussed the idea of GTAs, as inexperienced instructors-of-record, positioning themselves in more of a facilitation role and doing less lecturing and modeling of problem-solving at the board than had been the norm. It was hoped that a "facilitation role" might relieve them of some of the burden of "teaching" while also deepening student learning, as was the aspiration with all flipped classrooms. The idea was settled on that GTAs would typically provide brief information in a lecture format at the beginning of class and then would spend the majority of time circulating as students worked toward their own definitions. A physics faculty member, who was sitting in on this project alongside math faculty, pointed out that in his department GTAs were not instructors of record, but were instead strictly teaching in recitations. So he began to reimagine the recitations where his GTAs were involved. Those GTAs, he decided, might talk for just ten minutes and then turn it over to students to do problems, which would be followed by cold calling on students and whole room voting on answers. The physics professor had also imagined doing "think-alouds" wherein students would rehearse their strategies by speaking concepts aloud to classmates. In such ways did both the math and physics classrooms become increasingly dynamic locations.

As these examples suggest, from the beginning, participating faculty in this writing intervention were discussing not only content but method. Faculty explained at one point that they were concerned that GTAs were likely to teach in ways that would fall back on what they had themselves experienced. WAC faculty pointed out that math is not alone in witnessing this so-called "apprenticeship of observation" (Lortie; Grossman) which holds that no amount of professional development is ever as strong in developing the teacher as are the years of experience and observation (as a student) that have preceded the teacher's entrance into the classroom as teacher. In fact, WAC faculty warned, given demands on GTA time, they were *more* likely than faculty to take shortcuts towards that which was familiar, and this might also translate into low effectiveness in giving feedback to students. The goal, therefore, was to counter that which was nearly inevitable and to realize that this would not be a simple, one-time fix. Ongoing professional development would be needed.

At the same time, the faculty themselves were re-examining their own methods. For instance, the physics professor, an award-winning teacher, started this conversation:

> Physics P: I asked students to describe a notion in words and not use numbers.
>
> Math P: Maybe the challenge is more with the intentionality of approaches and activities than with what it used.
>
> Physics P: Still, we need the students to do the talking and report back to the group.
>
> WAC Consultant: This is sometimes called "Write-Pair-Share."
>
> Physics P: I'm going to try that. I think you should try it.

As this example suggests, conversations were anecdotal but also moved toward the drawing of general conclusions across disciplines.

Settling on Prompts

As we approached November, the prompts were starting to come together and math faculty had begun doing a kind of pre-pilot of the questions within their own classrooms. As had been suggested by the assistant dean for instruction, the writing integration in psychology had involved a lot of small ideas, but in math and physics the idea was to focus on big concepts and break them down into manageable parts, as with, for instance, the important concept of limits. The group discussed that the prompts might therefore be sequenced to establish the principle and then working toward greater difficulty and variety, first referring to the typical case and then moving toward elaboration into new or novel contexts, and ultimately exploring counter-examples. This process, it was hoped, would avail students to multiple iterations of similar kinds of tasks—variations on a theme—so that students would become increasingly masterful and develop flexibility as they saw how a principle works in new, even contradictory, situations.

Two types of tasks in particular stood out for 1) being simple and easy to implement, 2) providing opportunity for rich group and whole-class discussion, and 3) highlighting student misconceptions. The first task involved graphs and stories. For example, students worked with the graph of a function (fig. 1) multiple times during the semester, but in different contexts. Each time students were asked to identify quantitative characteristics of the graph (e.g., largest position, maximum velocity, etc.). In the first iteration, the function represented the position of an object with respect to time, but in the second, the scenario changed to velocity. In both contexts, the students were asked to write a story to match the graph.

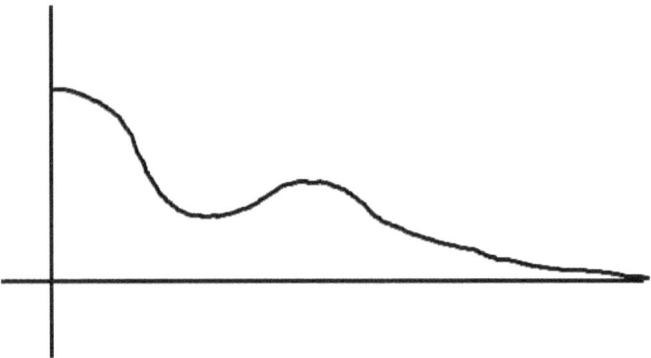

Fig. 1. The graph of a function changing with respect to time.

This prompt, it was determined, could be given to students at various points during the semester. When given at the beginning of the semester, student misconceptions could be quickly highlighted, which it was hoped would motivate rich discussions and early intervention. This prompt could then also be revised such that the graph represented velocity rather than position, or the graph could be modified so that it dropped below the x-axis, offering a new level of complexity. Typical student responses to the first prompt (not all correct) are below.

Selected student responses (when posed as a position graph) included:

- A ball is rolling down a hill, then it goes up a smaller hill then it rolls down some more.
- A skydiver jumps out of a plane and opens the parachute.
- I drive home but hit road construction so have to turn back and take an alternate route, then continue home.

To explain the differing quality markers of these responses, note that while the first response is correct, it does not indicate whether or not the student is correctly interpreting the horizontal axis as time or incorrectly perceiving the horizontal axis as horizontal distance. The scenario of a ball rolling down a hill is ambiguous and highlights a misconception that the student may or may not have. The third response, however, distinguishes itself from the first one because it illustrates a clear, correct interpretation of the horizontal axis. Such misconceptions can be teased out when the scenario changes to velocity with respect to time.

Selected student responses (when posed as a velocity graph):

- A ball is rolling down a hill, then it goes up a smaller hill then it rolls down some more.
- I was running away from zombies, and I was getting tired so I was running slower and slower. Then I noticed that the zombies were getting closer, so I started running faster. Then a zombie caught me and bit my leg off, and I fell down and crawled until I could crawl no longer.

In these explanations, faculty would note that a ball rolling down a hill does not match what is illustrated in the given graph. For it to be true, the graph of the velocity of the ball would need to be below the horizontal (and therefore depict negative velocity values). The zombie story, on the other hand, does demonstrate a clear understanding of velocity with respect to time—indicating the appropriate changes of running slower and faster—and it is also a creative story that demonstrates that the student could generate a fun correlative to the principle in question, thus suggesting confidence in the student's knowledge.

    To determine if students truly understood the relationship between object movement and time, this graph task was reversed. Students were given a story and then asked to draw the corresponding graph representing the position or velocity of an object with respect to time. For example, students were given the following prompt and then asked to draw the graph representing the scenario:

It took Ryan 15 minutes to walk from his house into campus on Tuesday. He needed to get to the Weber building. On his way, he walked past a coffee shop. He decided to turn around and buy a cup of coffee. After buying a cup of coffee he continued on toward campus, but was stopped by the train for three minutes. After the train passed by, he began walking again into campus and arrived at the Weber building. In the axes below, draw the graph that represents Ryan's position relative to the Weber building at time t.

Fig. 2 is a sample student response that correctly represents Ryan's position relative to the Weber building at time t.

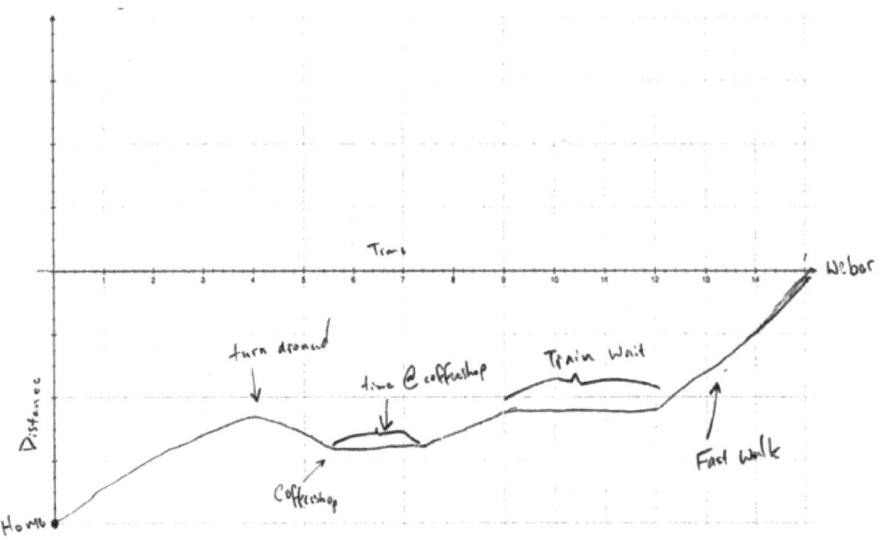

Fig. 2. A student's drawing of Ryan's position at time t.

A student who can correctly transition between different representations of mathematics (between words and graphs in this case) has a deeper understanding of concepts than a student who cannot. Further, such knowledge transfer illustrates that a student can make connections between different forms of mathematical concepts.

Additionally, in mathematics, understanding what does not "fit" or "work" demonstrates a deeper understanding of a mathematical concept. This notion is often referred to as the counterexample. To get students to think about counterexamples, we utilized true/false questions, which was the second type of writing task we employed and which involved more exposition than narration. Specifically, we asked students to consider statements, and if a statement was true, they had to explain why it was true. If a statement was false, they had to provide a counterexample. If utilized in a meaningful way, math faculty hoped that such tasks might promote thoughtful discussion and deeper knowledge.

This second approach also probed students' increasing sophistication with broad topics and variation and counterexample. We experimented with synthesis prompts that took the ideas that students had been exposed to and queried about via narrative prompts and brought them together through unifying, synthetic questions that took the conceptual level up a notch. For example:

1. Draw a concept map illustrating the ideas and concepts presented in this course. Explain how these concepts are connected.
2. Derivatives and integrals are two overarching topics in this course. However, we began the course with limits, which could be argued to be the theme of the course. Explain how limits connect to derivatives and integrals.

By the end of the first semester, we had a set of questions such as these that we believed we could pilot in the spring and then revise for fall instruction of GTAs.

Pilot Study and Results:

We piloted the prompts in two sections of Calculus I, and the sizes of these sections as well as the times of day each was offered were comparable. For purposes of the formal pilot, the classes were taught by two experienced GTAs, one of whom had six years of teaching experience. The other held a master's degree in mathematics and had three years of teaching experience. Both worked directly and substantially with the course director. Both GTAs met their classes four days a week, gave the same exams, assigned the same weekly homework, and achieved similar retention rates.

In the experimental group, referred to as the "Writing Section" (N = 36), students were provided minimal lecture time, and class consisted mainly of group activities with writing and discussion. In terms of writing, students in this section were given WTL activities. For group activities, groups were carefully constructed to achieve balanced ability groups. In the control group referred to as the "Standard Section" (N = 33), students were exposed primarily to traditional lecture with some worksheet activities provided that could be done individually or in groups, consistent with the course's traditional delivery.

Sample Writing Prompts and Responses

Students enrolled in the experimental section engaged in several discussions and writing activities. Students also participated in oral assessments before each of the four exams (three midterms and one final exam).

The prompts asking about graphs and stories as well as the true-false statements were among several of the prompts used for writing and discussion. Oral assessments were given to students in groups of three to four and were comprised of a variety of questions intended to prepare students for upcoming exams. Student responses to oral assessments provided additional insight into students' misconceptions and knowledge gaps, which would provide guidance in developing review content for exam preparation. Questions for oral assessments ranged from the procedural, such as taking the derivative of a function, to the conceptual, wherein students were asked to discuss the connection between continuity and differentiability. Students responded to questions as a group. For example, prior to exam two, students were given a graph (see fig. 3) and a list of stories. Students had to determine if a story represented position, velocity, or acceleration. One of the stories was: "Tatiana is jumping on a trampoline until her foot slips and she falls to the ground." Here is the conversation that followed:

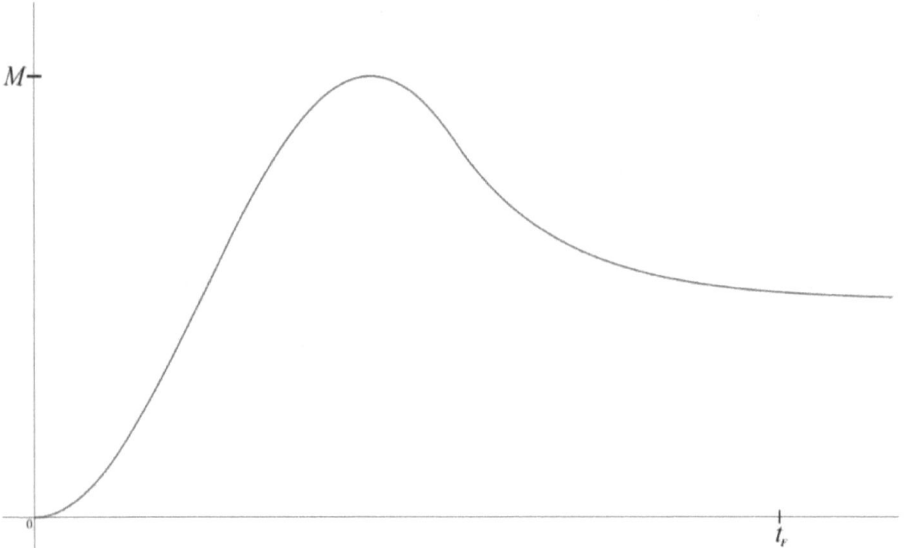

Fig. 3. The graph of a function with respect to time, t.

    Facilitator: Does the graph represent position?

    Student 1: It's not position because she doesn't hit zero when she falls down.

    Facilitator: Could it be velocity?

    Student 2: No. Just because she breaks her foot and immediately stops.

    Student 3: It'd be oscillating.

    Facilitator: For velocity, should the graph drop below the x-axis?

Student 3: Yeah, it should come back down the same way.

Student 2: Well, you can never get negative velocity.

Student 3: Yeah you can. When you start to fall down.

Student 2: Ohhhhh. Yeah.

Discussions such as this provided us with insight into students' knowledge of the physical quantities' position, velocity, and acceleration. The discussion also provided opportunity for a misconception to be resolved. By this point in the study, students had become comfortable weaving among the writing of stories to depict mathematical phenomena, the depiction of stories onto graphs, and the verbal narration of graphs. Discourse in varied forms had become mixed and complementary.

Findings

Students in the writing (experimental) section outperformed students in the standard (control) section for every exam (see table 1). The differences were at a level of statistical significance on the first exam and on the final exam, and the effect sizes (meaning the actual difference in performance as measured in terms of real world effect) were in the middle range, meaning that student grades were meaningfully influenced by these efforts and were not trivial differences—say, for instance, moving from a C to a C+ performance.

Table 1. Means of exam scores for Writing and Standard Calculus I sections.

	Writing Section N = 36	Standard Section N = 33
Exam 1:	82.8 $p = 0.03, d = 0.53$	76.1
Exam 2:	67.9	63.3
Exam 3:	64.2	60.8
Final:	71.6 $p = 0.03, d = 0.56$	62.1

One concern that had been voiced about this language-based intervention was that students might sacrifice "procedural skills" or fail to demonstrate mathematical processes and computational skills if their attention was focused on writing narratives or explanations. However, findings demonstrated that there was no loss of procedural skill. Instead, there were gains not only in conceptual understanding, at a statistically significant level, but also in procedural knowledge, although the latter was not at a statistically significant level (see table 2).

Table 2. Means of writing and procedural questions compared between Writing and Standard Calculus I sections.

	Writing Section N = 36	Standard Section N = 33
Conceptual Writing Question	4.44 $p = 0.002$	2.82
Procedural Question	13	11.9

While students in the writing section did not demonstrate the full extent of deep understanding that we aspired to obtain through the intervention, they nonetheless had responses that were better than those from students in the standard section.

Written responses were coded based on how students used mathematical ideas, vocabulary, and notation. So additionally, it was noted if a response contained pronouns in such a way that the corresponding noun could not be identified. Examples of correct and incorrect use of ideas, vocabulary, and notation are provided in table 3.

Table 3. Examples of qualitative data coding.

	Correct	Incorrect
Ideas	"The equation [for] $f'(a)$ is the slope of the tangent line at a given point."	"The equation is for tangent lines and secant lines at any given point on the graph."
Vocabulary	"The equation describes the slope of the tangent line at point a."	"A secant line is the slope between a and b."
Notation	$(a,f(a))$ (in reference to an ordered pair)	$f(a)$ (in reference to an ordered pair)

Our findings from coding student responses show that the writing section had a higher percentage in the use of correct ideas, correct vocabulary, and correct notation than the standard section. In addition, the writing section had a lower percentage of incorrect ideas, incorrect vocabulary, and incorrect notation than the standard section.

The writing section also had a lower percentage use of pronouns. An overuse of pronouns often indicates that students are trying to use terminology but do not yet know how to link together ideas correctly. For example, a student may state, "The equation is the slope. The limit goes to 0, so it approaches the tangent line." While *limit, slope,* and *tangent line* may be correct vocabulary words to include in a response involving the discussion of the definition of the derivative, the use of the word *it* is unclear and does not indicate that the student understands the meaning of the use of a limit in terms of slopes of secant lines and a tangent line. Using correct vocabulary in a meaningful way rather than making vague use of pronouns indicates that a student has a clear understanding.

Coda: Implications for GTA Training

Our discussion of findings thus far has focused on student performance and faculty development. Like Grawe and Rutz, "Our experience has convinced us that engaging faculty directly in the assessment of student work provides the impetus for curricular change" (14), but we acknowledge significant constraints moving forward as implementation of the WTL integration moves into its next, full implementation phase. We hold that the effectiveness of this WTL initiative on student performance was likely caused by a combination of both deepened student engagement with calculus material and enhanced teaching efficacy. However, imaginings about a writing-enhanced math curriculum must take into account who will do the implementing of such efforts once the approach is settled upon. In other words, if the experienced and highly motivated faculty who undertook this project will not be its deliverers in classrooms, does the initiative have much hope of succeeding? What problems might be anticipated? And what might be done to address these challenges?

As stated earlier, our investigation was undertaken by experienced faculty with high interest in the scholarship on teaching and with deep knowledge of student strengths and shortcomings. These faculty went into the project with high motivation and intention. They knew there were problems in student learning and they had already spent some considerable time improving the curriculum, even investing in teaching expertise by hiring a tenure-track pedagogue whose main research interest was in thinking about improvement to student outcomes. Even then, the project of identifying foundational objectives for the introductory calculus course took the better part of a semester, with faculty meeting weekly. Once the group had settled on objectives, they then devoted weeks to clarifying the prompts that would be used to probe understanding of both small and large (synthetic) concepts. As the prompts were being developed, these experienced and highly motivated faculty tested and refined them. In addition, these faculty had already embraced active teaching methods which included the use of active (flipped) classroom techniques such as paired conversations, discussions, and collaborative, small-group problem-solving. Faculty were also including more and more student verbalization in pairs and small groups as well as instructor facilitation and they had become conscious facilitators who floated around the room to listen and intervene with particular students and groups of students. They were equally engaged with ongoing assessment that allowed them to adjust their instruction. They learned through the WTL intervention that they also had an obligation to provide ongoing formative feedback to students.

In moving forward with this initiative, it is important to note that most of the instruction was scheduled to be provided by GTAs, as is often the case in large R1 institutions. A key question then became, to what degree could GTAs be expected to deliver this kind of curriculum? We posited that while it is convenient and even seductive to assume that GTAs are ready for this work, generally speaking they are not ready for it and need a great deal of mentoring and supervision. Too often it is assumed that GTAs arrive ready to teach and to provide feedback on student work, having even been described by some scholars as expert graders (Pare and Joordens). Yet most GTAs lack preparation for teaching (McKeachie) and are generally unfamiliar with the scholarship on their own development as teachers and scholars (Nyquist, Abbott, Wulff, and Sprague). They are also quite early in career development (Eble), may be challenged by their proximity to undergraduates in terms of age and authority (although, as Doug Hesse suggests, proximity in age can also be a benefit), and are likely to experience interference between their roles as teachers and graduate students (Duba-Biedermann; Doe "Lived Experiences"). Furthermore, most are still developing a teaching identity (Schempp, Sparkes, and Templin), and all are still developing disciplinary expertise. The literature further establishes that there is generally a strong need for GTAs to be socialized into their roles and responsibilities as faculty—skill sets that are by no means tacitly understood (Slevin; Braxton, Lambert and Clark).

None of these are new challenges. In fact, in 1987, at a conference about revising calculus instruction for a new century, organized by the National Academy of Sciences and the National Academy of Engineering, Bettye Anne Case and Allan C. Cochran observed that "The role of teaching assistants . . . in the teaching of calculus . . . is of serious concern" (76). Their preparation, they argued, requires considerable expense in terms of time and resources and requires ongoing training and the preparation of demonstrations and materials (77). Similarly, Eison and Vanderford argue for ongoing pedagogical instruction of GTAs, including observations of teaching, engagement with teaching theory, and faculty development in regard to the unique features of each discipline's pedagogical traditions. On the bright side, research by Doe and Gingerich suggests that while GTA grading and responding remains short of the standard set by experienced faculty, even when accompanied by rigorous training, GTAs do show impressive growth with just one semester of carefully planned pedagogical instruction.

In the current study, a first semester of piloting was conducted by faculty and a second by experienced GTAs with substantial teaching experience. It seems reasonable to assume that different problems will surface when new GTAs are attempting to integrate writing for purposes of learning mathematics. Given the challenges facing GTAs in every setting, it is likely that a quite substantial task remains to be addressed at the close of this project in regard to preparing calculus GTAs for the work that lies ahead. We therefore conclude our paper by providing some early observations about how GTAs fared in this context during the first year.

GTAs in the First Semesters of Implementation

GTA training improvements were first implemented prior to the start of the fall 2015 semester and have continued since. The work with GTAs began with the assumption that they need a realistic understanding of the students who will be in their classrooms and have the ability to provide instructional support for students who are learning to communicate and write mathematics at the university level. We find that GTAs typically begin with the assumption that their Calculus I students are just like them and can easily understand mathematical concepts and have the natural ability to connect mathematical ideas. However, this is not the case, of course, and GTAs typically discover the actual situation when grading their students' first exams. Unfortunately, though, this is often too late for students who can quickly become discouraged by early failure and wash out prematurely. To address this problem, we sought to help GTAs develop a better understanding of their Calculus I students and therefore developed WTL activities with corresponding sample student responses as part of training activities.

GTAs worked through a variety of student activities, including WTL prompts. They then discussed potential student responses as well as implications for the classroom. This exercise stimulated an extensive discussion around pedagogy with questions such as "How should a task be implemented?"; "What are good facilitating questions?"; and "What are possible student misconceptions?" Following a rich discussion about how students might respond to questions and prompts, GTAs were provided with student writing that showed how students actually respond. This led to a deeper discussion about the students that take Calculus I—their typical knowledge gaps, mathematical misconceptions, and weaknesses in notation and vocabulary. GTAs were predictably surprised by the examples that illustrated the range and content of student writing, and these made them, we believe, more mindful of their instruction starting on the first days of classes rather than only after the first examination.

Of course, we were hopeful that such engaging conversations with GTA instructors-of-record would lead to immediate improvements in instruction that would in turn have a positive impact on student success. However, we also realized that another factor was at play: turnover in Calculus I GTAs occurs every semester, so sustaining pedagogical change immediately presented as a challenge. To address this issue, the tenure-track calculus course director successfully argued for creation of a calculus center, which very much resembled a writing center built for mathematicians. Opening in the fall of 2016, the CSU Calculus Center is positioned to lead efforts to improve instruction in all calculus courses, through GTA and faculty training, and is intended to build upon the recently developed efforts of this writing integration project. Specifically, training will focus on the use of evidence-based practices, such as WTL, and will include student data and responses as a way to give meaning to such practices. Students will lead the conversations, just as they do in writing center work, and additionally, the CSU Calculus Center is envisioned to provide GTAs and faculty with a repository of rich tasks and activities. Envisioned as a working pedagogical research center through which data can be collected in an ongoing way to assess the impact of these efforts, the CSU Calculus Center's primary purpose is to help the student—to develop better mathematicians, not just better math exams—echoing Stephen North's charge that writing centers develop better writers, not just better writing (438). It is hoped that research and scholarship on teaching and learning coming out of the center will also affect faculty instruction, much as writing center pedagogy has influenced writing classrooms.

One important outcome of this project is that a small professional learning community has begun to flourish between faculty in the university writing program and faculty in mathematics. Collaborative efforts between these faculty will continue with support and facilitation from the calculus center and from WAC-interested rhetoric and composition faculty, perhaps even connecting the CSU Calculus Center with the CSU Writing Center for cross-disciplinary professional development. Some joint GTA training efforts are already planned, and WTL workshops for mathematics will be developed and implemented. The Calculus Center will also act as a vehicle for getting other STEM faculty involved in writing and learning activities, similar to what has occurred in Carleton College's QuIRK program (Carlton College). Our collaboration offers an opportunity to raise awareness about and provide education on the power of using writing in STEM disciplines through faculty professional development in the Calculus Center, led by both English and Mathematics faculty.

Special Acknowledgments

The authors would like to acknowledge the following individuals and groups at Colorado State University for their involvement in this project: Kathleen (Kate) Kiefer, Professor Emeritus of English and University Distinguished Teaching Scholar; Lisa Dysleski, Assistant Dean of Undergraduate Programs, College of Natural Sciences; Hilary Freeman, Senior Teaching Faculty in Mathematics; Brian Jones, Senior Teaching Faculty in Physics and Director of Little Shop of Physics; The Institute for Learning and Teaching (TILT); Simon Tavener and the College of Natural Sciences, Professor of Mathematics and Associate Dean for Academics; Anton Betten, Associate Professor of Mathematics;Julie Maertens, Research Associate in Psychology and Evaluator for the CSU STEM Center.

References

Angelo, Thomas A., and K. Patricia Cross. *Classroom Assessment Techniques: A Handbook for College Teachers.* 2nd ed., Jossey-Bass, 1993.

Bangert-Drowns, Robert L., Marlene M. Hurley, and Barbara Wilkinson. "The Effects of School-Based Writing-To-Learn Interventions on Academic Achievement: A Meta-analysis." *Review of Educational Research,* vol.74, no. 1, 2004, pp. 29–58. *Sage,* doi: 10.3102/00346543074001029.

Bean, John C. *Engaging Ideas: The Professor's Guide to Integrating Writing, Critical Thinking, and Active Learning in the Classroom.* 2nd ed., John Wiley and Sons, 2011.

Bicer, Ali, Robert M. Capraro, and Mary M. Capraro. "Integrating Writing into Mathematics Classroom to Increase Students' Problem Solving Skills." *International Online Journal of Educational Sciences,* vol. 5, no. 2 (2013), pp. 361–69, www.iojes.net/userfiles/Article/IOJES_1118.pdf.

Bressoud, David M., et al. "The Calculus Student: Insights from the Mathematical Association of America National Study." *International Journal of Mathematical Education in Science and Technology,* vol. 44, no. 5, 2013, pp. 685–98. *Taylor and Francis Online,* doi: 10.1080/0020739x.2013.798874.

Bressoud, David, and Chris Rasmussen. "Seven Characteristics of Successful Calculus Programs." *Notices of the AMS,* vol. 62, no. 2, 2015, pp.144–46, doi: 10.1090/noti1209.

Braxton, John M., Leo M. Lambert, and Scott C. Clark. "Anticipatory Socialization of Undergraduate College Teaching Norms by Entering Graduate Teaching Assistants." *Research in Higher Education,* vol. 36 no. 6, 1995, pp. 671–86, doi: 10.1007/bf02208250.

Carlton College. *What Is QuIRK.* Nov. 2014, https://apps.carleton.edu/quirk/.

Case, Bettye Anne, and Allan C. Cochran. "Role of Teaching Assistants." *Calculus for a New Century: A Pump, Not a Filter,* edited by Lynn Arthur Steen, Mathematical Association of America, 1988, pp. 76–77, http://files.eric.ed.gov/fulltext/ED300252.pdf

Çavdar, Gamze, and Sue Doe. "Learning Through Writing: Teaching Critical Thinking Skills in Writing Assignments." *PS: Political Science & Politics,* vol.45, no. 2, 2012, pp. 298–306. *CambridgeCore,* doi: 10.1017/s1049096511002137.

Cummings, Karen, and Michael Murphy. "The Effectiveness of Incorporating Conceptual Writing Assignments Into Physics Instruction." *2006 Physics Education Research Conference,* vol. 883, no. 1. pp. 61–64, doi: 10.1063/1.2508691.

Dietiker, Leslie. "Mathematical Texts As Narrative: Rethinking Curriculum." *For the Learning of Mathematics,* vol.33, no. 3, 2013, pp. 14–19.

Doe, Sue. R. "The Lived Experiences of Teacher Formation Among 1st-year Graduate Teaching Assistants in a Composition Program." Dissertation, Colorado State U, 2001.

Doe, Sue R., Karla J. Gingerich, and Tracy L. Richards. "An Evaluation of Grading and Instructional Feedback Skills of Graduate Teaching Assistants in Introductory Psychology." *Teaching of Psychology*, vol.40 no. 4, 2013, pp. 274–80. *Sage*, doi: 10.1177/0098628313501039.

Duba-Biedermann, Lisa. "Graduate Assistant Development: Problems of Role Ambiguity and Faculty Supervision." *Journal of Graduate Teaching Assistant Development*, vol. 1, 1994, pp. 119–26.

Eble, Kenneth E. *Career Development of the Effective College Teacher*. American Association of University Professors, 1971. *ERIC*, files.eric.ed.gov/fulltext/ED089630.pdf.

Eison, James, and Marsha Vanderford. "Enhancing GTA training in Academic Departments: Some Self-assessment Guidelines." *The Professional and Organizational Development Network in Higher Education*, vol. 12, 1993. To Improve the Academy, Paper 277, 1993, digitalcommons.unl.edu/podimproveacad/277.

Emig, Janet. "Writing as a Mode of Learning." *College Composition and Communication*, vol. 28, no. 2, 1977, pp. 122–28. *JSTOR*, doi: 10.2307/356095.

Flash, Pamela. Email with co-author, Sue Doe. 7 July 2016.

Fleron, Julian .F., and Philip K. Hotchkiss. "First-Year and Senior Seminars: Dual Seminars=Stronger Mathematics Majors. *Problems, Resources, and Issues in Mathematics Undergraduate Studies*, vol. 11, no. 4, 2001, pp. 289–325. *Taylor and Francis Online*, doi: 10.1080/10511970108984007.

Flores, Alfinio, and Carmina Brittain. "Writing to Reflect In a Mathematics Methods Course." *Teaching Children Mathematics*, vol. 10, no. 2, Oct. 2003, pp. 112–18. *JSTOR*, jstor.org/stable/41198093.

Ganguli, Aparna B. "Writing to Learn Mathematics: Enhancement of Mathematical Understanding." *AMATYC Rev*, vol 16, no.1, Fall 1994, pp. 45–51. *ERIC*, EJ512540.

Gingerich, Karla J., et al. "Active Processing Via Write-to-Learn Assignments: Learning and Retention Benefits in Introductory Psychology." *Teaching of Psychology* vol. 41, no. 4, Sept 2014, pp. 303–08. *Sage*, doi: 10.1177/0098628314549701.

Grawe, Nathan D., and Rutz, Carol A. "Integration with Writing Programs: A Strategy for Quantitative Reasoning Program Development," *Numeracy* vol. 2, no. 2, 2009, doi: 10.5038/1936-4660.2.2.2.

Grossman, Pamela L. "Overcoming the apprenticeship of observation in teacher education coursework." *Teaching and Teacher Education*, vol. 7, no. 4, Jan. 1991, pp. 345–57. *ScienceDirect*, doi: 10.1016/0742-051x(91)90004-9.

Heckelman, Ronald J., and Will-Mathis Dunn, III. "Models in Algebra and Rhetoric: A New Approach to Integrating Writing and Mathematics in a WAC Learning Community." *Language and Learning Across the Disciplines,* vol. 6, no. 3, Aug. 2003, pp. 74–88, wac.colostate.edu/llad/v6n3/heckelman.pdf.

Hesse, Douglas. "Teachers as Students, Reflecting Resistance." *College Composition and Communication,* vol. 44, no. 2, May 1993: pp. 224–31. *JSTOR,* doi: 10.2307/358840.

Lortie, Daniel. *Schoolteacher: A Sociological Study Learned Through the Apprenticeship of Observation.* University of Chicago Press, 1975.

Kittleson, Julie M., and Sherry A. Southerland. "The Role of Discourse in Group Knowledge Construction: A Case Study of Engineering Students." *Journal of Research in Science Teaching,* vol. 41, no. 3, Mar. 2004, pp 267–93. *Wiley Online Library,* doi: 10.1002/tea.20003.

Manouchehri, Azita, and Dennis St John. "From Classroom Discussions to Group Discourse." *Mathematics Teacher* vol. 99, no. 8, Apr. 2006, pp. 544–51. *JSTOR,* jstor.org/stable/27972052.

McCormick, Kelly. "Experiencing the Power of Learning Mathematics Through Writing." *Issues in the Undergraduate Mathematics Preparation of School Teachers: The Journal,* vol. 4, Sept. 2010, http://www.k-12prep.math.ttu.edu/journal/4.curriculum/mccormick01/article.pdf

McKeachie, Wilbert J. *Teaching Tips: Strategies, Research, and Theory for College and University Teachers,* 14th ed., Houghton Mifflin Company, 2014.Meier, John and Thomas Rishel. *Writing in the Teaching and Learning of Mathematics.* MAA Notes No. 48, Cambridge UP, 1998. Michigan Council for Teachers of Mathematics. National Council of Teachers of Mathematics. "Reading and Writing Across the Curriculum: A Policy Research Brief Produced by the NCTE." NCTE, 2011, www.ncte.org/library/NCTEFiles/Resources/Journals/CC/0203-mar2011/CC0203Policy.pdf.

North, Stephen M. "The Idea of a Writing Center." *College English.* vol. 46, no. 5, Sept, 1984, pp. 433-46. doi: 10.2307/377047.

Nyquist, Jody D. *Preparing the Professoriate of Tomorrow to Teach. Selected Readings in TA Training.* Kendall/Hunt Publishing, 1991.

Paré, Dwayne E., and Steve Joordens. "Peering into Large Lectures: Examining Peer and Expert Mark Agreement Using peerScholar, An Online Peer Assessment Tool." *Journal of Computer Assisted Learning,* vol. 24, no. 6, Dec. 2008, pp.526–40. doi: 10.1111/j.1365-2729.2008.00290.

President's Council of Advisors on Science and Technology (PCASTO). *Report to the President: Engage to Excel: Producing One Million Additional College Graduates with Degrees in Science, Technology, Engineering, and Mathematics.* PCASTO, 2012, https://www.whitehouse.gov/sites/default/files/microsites/ostp/pcast-engage-to-excel-final_2-25-12.pdf.

Pugalee, David K. "Writing, Mathematics, and Metacognition: Looking for Connections Through Students' Work in Mathematical Problem Solving." *School Science and Mathematics,* vol.101, no. 5, May 2001, pp. 236–45. *Wiley Online Library,* doi: 10.1111/j.1949-8594.2001.tb18026.

Reynolds, Julie A., et al. "Writing-To-Learn in Undergraduate Science Education: A Community-Based, Conceptually Driven Approach." *CBE-Life Sciences Education,* vol. 11, no.1, Mar. 2012, pp. 17–25, doi: 10.1187/cbe.11-08-0064.

Rivard, Lé Onard P. "A Review of Writing to Learn in Science: Implications For Practice and Research." *Journal of Research in Science Teaching* vol.31, no.9, Nov. 1994, pp. 969–83. *Wiley Online Library,* doi: 10.1002/tea.3660310910.

Schemjrp, Paul G., et al. "Identity and Induction: Establishing the Self in the First Years of Teaching." *The Role of Self in Teacher Development,* edited by Richard Lipka, State University of New York Press, 1999, pp. 142–61.

Seymour, Elaine, and Nancy M. Hewitt. *Talking About Leaving: Why Undergraduates Leave the Sciences.* Westview Press,1997.

Slevin, James F. *Next Generation: Preparing Graduate Students for the Professional Responsibilities of College Teachers.* Association of American Colleges, 1993.

Sorrell, Jeanne. "Stories in the Nursing Classroom: Writing and Learning Through Stories." *Language & Learning Across the Disciplines,* vol. 5, no. 1, May 2001, pp. 36–48, http://wac.colostate.edu/llad/v5n1/sorrell.pdf.

Steen, Lynn Arthur. "Calculus for a New Century: A Pump, Not a Filter. Papers Presented at a Colloquium." *MAA Notes Number 8,* Mathematical Association of American, 1988.

Stockton, Sharon. "Students and Professionals Writing Biology: Disciplinary Work and Apprentice Storytellers." *Language and Learning across the Disciplines,* vol.1, no. 2, Oct. 1994, pp. 79–104, wac.colostate.edu/llad/v1n2/stockton.pdf.

Thaiss, Chris, and Susan H. McLeod. "The Pedagogy of Writing Across the Curriculum." *A Guide to Composition Pedagogies,* 2nd ed., edited by Gary Tate et al., Oxford UP, 2014, pp. 283–300.

Urquhart, Vicki. "Using Writing in Mathematics to Deepen Student Learning." Mid-Continent Research for Education and Learning (McREL), 2009. *ERIC,* files.eric.ed.gov/fulltext/ED544239.pdf.

"Writing Across the Curriculum." Michigan Department of Education, www.michigan.gov/documents/mde/Writing_to_Learn_Mathematics_306722_7.pdf.

Of Evolutions and Mutations: Assessment as Tactics for Action in WAC Partnerships

FERNANDO SÁNCHEZ AND DANIEL KENZIE

In "A Taxonomy of WAC Programs," William Condon and Carol Rutz recently put forth a typology built on location and momentum for understanding WAC programs. Location, the authors explain, "is all about where WAC is: who is doing it, what courses it affects, where to find it in assignments, what resources it consumes, and so forth—the identity of the WAC program" (360). Momentum instead "involves outcomes; it is WAC in action, located in widely disparate sites, moving on many fronts at once—momentum is what WAC *does*" (360). Throughout this typology, we can see a natural progression that programs make as they evolve from a foundational type, to an established type, to an integrated type, to finally an institutional change agent type across five dimensions such as primary goals, organization, and indicators of success. It is clear that as a WAC program moves (or evolves) across this typology from a foundational type to an institutional change agent, the level of autonomy and influence expands, meaning that its work becomes more distributed across an institution.[1]

Ostensibly, this metamorphosis from one end of the spectrum to the other requires a slow, long-term, strategic plan for acquiring resources and expanding. Indeed, most of the literature involving WAC evolution and sustainability evokes this language of strategy and strategic efforts. This focus makes sense given that administrative endeavors typically involve shoring up resources and expanding programs. However, we think that there remain salient benefits to adding tactical thinking to strategic planning in WAC work. Borrowing from Michel de Certeau's framework on strategies and tactics, we argue that thinking tactically can 1) lead to increased administrative agency—particularly for WPAs and graduate WPAs (gWPAs) who spearhead WAC programs that are not on the path towards evolving—and 2) reveal new strategies that can aid in administrative work as particular WAC programs and partnerships mutate (rather than evolve). We begin by providing a brief overview of how strategies have come into play in WAC scholarship and then discuss examples from our own experiences of how we have brought tactics into our WAC contexts—both involving assessment work. We end with a discussion of what thinking tactically might mean more broadly.

WAC Strategies toward Expansion and Evolution

In *The Practice of Everyday Life*, Michel de Certeau makes the distinction between strategies and tactics. A strategy, he writes, is "the calculation (or manipulation) of power relationships that becomes possible as soon as a subject with will and power (a business, an army, a city, a scientific institution) can be isolated. . . . As in management, every 'strategic' rationalization seeks first of all to distinguish its 'own' place, that is, the place of its own power and will, from an environment" (36). Strategies aim to create a space that one can call his or her own from which to plan further strategies. Moreover, once a place has been established—whether this place is physical (for example, space for the writing center on campus) or figurative (room in the general education curriculum for first-year English)—strategies are enacted that look to the future and impose a careful management of power relations to protect the space that has been secured and plan for future growth. As Lauren Andres notes, "Strategies are related to determinism and regulation [in that] they have an explicit aim in the production of space and the realisation of a set of objectives and of a specific action plan" (764).

Historically, WAC work has been focused on finding strategies to do just that. James Kinneavy, writing in 1983, when *writing across the curriculum* was a fairly new term in writing studies and across institutions, states that WAC was best situated to tackle the literacy crisis of the time because unlike the "Band-Aid" approaches that had been tried previously, WAC could "be a total immersion, horizontally across all departments and vertically at all levels of high school and college" (13). And of course, one would need careful planning and vision in order to create such an immersive experience far and wide. Much like de Certeau's description of strategy, which is "a triumph of place over time," we can see how WAC had/has the potential of carving out its own place spatially (across all departments) and temporally (at all levels of education).

Indeed, by 1989, Susan H. McLeod wrote that she was beginning to see WAC entering a new stage in its development—one in which programs were "moving toward permanence in their institutions" (338). Not surprisingly, this permanence takes place by expanding—for example, reaching out to both newcomers and veterans on campus to attend workshops and requiring a number of writing intensive courses in the general education curriculum (339). And in order to create permanent curricular implementation, WAC requires faculty to integrate writing into their courses. To illustrate, the University of Chicago's Little Red Schoolhouse has acted as a WAC resource on campus for several decades. In describing their WAC program in 1990, Joseph M. Williams and Geoffrey G. Colomb state that future work will focus on "expanding the size of the Schoolhouse in order to expand the pool of experienced graduate student lectors" as well as "hiring more faculty to train these programs"

(109). This last point is particularly important for Williams and Colomb given that they state that "unless we expand the number of faculty either by persuading others to participate (unlikely) or hiring new faculty, we will necessarily grow smaller because the faculty now involved in the program are overextended" (109). Such issues have continued to be relevant in all of WAC work across many institutions, not just at the University of Chicago.

Two things are salient here in this drive to increase size by getting more faculty on board WAC programs, which will allow WAC to spread across campus. The first is a move toward accomplishing the vision of WAC and gaining what de Certeau would describe as a *panoptic practice*. When McLeod and others discuss successful WAC programs as those that have cultivated a permanent presence on campus by becoming accepted and integrated throughout the curriculum or when Williams and Colomb visualize the resources that are necessary to enact a far-reaching WAC program, we are reminded that effective strategies not only create a vision but also take view of an entire terrain and learn how to "transform foreign forces [i.e., funding, faculty, curricula, etc.] into objects that can be observed and measured, and thus control and 'include' them within [this] scope of vision" (de Certeau 37).

Second, this effort for continual growth remains with us today. As we can see, this language is embedded within the evolutionary framework that Condon and Rutz use. In describing the differences between foundational, established, integrated, and institutional change agent WAC programs, they note the shift in goals, funding, and structures that embody each particular type of program. For example, in terms of funding, an established WAC program "has [its] own budget, though often on temporary budget" and uses this funding to make its presence visible in terms of space, staffing, and programming (362). An integrated program, on the other hand, has a budget that "grows to support a more substantial presence" in that an integrated WAC program "is able to become important to other efforts, other programs, other agendas" on campus (371).

And by the time a program evolves into an institutional change agent, it has a very large reach indeed. When describing Washington State University's Critical Thinking Project, the two writers state: "During four years of grant supported activities, the project reached more than 350 individual faculty and helped more than a dozen departments and programs redesign all of parts of students' critical thinking abilities in those concentrations" (375). Other programs such as the University of Minnesota's Writing-Enriched Curriculum project, also "infuse" writing throughout an institution by "engaging each and every department in designing curriculum reform" (375). Evident in both of these examples is the far reach that evolved WAC programs have and the ways in which otherwise foreign spaces are made readable in the pursuit of strategic moves that will help WAC grow.

More recently, Laura Brady has used this evolutionary framework to explore the concept of growth itself in WAC models. In "Evolutionary Metaphors for Understanding WAC/WID," she notes that "[e]volutionary metaphors [such as Condon and Rutz's] help explain and explore patterns, interrelationships, and the conditions under which a program can thrive. The metaphor can also help us understand that not all mutations are adaptive or successful, and that certain conditions threaten a program's survival" (8). That is, as important as developing a portable model for understanding WAC programs (one that can be applied from one institution to another) is tracking the local circumstances that give rise to programs. As Brady notes, "WAC programs do not spring forth fully formed" (11), and to explore how WAC programs change—whether through grand evolutionary transformations or as localized mutative innovations—she proposes a heuristic for exploring the genealogy of WAC programs. Not surprisingly, one of Brady's questions for such exploration focuses squarely on strategic alliances.

This is, of course, as it should be, given that WAC depends on strategic endeavors. However, in this article, we show that despite the necessities for enacting strategies, tactics can also serve as topoi for sustaining WAC partnerships—particularly when WAC initiatives on campus are formative. Some WAC initiatives, after all, may not necessarily "evolve" from one type to another. Rather, some foundational or established WAC initiatives may continue to change—or "mutate"—without necessarily evolving, despite the long-term strategic planning that Condon and Rutz mention (360).

Tactics and Space

That said, directors and coordinators of foundational or established WAC programs may find it useful to adapt a strategic lens when viewing their positionality. According to de Certeau, unlike strategies, which shore up resources and claim space, tactics are short-term bursts of "isolated actions" that capitalize on opportunities rather than on an extended vision (36). Moreover, tactics are connected to *kairos* in that one must have the wherewithal to identify and take advantage of the opportunities afforded by a particular situation (xx). This makes sense. One cannot plan for every eventuality. And in those moments that are out of one's control, one needs to be ready to seize the opportunity to gain an advantage.

In comparison to strategies, tactics are spontaneous and "based on the re-use and on the non-possession of space whose regulation and control is ensured by other stakeholders" (Andres 764). Tactics also do not promise anything over a long period of time; they are opportunistic, temporary, and lack what de Certeau refers to as "a proper locus" (37). Thinking of WAC work in this way changes how we approach long term (and short term) goals for our programs. If we expand our focus beyond accumulating and redefining spaces into readable loci across campus, what exactly would that mean for administrators of WAC programs?

Recently, Elizabeth Wardle has noted how writing program administrators can benefit from paying attention to and seizing opportune moments that develop within their institutions. Specifically, Wardle details how the English department at the University of Central Florida was able to take advantage of a kairotic moment to implement a new "Writing about Writing" (WAW) curriculum and, at the same time, reduce class size, in large part due to the opportunities created by UCF's president to improve undergraduate education. Wardle's experience at UCF was not too different from what we would find at other institutions: first-year English courses were over-enrolled and taught by contingent faculty, and they covered a wide swath of content from course to course. Wardle's arguments to administrators allowed instructors to attend workshops on WAW pedagogy, which helped to mitigate the belief that any-one can teach writing, regardless of training and experience in studying writing; this change had the simultaneous effect of helping to create a more consistent curriculum. And Wardle is quick to note that such changes occurred in large part to being attuned to kairos. "Sometimes there are moments," she writes, "when change is more possible than usual, and as rhetoricians and writing program administrators, we can and must be prepared to take advantage of them" (n. pag.).

Although Wardle's example stems from first-year writing program administration, it does highlight how thinking tactically might look in broader writing administration contexts. Tactics may not necessarily come directly from the work one has invested in a program. Rather, the opening can emerge from outside circumstances beyond the immediate control of WAC administrators and WPAs. We expand on Wardle's experience by highlighting how tactical actions might look in a WAC context.

Animal Sciences WAC Partnership

There is no officially recognized WAC program at Purdue University, where both authors earned their doctorate degrees. We do not have a director of WAC nor writing workshops that faculty from other disciplines take to introduce writing concepts and assignments into their courses. Few campus-wide structures of this kind exist at Purdue because its individual colleges have traditionally established their own degree requirements. While Purdue instituted a core curriculum in 2013, establishing a mechanism for campus-wide requirements, the robust infrastructure required by a formal WAC program is not part of the history or culture of the institution. As founding Purdue Writing Lab director Muriel Harris puts it, faculty who do assign writing do so with "varying goals and varying awareness of what writing can do to enhance learning" (90).

In lieu of a formal WAC program, faculty and graduate students from the English department collaborate frequently with other departments on campus. Many of these collaborations involve the Writing Lab, which, as Harris wrote in 1999, often functions as a "de facto WAC Center." Harris argues that, while writing centers can take on a degree of faculty development work on campuses with no WAC program, limitations on their resources mean they cannot replace a WAC program. That said, she maintains that "there should be some recognition that there is merit in assisting with small changes even when there may be no likelihood of large-scale ones" (Harris 101). In the past, Writing Lab staff have consulted faculty in curriculum development, led classroom-based workshops, and given these collaborations a degree of permanence by hosting materials on the Purdue Online Writing Lab (OWL).[2]

Sometimes, ad hoc collaborations between the English department and other departments grow into long-term partnerships. However, because these partnerships have developed organically and not through any official, centralized program, they look very different depending on the department. For example, graduate students in rhetoric and composition have been able to serve as WAC coordinators for the School of Mechanical Engineering for the last several years, a relationship that grew out of Writing Lab-led workshops. In this role, a graduate student is responsible for leading workshops on writing instruction and evaluating writing assignments for teaching assistants who teach several sections of mechanical engineering courses.

While the School of Mechanical Engineering has instituted a workshop model of WAC, the partnership with the animal sciences (ANSC) department on the other hand has taken on a service model of WAC (see Jablonski 104–10 for the distinction between these types of WAC programs). This program has been described elsewhere (Sánchez and Nall) so we will not spend too much time detailing its intricacies or history here except to point out the following:

- This partnership has entered its second decade.
- Two graduate students serve as WAC consultants who are embedded in a specific ASNC course on Animal Breeding and Genetics (ANSC 311).
- Consultants are responsible for developing and grading student assignments in this course (such as professional memos, letters, and emails) as well as providing workshops and presentations on specific writing aspects (such as the language used in a beef simulation technical report).
- Graduate students typically spend two semesters in this role, but sometimes have stayed on for up to four semesters, which differs significantly from the mechanical engineering partnership, in which graduate students have stayed on for multiple years at a time.

In both of these roles (ANSC and mechanical engineering), graduate students are paid for their work through the different departments that are requesting WAC work. Goals for the WAC partnership are decided on collaboratively with faculty stakeholders. ANSC WAC coordinators do not have supervisors and are responsible for finding their own replacements once they have decided to move on. Seemingly, this partnership can be most closely classified as foundational, according to Condon and Rutz's taxonomy. In terms of its primary goals, it came about because faculty saw a need for incorporating more writing in the curriculum (365); its source of funding comes from the goodwill of an administrative entity (362); and its structure depends on a "small group of collaborators" to keep it going (362).

Below, we discuss how we each seized kairotic moments in deploying assessment and evaluation processes in tactical ways—not to expand the spaces that our WAC partnership with ANSC occupied (and thus shift how it can be categorized according to Condon and Rutz's typology)—but to safeguard it as it continued to mutate over time. A few pieces of information should be given before we proceed. First, to avoid confusion, it is important to mention that although we each served as coordinators for the ANSC WAC partnership, we did so during different time periods and with different colleagues as the second coordinator. Fernando served for three semesters from the fall of 2013 to the fall of 2014, and Daniel held the position immediately beforehand between fall of 2012 and spring of 2013. Additionally, we would like to point out that our primary intention in discussing these experiences is to showcase the work that can take place by thinking tactically. Even though our examples showcase the at times complicated and even frustrating work of handling formative WAC partnerships, we do not wish to use this piece to highlight the benefits of writing instruction to Purdue students or advocate for a more formal WAC program. Rather, our goal is more portable: namely, to showcase the strength of using resources from a liminal position of power in the face of larger structural threats within the context of shepherding formative WAC programs, which can be useful within other institutional contexts.

Tactics in Play

Fernando

Although lacking a centralized WAC program affords ANSC WAC coordinators the ability to create their own power structures on a micro-scale (developing curricula on their own with input from content faculty and making personnel decisions about replacements, for example), such a vacuum leaves the partnership susceptible to macro-level power structures. To illustrate, in the Spring of 2014, there was much discussion throughout our campus—a four-year public institution with an undergraduate student population of approximately thirty thousand—that our new president would like to implement standardized assessment to measure how much our students were learning. In his discussions of student learning, our president had professed to subscribe to the points made by Richard Arum and Josipa Roska in *Academically Adrift*. Briefly, Arum and Roska argue that students are only learning minimally in college because they are not being asked to read and write enough. Many have taken issue with the authors' methods and findings, for example, in that they do not operationalize their terms sufficiently, make errors in statistical analysis, make sweeping claims, and rely solely on the Collegiate Learning Assessment exam for their data (Haswell; Gunner; Addison and McGee).

My major concern at the time was that if such standardized assessment were to be implemented across campus, it might occlude students' learning about writing in this ANSC course and the WAC component could thus be seen as disposable from a budgetary standpoint. As Martha Townsend has noted, WAC scholarship often cites the lack of programmatic and administrative support structures as a reason for why WAC programs struggle or fail . While the ANSC department has been willing to maintain a budget for WAC instruction, the lack of institutional or even English department investment in our WAC instruction means that we are vulnerable to outside forces attempting to eliminate the work of graduate student WAC coordinators if it is viewed as nonessential.

Without the layer of tenured faculty who are experts in writing to make arguments for the longevity of WAC on campus, I knew that our partnership with ANSC would be vulnerable when discussing it with upper administrators. Turning to de Certeau's conceptualization of tactics would be especially helpful in this particular instance given that de Certeau discusses these terms within the larger context of uneven power structures. Using urban planning, linguistics, and war as a few backdrops, de Certeau showcases how users within systems develop and use their own methods for accomplishing goals in the face of established and intended rules and regulations. This action characterizes a manipulation of a system "by users who are not its makers" (xiii) in the pursuit of a task.

A "way of operating" within a spatial and linguistic power structure might be reflected in the following example.

> . . . a North African living in Paris or Roubaix (France) insinuates *into* the system imposed on him by the construction of a low-income housing development or of the French language the ways of "dwelling" (in a house or language) peculiar to his native Kabylia. He superimposes them and, by that combination, creates for himself a space in which he can find *ways of using* the constraining order of the place or of the language. Without leaving the place where he has no choice but to live and which lays down its law for him,

he establishes within it degrees of *plurality* and creativity. By an art of being in between, he draws unexpected results from his situation. (30).

Within my context, the purpose, then, was to make the necessity of the WAC partnership visible should the need arise to justify it. Tactically, this would mean using methods that borrowed from the values of the imposing system (namely assessment), but which would allow me to create a space to find "a way of using" the constraining order to showcase counternarratives that could speak against any reductive "students did not score high on writing" arguments. I set about looking toward the future of the partnership and to answer questions that spoke to WAC's relevance within the ANSC curriculum.

However, given my positioning as a transient graduate student with little authority, I had to, as de Certeau describes, "make do" with the few resources available to me. Specifically, this meant conducting a small-scale local assessment project which would connect the writing that students produce in the WAC classroom with the writing goals that are valued beyond the classroom. In this way, I could better showcase the ways in which the partnership addressed the values that the department placed on writing. And it would better showcase, in Condon's words, how "assessments designed locally to address local initiatives and contexts are more likely to portray those contexts accurately and treat the stakeholders fairly than are large-scale state, regional, or national assessments" (37).

The literature on approaches to WAC assessment has continued to expand in recent decades. In 1988, Toby Fulwiler argued that despite the fact that WAC programs had been around for over a decade, "no comprehensive evaluations of writing across the curriculum programs have been completed" (61), making it difficult for WAC directors and administrators to understand why programs succeed or fail. Since then, there have been a few more attempts to put forth robust conversations about WAC assessment. In 1997, Kathleen Blake Yancey and Brian Huot published their edited collection *Assessing Writing Across the Curriculum*. At the time, it was much needed, as one of the contributors, Meg Morgan reiterated Fulwiler's point, noting that "nothing much has happened in print that provides direction for WAC directors in their efforts to assess their programs" (143). While the collection indeed signaled a more focused attention to the issue of assessment in WAC, Bill Condon, writing four years later, lamented that "only two selections [in the collection] . . . address student outcomes from WAC, and only two others . . . address the administrative audience for WAC evaluation. The rest address the 'same old, same old' issues that surround faculty development *qua* curriculum reform" (32). Indeed, most of the texts on assessment did focus on WAC faculty and workshop evaluation and development.

More recently, however, there have been broader discussions of programmatic assessment in WAC. For example, in "Assessing Writing in Cross-Curricular Programs," Anson develops a model of WAC assessment that takes into account the contexts within which WAC programs exist—from an individual context where "a lone teacher who assigns and supports writing in his or her course, outside of any systematic emphasis on writing" (102) to an institutional context wherein institutions develop and regulate requirements for WAC instruction—and the levels of assessment that can take place (from instructional interventions in the classroom to more formal investigations). The goal, as Anson explains, would be to find appropriate alignments between these two axes depending on one's context in order produce appropriate assessment projects that focus on the outcomes of each particular WAC program. Adding to that, in 2009, the journal *Across the Disciplines* published a special issue specifically focused on WAC assessment. In their introduction to their issue, the editors, Kistler, Yancey, Taczak, and Szysmanski, note that as WAC programs have spread and grown, they have looked very different depending on their specific contexts and therefore WAC administrators have implemented "a diversity of methods to meet their particular WAC/CAC assessment needs" (n. pag.). Yet, behind the different data-gathering techniques—whether they be qualitatively or quantitatively driven—the editors emphasize that a recurring theme is an interest in documenting the value of these programs. This interest is not surprising given how invested WAC administrators can become in their programs and how motivated they can become to showcase the importance of their program.

With this in mind, my assessment work began by consulting with writing assessment professionals at national and international conferences such as the Council of Writing Program Administrators Conference in Bloomington, IL and the International Writing Across the Curriculum conference in Minneapolis, MN, both during the summer of 2014. Three goals generally came up in these discussions within the context of the ANSC partnership:

- Conducting a "genre reality check" by contacting current employers and seeing what genres employees are asked to compose in to help determine the viability and applicability of the genres that are taught as part of the WAC partnership
- Contacting recent alumni from the program to obtain the same information regarding genre and purposes for writing that they experience
- Bringing in outside animal sciences professionals who had graduated from Purdue's program and asking them to talk to current students about the type of writing that they perform on a regular basis.

In essence, my main research questions were how the WAC curriculum for Animal Science 311: Animal Breeding and Genetics was meeting the needs of animal science majors and what changes might be necessary to implement in order for it to align more closely with the types of writing that they may be asked to perform in the workforce. In this way, I wanted to collect data on a local level that would describe how our partnership functioned and could function in line with the goals of professionals in the field of animal sciences.

Human subjects approval was obtained to distribute surveys to employers and recent ANSC alumni who had taken ANSC 311 within the last ten years. A list of employer representatives (mostly recruiters) and alumni to contact were provided by the alumni coordinator. To further aid with response rates, the coordinator and I agreed that surveys to both populations should be kept short. Therefore, the following questions were asked to ANSC employers:

1. Name of your company (optional).
2. Please describe the type of work that your employees with backgrounds in animal sciences do on a regular basis at your company.
3. Please describe the writing that your employees with backgrounds in animal sciences have to do on a regular basis at your company.
4. Whom do your employees with a background in animal sciences have to write to on a regular basis in your company?
5. How often would you estimate that your recent employees with a background in animal sciences have to write to these people?
6. What writing skills or writing experiences do you look for when hiring new employees with a background in animal sciences?
7. What writing skills or experiences do you wish your new employees with a background in animal sciences learned while still in school?

ANSC alumni were asked the following questions:

1. Name (Will not be shared, will be de-identified)
2. What year did you graduate from Purdue?
3. What was your major at Purdue?
4. Briefly describe your job responsibilities and the type of company that you work for.
5. What types of writing do you do at work for your job?
6. Rank how much time you spend performing each of these types of writing.
7. Whom do you write to or for on a regular basis on the job?
8. Briefly explain why/what you write to each of the following people (from question 7).
9. What are your strengths as a writer?
10. What do you wish you could improve as a writer?

Initial requests to complete the surveys were sent out to both population groups during November 2014; a subsequent reminder was emailed in January 2015. In total, twenty employer surveys were sent and seven were received. Fourteen alumni were contacted and eleven responded.

While this article is not necessarily about the results of the assessment project, I include the results obtained from a few questions to highlight how those results will help to further the conversation about the value of WAC in ANSC—in essence, what was gained from this tactical work. In regards to what genres writers compose on the job, alumni noted that they wrote "medical forms" for certain audiences while others communicated that they wrote to a certain audience to "influence or explain." Much like animal science employers, alumni mentioned descriptive workplace genres or description itself as being valuable in the writing that they produce. However, alumni also indicated that persuasive writing was just as necessary for their writing in the workplace—much more than employers seemed to mention. I should note that there was nothing to link these particular alumni with the employers that responded, meaning that the alumni respondents could work for different companies from where employer respondents work. What became clear, however, was that ANSC 311 students will have to write for multiple purposes through various genres once they work in the professional world.[3]

Another notable finding is the split between the skills that alumni and employers value. In their responses, alumni mentioned a range of different skills that they use or wish that they could improve. These range from being "grammar-minded" to an ability to "speak to many audiences" in terms of current strengths (Appendix 1) and a desire for better stylistic clarity and creativity as far as strengths alumni would like to develop (Appendix 2). Employers, on the other hand, only seem to be concerned with graduates' grammatical abilities (Appendix 3). Clearly, based even on these few responses, we can already see the work that needs to be done from a pedagogical and an administrative perspective.

While this assessment tactic began as a way of reality-checking the genres that are taught in the WAC component of ANSC 311, the tactic changed over the course of the months when it was implemented. The fact that alumni, much like employers, reported a wide range of genres did not necessarily mean that we needed to teach students to compose for every eventuality. Rather, when it came to building arguments for the importance of the WAC partnership, we needed to shift gears and refocus on the overall skills that students reported using or desiring to possess. More so, with these sample responses (as limited as they might have been), future WAC coordinators would have a roadmap of what to concentrate on when they revised assignments or provided lesson plans. To illustrate, although we provided students with opportunities to write to different types of audiences—for example, the memos were written to inside supervisors, while letters were sometimes written to outside clients—could there be a way to expand on this need for students to practice reaching different audiences, which many alumni emphasized? Perhaps more could be done to connect students with actual scenarios that alumni experience in the animal science field rather than having the instructor of the class create a scenario for students to respond to. In this way, their writing might be seen as fitting an actual need in the community of practitioners where they may one day work.

Similarly, a takeaway from the data was that WAC coordinators should not overlook grammatical issues, as nearly all of the employer respondents stated that this was something that ANSC writers needed to improve. This takeaway poses the challenge of how to address grammar productively, as research indicates that grammar instruction is ineffective when taught without the proper context (see Hartwell; Harris and Rowan). At the same time, the responses from employers provide an opportunity to explore further what was meant by the term "grammar." This term could refer to spelling, mechanics, sentence construction, or even appropriate vocabulary and style. Having a more concrete understanding of what grammar errors occur most frequently, and how style may be implicated in this discussion, may help WAC coordinators prioritize instruction in a way that connects grammar and style to students' writing context. From an administrative and research perspective, future WAC coordinators could reach out again to employers and determine what exactly the term "grammar" might mean for this specific population. While the threat of standardized assessment still looms over the institution as a whole even after I have graduated and serve as assistant professor at another institution, I am confident that I have contributed to the tools that future WAC coordinators will need to argue for the continued funding of the ANSC WAC partnership should they need to.

Daniel

During roughly the same time, having already acted as a WAC coordinator for ANSC 311, I also became interested in how the partnership between English and animal sciences could continue to improve and to demonstrate its efficacy. With this goal in mind, I knew that agriculture and animal sciences scholarship primarily values writing instruction in terms of career preparation, in its promise to prepare students for workplace writing (Barry and Orth) and to instill the habits of mind needed to continue learning on the job (Orr). Given this priority, I, too, focused an inquiry on the college-to-career transition. However, while Fernando gathered survey data pertaining to writing skills and genres that employers and alumni value, my assessment project centered on collecting students' perceptions of how the ANSC 311 course was preparing them for their future careers. In this way, although these two projects were in no way coordinated, they provided complementary bursts of input that helped reveal a larger dimension of our WAC partnership.

I was mostly interested in studying student perceptions of their coursework's future relevance because much of the research on transfer of learning has demonstrated a connection between how undergraduates perceive the future relevance of writing assignments and their ability to transfer their learning across varied contexts (Yancey, Robertson, & Taczak; Driscoll & Wells). Moreover, as educational psychologists Kevin Pugh and David Bergin suggest, motivational factors influence transfer in terms of initial learning, the initiation of transfer attempts, and persistence on transfer tasks (156). This meant devising a protocol that would assess both perception and motivation in ANSC students on the coursework that they produced. As mentioned previously, students in the course produce a technical report, which seemed like the most appropriate assignment about which to collect information given that it occupies a very discipline-specific place in the curriculum. This beef simulation report, or "beefsim," as a simulation, is meant explicitly to replicate an out-of-school experience with animal breeding. In the simulation, students are given a "herd" of cattle and make selection decisions over ten "years" with the goal of increasing yearling weight. Students then report on their selection process and findings in a technical report. Through focus groups, I wanted to learn what connections students were making between this classroom simulation and their future work on the job. I also wanted to begin to see whether those perceptions of relevance affected students' approaches to completing the work. My overarching goal was to help future WAC coordinators identify existing successes and marshal students' own language about college-to-career transitions to better support this transition.

Focus groups were a natural choice for this inquiry because they allowed me to elicit opinions and memories participants would not think of on their own and broadly ascertain consensus. More importantly, they provided an opportunity to collect data from a large number of participants in a short time, to take the pulse of as many students in ANSC 311 as possible in order to relay that input to the program and ask new questions. In April 2014, I conducted focus groups with twenty-one out of sixty-two enrolled ANSC 311 students. All participants were juniors or seniors majoring in animal sciences. At the time, students had just submitted their beefsim reports less than a week before and had not yet received grades. I developed these focus groups with three research questions:

1. What connections, if any, do students see between their work on the beef simulation assignment and their future professional work?
2. How do students use resources, particularly teacher talk, to complete the beef simulation assignment?
3. How do students' perceptions of future transfer relate to their resource use, if at all?

I asked questions such as:

- Tell me about your future career goals.
- How do you see your beefsim work applying to or preparing you for your future work?
- Think back to when you were working on the beefsim project. What was it like?
- What was the most helpful in completing the report?
- What would you want future students to know about the beefsim project?

Here, I will highlight a few key points from the results that might help future WAC coordinators make situated judgments. First, participants disagreed considerably about the beefsim's relevance to their careers. This is perhaps unsurprising given the variety of career goals they reported: most said they plan to attend veterinary school after graduating, while others said they want to attend graduate school in animal nutrition, return to their family farms, pursue sales, or do agricultural extension work, while a few said they were undecided. This means that a majority of participants do not plan to be breeders (or "producers," terms they used interchangeably), though they expect to have varying degrees of contact with breeders.

There was also significant disagreement about relevance even within a pre-vet track. These students connected the relevance of the beefsim to the ways they expected to work with breeders and how they saw the relationship between breeding and care. The focus groups contained multiple exchanges in which participants debated whether, as veterinarians, they would only need to understand general breeding concepts such as "knowing what affects what" or if the more advanced quantitative analysis required by the beefsim would also be useful when working with breeders.

In addition to seeing vet/breeder relationships and the value of quantitative knowledge differently, participants also understood relevance in terms of the genre of the research report. Many participants did not expect to write a similar scientific report in the future, leading them to adamantly reject the assignment, while a few did expect to write more, such as one student planning to attend graduate school for animal nutrition. Whether they valued the report assignment or not, they widely understood genre acquisition and transfer as one-to-one application.

The participants with the most negative feedback demonstrated an underlying rejection of ANSC 311 even having a writing component. A few particularly vocal participants suggested that any "bad writers" who still needed feedback on their writing as juniors and seniors should seek it on their own time. Good writers, in contrast, should not need writing instruction at this level, and forcing it on them is a kind of punishment. These attitudes are a reaction not only to specific assignments but also to the very premise of WAC and suggest a view of writing as a basic skill.

Other participants expressed a milder resistance to the WAC component, suggesting instead that the connections between course content and writing assignments were not always clear, and some assignments might better fit courses earlier in the animal sciences curriculum. This discussion provided a window into students' larger experience of writing in their major, however brief or subjective. Such insight is vital to making informed judgments when presenting the WAC curriculum to students and administrators.

The focus groups were not intended to answer big questions conclusively, but rather to get a quick snapshot of what students that semester were experiencing and thinking. They did not motivate large scale redevelopment of the ANSC 311 writing curriculum, but instead small adjustments to the assignments' rhetorical situations and to how writing was "pitched" to students. These adjustments were made in order to make connections to workplace needs more tangible. Moreover, the focus groups provided insight into many students' fundamental beliefs about writing instruction, such as writing as a basic skill and genre acquisition and transfer as one-to-one application. These beliefs are beyond the reach of pedagogical interventions to neatly resolve. However, an understanding of these beliefs and students' language to describe them can inform WAC coordinators' judgments when making in-the-moment, tactical decisions while meeting with students and faculty, providing written feedback, or arguing for the value of the WAC partnership.

Discussion

By engaging in short, isolated, and uncoordinated bursts of activity, we were able to contribute to the WAC partnership in unique ways from different perspectives. While we had discussed the projects related to the ANSC WAC partnership in passing, we were independent in the work we undertook. This was most likely because of the different roles that we held at the time of each of these projects. Fernando was still a WAC coordinator and thus had a different interest in the future curriculum of the partnership before leaving. Daniel had stepped down as WAC coordinator a year prior to the time of his project. It was only during a meeting in the spring of 2015 with the ANSC instructor and coordinators that we produced our results and began to talk about our work as tactical. Fernando brought up five recommendations which included being aware of grammatical concerns, developing assignments that were descriptive rather than focusing entirely on any particular genre, and emphasizing rhetorical awareness, among others. Daniel's primary recommendations were to frame school-to-work transitions directly and deliberately, tweak assignment guidelines to make relevance explicit, emphasize transferable skills and knowledge, and present genre acquisition and transfer in a nuanced way. Reporting findings to ANSC faculty and then-current WAC coordinators provided an occasion for both groups to confer on matters of shared concern and discuss each of our perspectives on the issues raised. Our conversation was particularly empowering given the little power we had as graduate students to help the WAC partnership evolve into something other than a foundational enterprise. In this way, we were able to showcase the expertise that we had developed by, as de Certeau describes, converting our competence into authority (7). The knowledge that we had gained about ANSC students and the WAC partnership through our tactical assessment work allowed us to speak with authority and to advocate for certain changes going forward.

Such issues of building authority should not be overlooked within contexts where coordinators have minimal influence within larger power structures. To illustrate, in "Thinking Liminally," Phillips, Shovlin, and Titus argue that graduate WPAs usually occupy a paradoxical space of lack. This means that graduate WPAs lack the "status markers such as a terminal degree, a job description, or a permanent position" (42) that typically come with WPA positions. Such liminal positions might take the form of graduate students having access to writing program budgets but not being able to use those funds or a faculty member with a master's degree running a writing center despite a lack of credentials. Occupying a space of lack (a no-place), the writers note, can result in feelings of powerlessness for liminal WPAs in these various writing program administrative roles. Phillips, Shovlin, and Titus offer a few recommendations for thinking liminally in these instances—assessing how much power one has, assessing other available power, and using institutional impermanence and invisibility to one's advantage (55). These are certainly important suggestions to keep in mind, particularly when positions offer little room to exert institutional power. However, we hope that thinking tactically can help to expand this particular framework—for liminal WPAs or otherwise.

That is, adopting a tactical lens provided us with a larger sense of agency, as we were able to work within our limitedly defined job description and determine how much power we could exert for the sake of helping preserve and improve a writing partnership. As WAC coordinators, we worked with and for the ANSC department but as consultants whose positions could be terminated at any point. We also coordinated with the ANSC 311 faculty member, but we lacked any infrastructural guidance from the English department. Given that tactics naturally spring from an absence of a "proper locus" to call one's own (de Certeau 37), it isn't surprising that we turned to thinking tactically to create knowledge and new narratives about our WAC partnership.

At no point, however, were we under the impression that our work would evolve the writing partnership with ANSC 311 into a something that was more established, or that we would strategically expand into new territory via our methods. Indeed, Fernando undertook his project to help accumulate evidence that the program should remain the same. While it would be tremendously helpful if more resources were put in place to expand WAC to truly reach across the curriculum, the infrastructure is simply not there. Given that there is no supervisory body composed of established and long-standing associate or full professors overseeing this partnership and that a revolving door of graduate students have been responsible for maintaining it, we saw value in thinking tactically to help keep our partnership viable in the long-run (and to allow for more strategic thinking in the long run). We should be clear that we do not view this partnership in any negative light. While forces beyond our control may improve or worsen the conditions of our WAC partnership, our tactical assessment projects remind us to accept the current circumstances of our WAC work as they are and to remember the constraints within which we navigate.

Since our meeting with ANSC faculty and administrators, some of our recommendations have been implemented and some have not, but our tactics have added to the conversation surrounding the ANSC WAC partnership. Taking advantage of an opening allowed us to showcase the work that still needs to happen within our partnership and continue our discussions of how it might change in the future—without any illusions that it would expand beyond what it already is. Indeed, to illustrate how this partnership continues to change, changes in ANSC faculty availability have caused the WAC component to shift from being embedded in the Animal Breeding and Genetics course to the senior seminar. WAC coordinators teach the same number of students, and teach mostly the same types of assignments, but the context of their work is different now. At the same time, the College of Liberal Arts has begun to take steps toward a writing intensive requirement within the college. Because the English department is housed within Liberal Arts, time will tell how this change will affect its partnerships across campus—whether this means the ANSC WAC partnership will evolve or mutate we cannot tell at this point.

We end by cautioning that thinking tactically does not mean being sloppy with one's methods for engaging in this work. We should keep in mind Toby Fulwiler's cautious words that "measures that are quick and dirty do not seem to prove much" (63). Although Fulwiler is speaking mainly of using qualitative measures to "prove" that WAC initiatives are improving student writing, it is still important to stress the importance of adopting methods that are holistic, robust, and non-reductive across all assessment-based endeavors. Within our particular context of tactical assessment, this meant taking the time to be inclusive of various viewpoints and perspectives, collecting as much data as we could without overwhelming our participants, and listening to the stories that emerged from our results in order to push forward with recommendations.

Local assessment measures can act as tactics that can both help give more valid information on what students value when it comes to writing and be more inclusive of stakeholders beyond students and administrators. What we have tried to show through these particular interventions is how we, as McLeod and Miraglia encourage, can "jump on the assessment bandwagon and attempt to steer it in the right direction. The danger of all assessment initiatives in education is that they become reductive" (6). WAC programs need to balance stakeholder needs with collecting data that "reflect the complexity of both student learning and the WAC programs, which are structured to facilitate that learning" (6–7).

We have focused in this article on one particular case, but from here we can argue that all WAC administrators and WPAs in general—especially those liminal and graduate WPAs serving in constrained positions—should pay close attention to infrastructural opportunities that present themselves to form meaningful tactics for obtaining stakeholder buy-in; particularly, as Barbara Walvoord has mentioned, when the future of WAC looks to be highly dependent on securing funding and concentrating on institutional concerns (69–70), we may need to look for momentary bursts of activity to help guide our programs along. While thinking tactically may not necessarily allow a WAC program to gain new ground and evolve (as de Certeau notes, a space of tactics cannot build on its own position, as "what it wins, it cannot keep" [37]), it can coordinate rather than distribute—meaning that it can rely on multiple temporary yet deliberate actions to show long-term value.

Acknowledgments

The authors would like to thank Roy Andrews and our three anonymous reviewers for all of their insightful comments and suggestions on our manuscript. We also thank Animal Sciences professor Terry Stewart for his strong commitment and dedication to writing across the curriculum and for providing English graduate students at Purdue the great opportunity to teach his Animal Sciences students about the importance that writing and rhetoric play in their current coursework and in their future workplace communication.

Notes

1. While we do not have enough space here to explain in detail the four different types of WAC programs that Condon and Rutz describe in their taxonomy, we provide an overview of each. Foundational programs take hold when the need for more writing instruction is identified; funding for these types of programs largely depends on upper administration; faculty workshops are voluntary. Established WAC programs have their own (often temporary) budget; may have a more visible WAC office space and support staff and may even have course offerings in the curriculum institution-wide. Integrated WAC programs function as part of an institution; they are regularly assessed and have a growing budget; more so than with the previous two types, these programs upper administration

sees the value of integrating and requiring WAC throughout the curriculum. Institutional change agents can drive change on campus independent of upper administration; faculty outside of WAC turn to the WAC program as an entity for guidance (see Condon and Rutz 362–79 for a more detailed account of these types).

2. For further discussion of WAC on Purdue's campus, see Rutz, "Considering WAC from Training and Hiring Perspectives: An Interview with Irwin 'Bud' Weiser of Purdue University" and Bergmann, "The Writing Center as a Site for Engagement."

3. Among the genres reported by ANSC employers and hiring managers were: emails, project plans, Prezis and other presentations, reports, Excel spreadsheets, permits, popular articles, operating procedures, job descriptions, summaries, abstracts, and scholarly peer reviewed papers.

References

Addison, Joanne, and Sharon James McGee. "To the Core: College Composition Classrooms in the Age of Accountability, Standardized Testing, and Common Core State Standards." *Rhetoric Review*, vol. 34, no. 2, 2015, pp. 200–18.

Andres, Lauren. "Differential Spaces, Power Hierarchy and Collaborative Planning: A Critique of the Role of Temporary Uses in Shaping and Making Places." *Urban Studies*, vol. 50, no. 4, 2012, pp. 759–75.

Anson, Chris. "Assessing Writing in Cross-Curricular Programs: Determining the Locus of Activity." *Assessing Writing*, vol. 11, no. 2, 2006, pp. 100–12.

Arum, Richard, and Josipa Roska. *Academically Adrift: Limited Learning on College Campuses*. U of Chicago P, 2010.

Barry, Teresa Trupiano, and Michael Orth. "Designing Effective Writing Assignments for Students in the Animal Sciences." *Natural Sciences Education*, vol. 42, no. 1, 2013, pp. 137–44.

Bergmann, Linda. "The Writing Center as Site for Engagement." *Going Public: What Writing Programs Learn from Engagement*, edited by Shirley Rose and Irwin Weiser, Utah State UP, 2010, pp. 160–74.

Brady, Laura. "Evolutionary Metaphors for Understanding WAC/WID." *WAC Journal*, vol. 24, 2013, pp. 7–27.

Certeau, Michel de. *The Practice of Everyday Life*. U of California P, 1984.

Condon, William. "Accommodating Complexity: WAC Program Evaluation in the Age of Accountability." *WAC for the New Millennium: Strategies for Continuing Writing-Across-the-Curriculum Programs*, edited by Susan H. McLeod, Eric Miraglia, Margot Soven, and Christopher Thaiss, NCTE, 2001, 28–51.

Condon, William, and Carol Rutz. "A Taxonomy of Writing Across the Curriculum Programs: Evolving to Serve Broader Agendas." *College Composition and Communication*, vol. 64, no. 2, 2012, pp. 357–82.

Driscoll, Dana Lynn, and Jennifer Wells. "Beyond Knowledge and Skills: Writing Transfer and the Role of Student Dispositions in and Beyond the Writing Classroom." *Composition Forum*, vol. 41, no. 3, 2012, n. pag.

Fulwiler, Toby. "Evaluating Writing Across the Curriculum Programs." *Strengthening Programs for Writing Across the Curriculum*, edited by Susan McLeod. Jossey-Bass, 1988, pp. 61–75.

Gunner, Jeanne. "Everything That Rises . . ." *College Composition and Communication*, vol. 63, no. 3, 2012, pp. 491–95.

Hartwell, Patrick. "Grammar, Grammars, and the Teaching of Grammar." *College English*, vol. 47, no. 2, 1985, pp. 105–27.

Harris, Muriel. "A Writing Center without a WAC Program: The De Facto WAC Center/Writing Center." *Writing Centers and Writing Across the Curriculum Programs: Building Interdisciplinary Partnerships*, edited by Robert W. Barnett and Jacob S. Blumer, Greenwood Press, 1999, pp. 89–103.

Harris, Muriel, and Katherine E. Rowan. "Explaining grammatical concepts." *Journal of Basic Writing*, vol. 8, no. 2, 1989, pp. 21–41.

Haswell, Richard. "Methodologically Adrift." *College Composition and Communication*, vol. 63, no. 3, 2012, pp. 487–91.

Huot, Brian, and Michael Williamson. "Rethinking Portfolios for Evaluating Writing: Issues of Assessment and Power." *Situating Portfolios: Four Perspectives*, edited by Kathleen Blake Yancey and Irwin Weiser, Utah State UP, 1997, pp. 43–53.

Jablonski, Jeffrey. *Academic Writing Consulting and WAC: Methods and Models for Guiding Cross-Curricular Literacy Work*. Hampton Press, 2006.

Kinneavy, James L. "Writing Across the Curriculum." Profession, 1983, pp. 13–20.

Kistler, Ruth, Kathleen Blake Yancey, and Kara Taczak, with Natalie Szysmanski. "Introduction: Writing Across the Curriculum and Assessment." *Across the Disciplines*, vol. 6, 2009, n.pag. WAC Clearinghouse, http://wac.colostate.edu/atd/assessment/kistleretal.cfm.

McLeod, Susan H. "Writing Across the Curriculum: The Second Stage and Beyond." *College Composition and Communication*, vol. 40, no. 3, 1989, pp. 337–43.

McLeod, Susan H., and Eric Miraglia. "Writing Across the Curriculum in a Time of Change." *WAC for the New Millennium: Strategies for Continuing Writing-Across-the-Curriculum Programs*, edited by Susan H. McLeod, Eric Miraglia, Margot Soven, and Christopher Thaiss, NCTE, 2001, pp. 1–27.

Orr, Carolyn L. "Communication across the Curriculum in Animal Science." *Journal of Animal Science*, vol. 74, 1996, pp. 2828–34.

Phillips, Talinn, Paul Shovlin, and Megan Titus. "Thinking Liminally: Exploring the (com) Promising Positions of the Liminal WPA." *WPA: Writing Program Administration*, vol. 38, no. 1, no. 2014, pp. 42–64.

Rutz, Carol. "Considering WAC from Training and Hiring Perspectives: An Interview with Irwin "Bud" Weiser of Purdue University." *WAC Journal*, vol. 19, 2008, pp. 73–84.

Sánchez, Fernando, and Stacy Nall. "Crossbreeding Disciplines: Collaboratively Developing a Writing Culture in Animal Sciences Courses." *Writing Program and Writing Center Collaborations: Transcending Boundaries*, edited by Alice J. Myatt and Lynée L. Gaillet, Palgrave Macmillan, 2017, pp. 95-116.

Townsend, Martha. "WAC Program Vulnerability and What to Do about It: An Update and Brief Bibliographic Essay. *WAC Journal*, vol. 19, 2008, pp. 45–61.

Walvoord, Barbara. "The Future of WAC." *College English*, vol. 58, no. 1, 1996, pp. 58–79.

Wardle, Elizabeth. "Intractable Writing Program Problems, Kairos, and Writing about Writing: A Profile of the University of Central Florida's First-Year Composition Program." *Composition Forum*, vol. 27, 2013, n.pag.

Williams, Joseph M., and Gregory G. Colomb. "The University of Chicago." *Programs that Work: Models and Methods for Writing Across the Curriculum*, edited by Toby Fulwiler and Art Young. Portsmouth, Boynton / Cook Publishers, 1990, pp. 83–114.

Yancey, Kathleen Blake, Robertson, Liane, and Kara Taczak. *Writing across Contexts: Transfer, Composition, and Sites of Writing*. Utah State UP, 2014.

Appendix 1. Self-reported Strengths of ANSC Graduates.

Detail-oriented; punctuation and grammar-minded; thoroughness; able to express in an articulate manner via written word; professionalism; combining scientific conversation with understandable language.
Concise and literal writing that is easy to understand. Elaborate on activites [sic] when needed
Word structure, choice of words
Ability to articulate my point, and provide great detail. I am also able to speak to many audiences, and use interpersonal savvy to allow communincations [sic] to be understood and not taken the incorrect way.
I believe I have strong content to my pieces of writing.
Technical communication comes easily to me—breaking down a complex subject and making it easier for farmers and producers to understand why they should know about a topic.
I had 7 semesters of Latin in high school and received A's in my English and communications classes. I feel that I am an around decent writer.
I am never at a loss for words
Making difficult or more scientific topics easy to understand.
Being able to relate complex information in an understandable manner.

Appendix 2. Self-Reported Areas for Improvement as Reported by ANSC Graduates.

So much email can be misconstrued—I am constantly trying new ways to bring clarity and focus to the exact meaning of my messages.
Writing more articles instead of just policies and lesson plans
Communicate my thoughts better
The ability to write more scientifically. A larger vocabulary.
I wish to improve spelling and sentence structure.
I wish I had more experience in a diversity of writing styles. My strength in writing lies in technical communications, but I wish I had more creative writing work to showcase for clients.
The ability to write abstracts is always a challenge.
To be able too [sic] flawlessly have a better wording and to be able to communicate my emotions through the message that I am trying to relay.
Specific types of writing—writing for the web, for example, is a different skill than writing for a display or writing for a news release. It would be nice to have a refresher of each of these types.
I wish I was better at technical writing. The most difficult part for me is how simple and boring it is. I like to utilize more complex writing.

Appendix 3: Necessary ANSC Writing Skills as Reported by ANSC Employers.

How to properly address and write, grammar, proper use of punctuation
Grammar, sentence structure, proper punctuation, and writing to different comprehension levels
AS LONG AS REPORTS UTILIZE GOOD GRAMMER [sic], SPELLING AND PUNCTUATION WE ARE GOOD TO GO
New employees that possessed the ability to think and write critically would be an asset. The ability to read, understand, write company policy and enact new regulatory guidelines throughout the company or a department will be an important aspect of our company moving forward.
GOOD GRAMMAR
Business writing
Although this is looking backward, I wish I had more practice writing business and marketing pieces, or even how to structure contract language. Most of the stuff I had to do was pretty scientific in nature. However, perhaps some of this is due to the "Science" emphasis and not the "Agribusiness" emphasis? Perhaps there is more cross-training now. Side note on generalized communications.... Maybe there is a need for basic refresher courses/classwork geared toward basic writing skillsets? (Ex/Emails should not be written like an informal texts). Hypocritically and ironically, please ignore the poor grammar usage in this survey.

Community College STEM Faculty Views on the Value of Writing Assignments

KOSTAS D. STROUMBAKIS, NAMJONG MOH, AND
DIMITRIOS KOKKINOS

Introduction

Writing, as a pedagogical strategy, has been advocated, supported, and implemented in higher education for several decades, and its presence is on the rise. Thaiss and Porter (2010), having surveyed 2,034 postsecondary institutions, report 51% of 1,126 United States respondents have a writing program, typically called "writing across the curriculum" or "writing in the disciplines" (WAC/WID) (p. 562). This is a 33% increase over the past twenty years. Moreover, 27% percent of institutions that reported not having a WAC/WID program were planning for one (p. 541). As additional evidence of the vibrancy of WAC/WID, Thaiss and Porter (2010) report that funding for writing programs was "at the school's dime" with at most 21% of funding reported as not internal (p. 536)

This pedagogy has not been challenge-free. Though assertions regarding the effectiveness of writing are numerous, also common are assertions about the lack of evidence, in terms of large data, to support its effectiveness. For example, in Ackerman (1993) a review of thirty-five studies does not find "empirical validation of writing as a mode of learning" (p. 334). More recently, in a meta-analysis of forty-eight writing-to-learn treatments Bangert-Drowns et al. (2004) report that "writing can have a small positive impact" compared to conventional instruction. In their review of learning techniques, Dunlosky et al. (2013) rate summary writing as an overall low-utility technique. Sprigel and Delaney (2014) report they found no evidence that summary writing is more effective than restudying. More narrowly focused on the performance of calculus students, Porter and Masingila (2000) associate a positive impact with writing but could not determine if the difference is attributable to writing itself or to the additional time-on-task.

In addition to the financial cost of running a writing program, implementation can be resource intensive for both instructor and student, and both parties often need a degree of persuasion in order to engage. Faculty has often been reported as skeptical and resistant with regard to writing assignments (McLeod & Miraglia, 1997; Zhu, 2004; Salem and Jones, 2010). The time required to make, write, comment on, revise, and grade a typical writing assignment makes it an inefficient tool. Among science, technology, engineering and mathematics (STEM) departments, writing faces additional challenges. The fact is, STEM fields use considerably less writing than other fields do. More so, writing is typically associated with staples such as the essay or the term paper that are common in the humanities but not common in STEM. The association is traditional but can be evidenced by the dimensions of writing rubrics, which can serve as operational definitions of writing. This association contributes to the perception that STEM may not be the best place to practice writing.

It is difficult to measure the impact these challenges have on the acceptance of writing pedagogy across fields. At least for mathematics, data from the Conference Board of the Mathematical Sciences, CBMS (2010), suggest low usage of writing. CBMS (2010) reports mathematics enrollment accounting for more than 25% of course enrollment in four-year colleges and close to 30% in two-year colleges. A large majority of these courses are below the calculus level. Yet, only about 16% of sections, for four-year schools, report including writing assignments in the instructional methods. Accordingly, at least one in five undergraduate courses are essentially writing-free. There is evidence that brief writing segments focusing on communicating knowledge about the material can reinforce learning (Bangert-Drowns et al., 2004). Such assignments could also benefit students' communication and writing skills, and if the purpose of writing were narrowed to communicating concepts, we believe writing assignments would have wider acceptance.

Purpose of the Study

The purpose of this study is to investigate how STEM faculty, at a large urban community college, value writing assignments as a pedagogical tool and to examine their practices regarding such assignments. Literature shows there are several, widely relevant factors that make it important to know the positions of practitioners wherever WAC is implemented. Among these factors are:

- The pedagogy's potential to impact large numbers of students: the impact can be positive, if indeed writing can be used effectively, and negative otherwise. At our school, in Spring 2015, over 2,000 students were enrolled in WI STEM courses. Given the rise of WAC/WID (Thaiss & Porter 2010), such large enrollments are likely not limited to our school.
- The potential for negative impact increases with underprepared students. At our school, 70% of incoming freshmen require at least one remedial course (reading, writing, or mathematics), and the national picture, for community colleges, is similar (Bailey et al., 2010). Attrition rates, for mathematics in particular, are very high with negative consequences towards graduation rates (Bailey et al., 2010). If writing can be effective towards learning mathematics at all levels, we need to articulate measurable implementations lest we risk unnecessarily adding to the load of students who are already at risk.

- Practitioners provide important information on what works and their support is critical to the success of any pedagogical model (McLeod & Miraglia, 1997). Given the conflicting evidence regarding the efficacy of writing assignments, knowing what STEM faculty value can help toward a more effective pedagogy that is easier to adopt.

STEM instructors were invited to participate in an online questionnaire and express their views on the effectiveness of writing assignments as teaching and learning aids. Participants were asked to indicate agreement, using a 1-5 Likert Scale, with claims in the literature, as found for instance in Ackerman (1993), regarding benefits of writing assignments as experienced in their STEM courses, and the extent to which such benefits should serve as a primary goal of writing assignments in STEM courses. Additional questions addressed both views and practices on the amount and frequency of writing and also components of the writing-intensive paradigm, such as revision, peer review, low-stakes writing and high-stakes writing.

Each department has courses with the designation WI ("writing intensive"). These courses follow the college's guidelines on WAC/WID pedagogy and have a required writing component, which is weighted significantly in the calculation of the course grade. The college requires a minimum of two WI courses for graduation. Instructors who teach WI courses have completed a related workshop with general guidelines on the nature of the writing component.

Participants in this study self-identified either as "having WI experience," i.e., had taught a WI course, or not. Instructors with WI experience were also asked about their practices in non-WI courses. The survey was designed by the authors and revised based on comments from the school's assessment office and from supportive faculty.

Through the school's email system, STEM faculty were invited to participate in the online survey. The population of full-time STEM faculty was estimated to be at most 100. Two reminders were sent over a period of four weeks. In total, 65 invitees self-identified as STEM faculty responded to the survey. Of the 65 participants, 39 reported having WI experience at the school and 26 reported not having such experience. A total of 6 participants did not respond to all questions. Consequently, the summary results that follow use the response count for each survey item. All five STEM departments were represented: biology, chemistry, engineering, physics, and mathematics. Mathematics faculty represented roughly 45% of participants with the remaining 55% distributed rather evenly among the other four departments. These ratios are consistent with the relative sizes of the departments. About 8% of all participants reported their status as part-time faculty and the remainder as full-time. Through a survey question, 26 participants volunteered for a follow-up interview. Based on comments participants made in the survey, a stratified sample of 11 was selected for interviews. The goal of the interviews was to have participants elaborate on their responses and to seek additional confirmation that closed responses were interpreted correctly.

Summary of Results

STEM instructors believe in the potential of writing assignments as indicated by the high ratings of statements in Table 1. Comparisons through Mann-Whitney tests revealed no significant differences in the ratings of these questions between faculty with WI experience and faculty without WI experience.

Table 1. Mean ratings of potential benefits of writing assignments (1 = strongly disagree; 5 = strongly agree).

Statement	WI Experience (n = 39)	No WI Experience (n = 26)
WI assignments are an effective means for students to improve their writing skills	3.74	3.96
WI assignments are an effective means for students to learn course content	3.62	3.96
Note: For faculty who did not report having WI experience, the wording of the questions differed slightly from ". . . are an effective . . ." to ". . . can be an effective . . ."		

A majority, 66% (n = 65), of participants agreed or strongly agreed that activities other than WI assignments are as effective in helping students learn content. Alternatives offered as equally effective assignments included projects, presentations, discussions, and lab reports, most of which involve some form of writing. A majority of participants (n = 65) thought the added effort for teaching a WI course was worth the payoff, as indicated by the high ratings of statements in Table 2. No significant differences were found between the two groups on the questions of cost effectiveness through comparisons with Mann-Whitney tests.

Table 2. Mean ratings of cost effectiveness of writing assignments (1 = strongly disagree; 5 = strongly agree).

Statement	WI Experience (n = 39)	No WI Experience (n = 26)
If the effort for teaching a WI course were the same as that for a non-WI course, I would prefer to teach a WI course.	3.54	3.42
The effect of WI assignments on students' learning justifies the amount of student effort required to complete the assignments.	3.49	3.81
The effect of WI assignments on students' learning justifies the effort I put to prepare and administer the assignments	3.23	3.69

The two groups also agreed with what ought to be primary goals of writing assignments. These are summarized in Table 3. More so, there was strong agreement that these should be primary goals of writing assignments. Such goals are commonly discussed in the literature, Ackerman (1993), as potential areas of benefit from WI assignments.

Table 3. Mean ratings of primary academic goal of assignments (1 = strongly disagree; 5 = strongly agree).

Goal	WI Experience (n = 37)	No WI Experience (n = 26)
Discipline-Related Writing Skills	4.15	4.08
Critical Thinking	4.15	4.00
Reinforce Class Lessons	3.96	4.08
Make Connections	3.92	4.00
Learn New Content	3.88	3.81
General Writing Skills	3.46	3.69
Research	3.38	3.69

The one area where the two groups differed was on their ratings of students' writing skills when asked to show agreement with the following statement: "The writing skills, of students in my course(s), are adequate for the challenge of effective writing assignments." A Mann-Whitney test indicated that faculty with WI experience assessed students' writing skills significantly higher, $U = 94.5, p = 0.001, r = -0.76$, than faculty without WI experience. However, only a minority (32%) of WI faculty agreed or strongly agreed that students in WI courses had writing skills adequate for effective writing assignments.

Of those who had taught a WI course (n = 39), a majority, 57%, reported often or almost always giving revision opportunities. However, only 30% agreed that a majority of revised work showed significant improvement over the first draft. Only 6% reported using peer-review often or almost always. Revision and peer-review questions were not posed to faculty without WI experience.

WI Practices in Non-WI Courses

In addition to their general views on WI assignments, participants were asked about their practices in non-WI courses. For faculty without WI experience, presumably all of their courses would have been non-WI. In non-WI courses, inclusion of a writing component is at the instructor's discretion.

Among faculty with WI experience, reporting on practices in non-WI courses was significantly different from reporting on best practices for WI courses on the amount of writing, the number of assignments, and the percentage of each course grade allocated to the assignments. Table 4 summarizes the practices and median amount for each type of course.

Table 4. Median amounts reported by faculty with WI experience (n = 33).

High Stakes Assignments	
Best for maximizing effect to students in WI courses	
Number of Assignments	5
Total Writing (pages)	6
% Course Grade	20
Use in non-WI courses	
Number of Assignments	1
Total Writing (pages)	3
% Course Grade	10

Within WI reporting, total writing had low to moderate correlation with percentage of course grade, Spearman ρ(31) = 0.476, p = 0.005, whereas within the non-WI data these two variables were moderately correlated, Spearman ρ(31) = 0.700, p = 0.001. Faculty without WI experience were not asked for practices that would maximize the effect to students in WI courses. For non-WI courses, both groups were asked about practices mentioned in Table 5.

Table 5. Practices used in non-WI Courses on a 5-point scale (1 = "never" and 5 = "always").

Practice	Faculty With WI experience (n = 33)	Faculty Without WI experience (n = 26)
Mention in Syllabus	3.30	2.08
Opportunity to Revise	2.82	1.54
Use High-Stakes	3.09	2.08
Use Low-Stakes	3.12	2.04
40% of respondents reported low return value as a primary reason not to use writing assignments in non-WI courses.		

Through responses, such as "too much work," "not appropriate for the course," and "not enough value added," about 40% of participants gave low return value as a primary reason for not using writing assignments in non-WI courses. This was followed by "not enough time" at 38%.

Faculty with WI experience were not asked about these practices for their WI courses. Because of the guidelines discussed in the WI workshop, we presumed the answers regarding these practices in WI courses would be consistently "almost always." Consequently, on these variables, we could not make a direct comparison of what these faculty practices were in WI courses and what they practice in non-WI courses.

In non-WI courses, writing assignments are used at the instructor's discretion. We thought the percentage of faculty who reported low return value (see note to Table 5) as the primary reason to not use writing assignments was very high. This reporting was true for both groups of faculty and was at odds with the results in Table 2, which show high levels of agreement that writing assignments were cost effective. To explore the apparent inconsistency, we made a comparison between the reported return value of writing assignments and use of assignments in non-WI courses. For each participant, we constructed a *return value* score by averaging the participant's levels of agreement to the statements in Table 2 on the cost effectiveness of assigning writing. We also constructed a *usage* score, for each participant, by averaging the participant's reported use of low-stakes and high-stakes assignments. The scores are summarized in Table 6. A comparison of the two scores, using a Wilcoxon signed-ranks test, indicated *return value* was significantly higher than *usage* $Z = 4.23$, $p < .001$, $r = .38$. That is, faculty usage of discretionary writing is significantly lower than their reported return value of writing assignments.

Table 6. Return value and use.

Composite Score (n=33)	mean	SD
Perceived "return value" of writing assignments	3.54	1.09
Actual use of high and low stakes writing assignments in non-WI courses	2.62	1.09

Discussion

This study provides further evidence of conflicting positions among faculty regarding the value of writing assignments. We found high appreciation of good writing, belief in the potential of writing to help students learn, but also found significantly lower levels of writing in courses where writing is discretionary and where low return value was the primary reason for the low levels of usage. These conflicting positions are laid over numerous calls for large-data evidence regarding the widespread effectiveness of writing and contrasting conclusions of this effectiveness in studies of smaller scale. Identifying and addressing conflicting positions are important elements for arriving at a model that optimizes the effectiveness of writing assignments.

Participants reported low use of writing in discretionary cases coupled with low return value as the most frequent reason reported for such low use. This is contrary to the highly rated potential and cost-effectiveness of assignments in WI courses. It is reasonable for writing to have a stronger presence in WI courses. However, given that questions were phrased in terms of maximizing benefit to students, it would also be reasonable to expect comparable levels of writing in non-WI courses. Although we do not have strong evidence to support or refute an explanation for the discrepancy, below we offer several possibilities.

Workshop Influence

It is possible that guidelines and training of the WAC workshop offered at the school had influence on responses pertaining to questions about WI courses. There is evidence in favor and against this explanation. For example, responses aligned with workshop recommendations on use of revision and the percentage of grade assigned to writing but differed significantly from the workshop-recommended ten pages of writing.

Speculative and Self-assessment Questions

Questions pertaining to WI courses had a speculative and self-assessment aspect. For example, asking whether assignments in WI courses help students learn course content is asking for an assessment of one's own effort, and asking for the number of pages of writing to optimize effectiveness is asking for a speculation. It would be surprising to see faculty give low ratings to work in which they engage, particularly when no conclusive evidence exists on the lack of positive impact by WI assignments. In contrast, questions pertaining to non-WI courses were more factual—e.g., "do you use low stakes in non-WI?"—and for these questions it is easier to have more accurate ratings.

Program Assessment

Ratings for questions on the effectiveness of assignments in WI courses can be seen as indirect assessment of the school's WAC program. This is a university-wide initiative spanning over twenty years. Similarly to the previous possibility, high ratings may be expected on these questions partly because they can be seen as ratings of a group effort. Each respondent is a member of the group, both as a faculty member and as WI-certified, and it may be more difficult to give low ratings to one's own effort.

The very fact that there are WI and non-WI courses shows writing assignments are not placed uniformly across the curriculum. The rationale used to determine which courses receive WI designation may help explain the discrepancy that we found.

Writing Where It Is Most Effective

Another possibility, that could help explain the discrepancy, is that writing is indeed better-suited for courses that are designated as WI. This possibility would explain and justify higher usage and higher return value of writing in WI courses. However, this interpretation begs the question, "What criteria would make a course better suited for WI?" Accepting this interpretation would require reviewing the claim that every course stands to benefit more or less equally from writing.

Writing Where It is Least Disruptive

Similar to the previous interpretation, the low use of writing in non-WI courses may be due to the reasoning on which courses were initially designated as WI. A cursory search of several schools, as well as our school, suggests higher-level and for-majors courses are designated as WI at a much lower rate than introductory courses or courses for non-majors. This suggests writing is not thought of as equally suitable and used in courses where some reduction in content coverage may be acceptable.

Validation of Past Reasoning

Another possibility, which may help explain the discrepancy, is validation of a prior reasoning process. Among the participants were faculty who, over the years, helped their departments identify which courses to designate as WI. The designation was based on some criteria. The discrepancy found in the present study may be seen, at least in part, as an indirect validation of those criteria.

In additional findings, respondents to this survey offered alternative activities as equally effective equivalents to writing. This is consistent with other findings and theoretical reports on active learning, which position writing as one tool among many equal alternatives, e.g., verbal communication and collaboration. (Bullock Report, 1975; Penrose, 1992; Spirgel and Delaney, 2014; Bangert-Drowns et al., 2004; & Dunlosky et al., 2012.) However, the alternative activities offered in this study involved some form of writing. There is some inconsistency in suggesting poster presentation as an alternative to writing. We think this in part due to writing, as an academic task, being associated more with the essay or the term paper. These are not as common in STEM and particularly in mathematics. Such an association would reduce the perceived relevance of writing in STEM and could deter faculty from using it frequently.

Consistent with the schools' remediation needs, participants did not think students' writing skills were adequate for assignments to be effective. However, in relation to writing practices, a low skill level can be cause for concern because writing assignments have been reported as potentially counterproductive for low-skilled writers (Penrose, 1992; Bangert-Drowns et al., 2004.) The majority of our writers need improvement at the paragraph level before addressing the level of an article or report.

The low use of discretionary writing is consistent with reported skepticism regarding the effectiveness of the pedagogy and the appropriateness of having "non-writing" faculty give writing instruction. Ground for such skepticism is provided by the lack of large-data support, particularly after decades of implementing the pedagogy; evidence that other treatments can be as effective as, or more effective than, writing; reports on writing's weak effects and in cases potentially negative effects; associations of writing with the essay or term paper; and the overhead required in implementing writing assignments. However, the perfect need not be the enemy of the good, and a case can be made for writing in early STEM courses.

A form of writing, focusing on effective communication of content, seems well suited to help students succeed. Yet, writing has not found wide acceptance as a pedagogical tool in STEM (CBMS, 2010). Algebra, for example, the mathematics course with the highest registration and notorious for high attrition rates, rarely gets a WI designation. We think one reason for the low levels of WI designation is that WAC pedagogy is presented mostly through the humanities lens, leading to faculty perceiving writing as a task of low relevance in STEM instruction. STEM is consistently part of the WAC/WID discussion, yet, we find the discussion pertaining considerably more to the humanities, with STEM, and mathematics in particular, looking for creative implementations. To quote from Fulwiler (1984), "As a group, mathematics teachers seem to have the hardest time figuring out how [WAC] workshop ideas apply to their teaching" (p. 116). Two innovative (but of uncertain scalability) approaches are discussed in Young (2011) and Bahls (2009). Young discusses a technique whereby students summarize a concept or lesson including associated difficulties they may have faced and then each exchange notes with another student, responding to each other. Bahls discusses using poetry in calculus.

To increase meaningful engagement with writing assignments among faculty, and just as importantly among students, we believe a branching and possibly rebranding of WAC/WID pedagogy is in order. This branch would target STEM-type writing and could focus on (1) writing for effective communication and (2) quantitative writing. Communicating about quantities is at the core of STEM. Therefore, writing having these foci is readily identifiable as aligning with the purpose of STEM instruction and can become an attractive pedagogy even among faculty who would be otherwise skeptical.

Clear communication regarding a concept can be stronger evidence of understanding than solving exercises is. It also makes it easier to pinpoint problem areas. Assignments having communication as the primary goal can be designed for various levels of learning. Young (2011), for example, discusses a form of *writing to communicate*, in which assignments are "designed to expand and refine students' knowledge and mastery of the subject matter" (p. 47). However, as STEM content can be very dense with meaning, assignments through which students simply demonstrate their knowledge are an appropriate entry point.

Quantitative writing involves the use of quantities to explain or support a conclusion. It encompasses quantitative reasoning, another critical skill, and typically involves real or realistic data. The explanation may rely on quantities ranging from simple percentages or averages to more complex relationships between variables. Quantitative writing is discussed in the literature, for example in Wolfe (2010), Grawe and Rutz (2009), Lutsky (2008), and Miller (2007). Notably, Wolfe (2010) makes a strong argument for bringing quantitative writing to the composition classroom. Laboratory reports asking students to communicate conclusions are examples of such writing, and any course that uses statistics would abound with quantitative writing opportunities.

In traditional mathematics courses, where abstractions are more frequent than measurements, there may be proportionally fewer opportunities for quantitative writing based on data. However, we think there are still plenty of opportunities and the writing can be based on abstract quantities as well as on real data. Beginning with entry-level mathematics, there are numerous concepts with applications that are accessible to students. For example, given a mathematical model, an assignment may ask students to interpret the components of the model and support conclusions based on these components. Conversely, given a scenario with competing explanatory models, students may be asked to compare the models for feasibility.

Assignments can also be structured on concepts that may not at first seem to have clear applications. Students may be asked to explain the rationale behind the steps of a procedure, rather than just stating the steps, to compare two alternative procedures, or even to paraphrase a textbook explanation. As writing assignments, these can be complex tasks, albeit of just a few sentences. As mathematics assignments, they can reinforce students' procedural fluency and conceptual understanding. For example, evaluating $\log 0.0001$ without a calculator may seem a tedious task. However, stating and justifying the steps requires considerable effort on the part of the writer along with knowledge of powers of ten, negative exponents, understanding the meaning of the expression $\log x$ and synthesis for a cohesive piece of communication.

A WAC branch focusing on communication and quantitative writing would differ from WID, which does address field-specific writing but is more relevant for the majors. For community college students in introductory STEM, students who will not become majors, it would probably be more beneficial to spend time on content and communication than on learning the writing nuances of a field. STEM faculty is already participating in WAC and the participation is considerable. However, reluctance to use writing remains, as does skepticism about its effectiveness. Writing that is more easily associable with the needs of STEM instruction, particularly for underprepared non-majors as may be found at a community college, is more likely to be tried and perhaps adopted as a pedagogical tool.

References

Ackerman, J. A. (1993). The promise of writing to learn. *Written Communication, 10*(3), 334–70.

Bahls, P. (2009). Math and metaphor: Using poetry to teach college mathematics. *The WAC Journal, 20*, 75–90.

Bailey, T., Jeong, D.W., & Cho, S. W. (2010) Referral, enrollment, and completion in developmental education sequences in community colleges *Economics of Education Review, 29*, 255–70.

CBMS (2010). *2010 CBMS survey of undergraduate programs*. Washington, DC: The Conference Board of the Mathematical Sciences. Retrieved from http://www.cbmsweb.org/

Bangert-Drowns, R. L., Hurley, M. M., & Wilkinson, B. (2004). The effects of school-based writing-to-learn interventions on academic achievement: a meta-analysis. *Review of Educational Research, 74*, 29–58.

Dansdill, T. T., Hoffman, M. E., & Herscovici, D. S. (2008). Exposing GAPS, exploring legacies: paradoxes of writing use in computing education. *Journal of Computing Sciences in College, 23*(5), 24–33

Dunlosky, J., Rawson, K. A., Marsh, E. J., Nathan, M. J., & Willingham, D. T. (2013). Improving students' learning with effective learning techniques: promising directions from cognitive and educational psychology. *Psychological Science in the Public Interest, 14*(1), 4–58.

Fulwiler, T. (1984). How well does writing across the curriculum work? *College English, 46*(2), 113–25.

Grawe, N. D. & Rutz, C. A. (2009). Integration with writing programs: A strategy for quantitative reasoning program development. *Numeracy, 2*(2), Article 2. doi: doi.org/10.5038/1936-4660.2.2.2

Lutsky N. (2008). Arguing with numbers: teaching quantitative reasoning through argument and writing. In B. L. Madison. & L. A. Steen (Eds.), *Calculation vs. context: Quantitative literacy and its implications for teacher education* (pp.59–74). Washington, DC: Mathematical Association of America.

McLeod, S. H. & Miraglia, E. (1997). Whither WAC? Interpreting the stories/histories of mature WAC programs. *WPA: Writing Program Administration, 20*(3), 46–65.

Ochsner, R. & Fowler, J. (2004). Playing devil's advocate: evaluating the literature of the WAC/WID movement. *Review of Educational Research, 74*(2), 117–40.

Penrose, A. M. (1992). To write or not to write: Effects of task and task interpretation on learning through writing. *Written Communication, 9*(4), 465–500.

Porter, M. K. & Masingila, J. O. (2000). Examining the effects of writing on conceptual and procedural knowledge in calculus. *Educational Studies in Mathematics, 42*(2), 165–77.

Salem, L. & Jones, P. (2010). Undaunted, self-critical, and resentful: Investigating faculty attitudes toward teaching writing in a large university writing-intensive course program. *WPA: Writing Program Administration, 34*(1), 60–83.

Spirgel, A. S. & Delaney, P. F., (2014). Does writing summaries improve memory for text? *Educational Psychology Review, 28*(1), 171–96. doi: 10.1007/s10648-014-9290-2

Thaiss, C. & Porter, T., (2010). The state of WAC/WID in 2010: Methods and results of the US survey of the international WAC/WID mapping project. *College Composition and Communication, 61*(3), 524–70.

Wolfe, J. (2010). Rhetorical numbers: A case for quantitative writing in the composition classroom. *College Composition and Communication, 61*(3), 452–75.

Young, A. (2011). *Teaching writing across the curriculum (4th ed)*. Fort Collins, CO: WAC Clearinghouse. Retrieved from http://wac.colostate.edu/books/young_teaching/. (Original work published in print in 2006 by Pearson Education, Upper Saddle River, New Jersey).

Zhu, W. (2004). Faculty views on the importance of writing, the nature of academic writing, andteaching and responding to writing in the disciplines *Journal of second language Writing, 13* (1), 24–48.

Review of *Toward a New Rhetoric of Difference*

TRAVIS GRANDY

Stephanie L. Kerschbaum. *Toward a New Rhetoric of Difference*. Urbana, IL: CCCC/NCTE, 2014. 187 pages.

The field of composition studies has interrogated questions of diversity, difference, and access for several decades. However, as institutions respond to calls to better include and represent people from backgrounds that have historically been excluded from higher education, we must continually revisit questions and contentions for how these power relationships affect our classrooms. How can we negotiate ways that university discourses construct student bodies and identities, how do we as educators understand differences in the lived experiences between us and our students, and how can we meaningfully engage with ways that difference and power are marked and enacted in our classrooms? Contributing to this conversation, Stephanie Kerschbaum's theoretical and methodological innovations in *Toward a New Rhetoric of Difference*, winner of the 2015 CCCC Advancement of Knowledge Award, provides us with a useful perspective to consider difference on the level of the microinteractions between teachers and students and how these are affected by institutional discourses about diversity.

For Kerschbaum, diversity is a much larger question than who gets a seat in the university classroom; rather, she is also concerned with how differences between teachers and students are enacted rhetorically and with how these interactions can be shaped by institution-wide discourses. Although composition studies has long debated the contact-zone as a model for negotiating difference in the classroom, Kerschbaum warns that this may perpetuate contact as a trope for conflict, when in fact such interactions are much more nuanced and socially contingent. Her study builds upon previous research that shows how identity and group affiliations are articulated through writers' lived experiences (LeCourt, *Identity Matters*; Royster), how markers of difference are constituted and valued within structures of power (Gonçalves; McRuer; Price), and utilizes strategies of critical discourse analysis as a way of connecting public, institutional, and classroom discourses (Huckin, Andrus, and Clary-Lemon). Additionally, as I discuss later in this review, Kerschbaum's orientation toward interaction and discourse provides the field with productive ways to reimagine our engagement in writing across the curriculum.

Kerschbaum provides us with several lenses to reconsider the ways diversity discourses enter the composition classroom through teacher and student talk. Driving this research are two central questions: "How is difference identified within classrooms? What conditions or factors motivate engagement with difference?" (15). In particular, she holds that the way that teachers understand difference affects the way they teach writing and interact with their students. For this reason, Kerschbaum seeks to "encourage heightened awareness of systematic patterns of ignoring, suppressing, and denying difference as well as of recognizing, highlighting, and orienting to difference" (15). Although critical writing pedagogies suggest ways that teachers can influence talk about difference in their classrooms, she argues that "attention to students' and teachers' classroom discourse must be considered within the context of the discourses that circulate at [an] institution" (18). Kerschbaum wants teachers to consider how institutional discourses shape their perspectives and to approach classroom interactions as places where both students and teachers enact differences, often strategically.

The study site was a large research university in the Midwest that Kerschbaum gave the pseudonym "Midwestern University" (MU). Drawing on multiple research traditions including grounded theory, dialogic discourse analysis, and critical discourse analysis, she observed and analyzed the writing and classroom talk of a FYC course linked with a psychology seminar. Over the course of the 2003 fall semester, she observed every class meeting, made video recordings, recorded ethnographic field notes, conducted a demographic survey, and collected classroom documents and student writing portfolios. Additionally, thirteen peer review sessions were taped for dialogic analysis. Of the nineteen students in the course, Kerschbaum selected four focal participants for interviews as well as interviewing the course instructor.

Following her introductory chapter, Kerschbaum examines the texts that constitute MU's diversity discourse, demonstrating how "diversity discourses reify and commodify race-ethinic difference" (32). In her analysis of texts such as university websites, brochures, and a ten-year diversity strategic plan, Kerschbaum finds three interdependent layers of this discourse: 1) diversity is linked to market values in ways that commodify "diverse" individuals; 2) definitions of diversity impact how students self-identify with their race and ethnicity; and 3) the discourse establishes relationships between who provides diversity and who benefits from it. For this third point, Kerschbaum analyzes the use of pronouns in MU's ten-year plan for diversity, such as the outcome statement, "to increase the depth of understanding by the large majority of us who are not in those groups for their values, customs, and experiences" (51). The "us" clearly benefits from having diversity, but the text never identifies who they are explicitly. Similar to studies that point to how linguistic difference can be encoded and racialized in composition studies (Clary-Lemon), Kerschbaum's analysis shows that "white students are implicit throughout the document only through their absence" (53). Through her analysis, she traces how tacit ideological commitments enacted through discourse are one iteration of larger social formations that exist across institutions and communities. In this case, the commodification of "diverse" students and the value they add to white students' educations demonstrates how neoliberal market values are intertwined with structural racism in education. These findings are in keeping with other discursive analyses of diversity statements and policies that demonstrate how "diversity" in university discourses is often structured to serve the social, cultural, and economic needs of middle-class white students (Ahmed; Iverson). This intersectional perspective can help teachers be sensitive to how institutions produce and maintain social inequality, especially when students are implicated by these discourses before they even enter a writing classroom.

In her subsequent chapters, Kerschbaum builds a model of difference as an interactional and rhetorical phenomenon through examining key moments from classroom observations. Her second chapter theorizes difference as a rhetorical performance and "resituates the problem away from *learning about*, and thus needing to know students, toward *learning with*, and thus always coming-to-know students" (57). As an example, Kerschbaum criticizes ways educators can rely on categories of student difference, such as the diagnosing of students on the autism spectrum, and how these can lead teachers toward making problematic assumptions about students' abilities and needs. Instead, she argues, differences should also be interpreted by how they emerge relationally in the unique social situation of the classroom and be interpreted as rhetorical performance. In her third chapter, Kerschbaum looks to classroom interactions, including peer review sessions, to appreciate how members of a classroom mark difference through their talk, noting that these processes "can help us recognize ways that we take up and respond to our own and others' positions" (80). For example, in an episode from a peer review session, a student, Blia, offers feedback on her peer Choua's writing, and each woman contests the change through how she constructs her authority through narratives about past education. Because this marking is always relational, individuals have agency "to contest or challenge identity constructions because personal experience is not generally treated as material available for disagreement" (111). Kerschbaum's fourth chapter distinguishes that even when teachers prioritize meaningful engagement with difference in their classrooms, "[r]ecognizing markers of difference can also be painful, especially when we acknowledge the values accorded to different ways of moving in the world" (118). To demonstrate this, she looks to moments of communicative failure to illustrate how individuals develop an understanding of identity in relation to others and may not always negotiate difference in productive ways. In a different peer review session, Timothy and Emily have a significant disagreement over one of Timothy's sentences, and in their talk about his writing, they "identify and signal differences between themselves" (120). From these moments of rupture that occur during student peer review sessions, she suggests the importance of accountability and engagement, fostering a learning space that is supportive of learning from mistakes, and "listening to conflict, difficulty, and resistance for the sense-making behind others' acts and responses" (149).

In conclusion, Kerschbaum suggests three key recommendations for how we conceptualize difference in the writing classroom:

1. Attention to markers of difference can help us resist simplistic generalizations about students (113).
2. Practices for marking difference can help us identify opportunities for rhetorical action and dialogue (115).
3. Attention to markers of difference can encourage us to recognize and revise how we engage with students in our classrooms (116).

While Kerschbaum illustrates her argument through several examples of student to student interactions, her case study does not provide similar detail for the course instructor, Yvonne. Illustrating the social conditions of the class through interactions with the instructor and other teaching moments, such as how the instructor facilitated peer review, could serve as a way to connect student interactions to their classroom or institutional frame. Kerschbaum's analyses of student interactions shows the promise of framing difference as rhetorical interaction and "attends to difference as it is performed during the moment-to-moment vicissitudes of communication" (67). Her choice to emphasize peer review episodes does not undermine her argument but rather leaves open further productive lines of inquiry for classroom interactions and discourses.

I admire how *Toward a New Rhetoric of Difference* helps us reread everyday interactions in the classroom to better understand what is at stake when we or our institutions talk about diversity. In particular, Kerschbaum offers a productive reformulation of identity politics in the classroom that emphasizes the dynamic and dialogic ways identities and social relations are produced and negotiated through everyday interaction. More broadly, she opens methodological approaches for composition studies to reexamine the relationship between classroom discourses and the institutional discourses that provide their frame. As Kerschbaum identifies in connecting MU's diversity discourses to values of neoliberalism, the influence of institutional discourses can pose significant challenges for critical writing pedagogies and their translation to teaching practice.

I find striking resonances between *Toward a New Rhetoric of Difference* and conversations in writing across the curriculum. Although WAC literature provides us with numerous ways to frame and engage with classroom discourses, it would benefit from more meaningful engagement with ways power and difference have social and material significance for WAC classrooms. To extend Kerschbaum's contributions to how we can frame difference as relational and iterative, I suggest two possible directions to further develop this line of research. First, WAC's literature on academic discourse communities should account for how power tied to difference influences how students enact academic literacies and acquire the worldviews of particular disciplines. Although scholars have productively explored these dynamics through genre studies (Carter; Clark and Hernandez), the field would also benefit from further naturalistic studies of students negotiating these literacies in classroom talk. Kerschbaum's positioning of classroom discourses alongside institutional discourses suggests composition researchers should account for this broad, if often tacit, ideological influence in the framing of writing pedagogies. WAC classrooms can function as a productive space for students to negotiate and criticize the discourses and power structures they encounter at school (LeCourt, "WAC as Critical Pedagogy"), and engaging students in discourse analysis can further learning goals already valued in composition studies (Huckin; McRuer; Powell).

Second, Kerschbaum's approach to discourse analysis provides a generative perspective on reinterpreting the ideological work of WAC programs. In their model of WAC as both location and momentum, William Condon and Carol Rutz suggest that we differentiate where we locate WAC programs from what programs impact through their work. This is especially useful in framing programs in relation to the unique conditions of institutions and broader interactions with institutional and public discourses. For example, the IWAC "Statement on WAC Principles and Practices" (2014) acknowledges how institutional, state, and national discourses on "accountability" are one of the drivers for assessment in WAC programs (6). These discourses operate in the background of reform work being undertaken by WAC programs (such as general education or faculty development). Attending to the relational and strategic dimensions of these discourses could help researchers identify ways WAC initiatives are influenced or appropriated by other discourses. For example, we could explore implications of these dynamics in discourses about transfer, accelerated curricula, and internationalization of WAC. The ways WAC programs take up or interact with these discourses have implications for how they construct the WAC classroom and possible identities and power relations for both teachers and students.

To conclude, Kerschbaum urges us to be critically engaged with ways identities and ideologies are enacted both through microinteractions in the classroom and through institutional discourses: "When social institutions create and perpetuate particular forms of language, that language is never disinterested" (29–30). As WAC programs adapt to the changing landscape of higher education, and as we seek to build classrooms that are supportive of the learning of *all* students, we must remain attentive to how our own talk and the talk between students are pivotal moments where identities are enacted, contested, and even silenced. Taken as relational phenomena, diversity and difference are not problems to be fixed, but rather points of contact with which we can engage. Kerschbaum leads us to a praxis of how we might try to learn alongside our students.

References

Ahmed, Sara. *On Being Included: Racism and Diversity in Institutional Life*. Duke UP, 2012.

Carter, Michael. "Ways of Knowing, Doing, and Writing in the Discipline." *College Composition and Communication*, vol. 58, no. 3, 2007, pp. 385–418.

Clark, Irene L., and Andrea Hernandez. "Genre Awareness, Academic Argument and Transferability." *The WAC Journal*, vol. 22, 2011, pp. 65–78.

Clary-Lemon, Jennifer. "The Racialization of Composition Studies: Scholarly Rhetoric of Race Since 1990." *College Composition and Communication*, vol. 61, no. 2, 2009, pp. W1–W17.

Condon, William, and Carol Rutz. "A Taxonomy of Writing Across the Curriculum Programs: Evolving to Serve Broader Agendas." *College Composition and Communication*, vol. 64, no. 2, 2012, pp. 357–82.

Glenn, Cheryl. *Unspoken: A Rhetoric of Silence*. Southern Illinois UP, 2004.

Gonçalves, Zan M. *Sexuality and the Politics of Ethos in the Writing Classroom*. Southern Illinois UP, 2005.

Huckin, Thomas. "Critical Discourse Analysis and the Discourse of Condescension." *Discourse Studies in Composition*, edited by Ellen Barton and Gail Stygall, Hampton Press, 2002, pp. 155–76.

—, Jennifer Andrus, and Jennifer Clary-Lemon. "Critical Discourse Analysis and Rhetoric and Composition." *College Composition and Communication*, vol. 64, no. 1, 2012, pp. 107–29.

International Network of WAC Programs. *Statement of WAC Principles and Practices*. February 2014, http://wac.colostate.edu/principles/statement.pdf.

Iverson, Susan V. "Constructing Outsiders: the Discursive Framing of Access in University Diversity Policies." *Review of Higher Education*, vol. 35, no. 2, 2013, pp. 149–77.

LeCourt, Donna. *Identity Matters: Schooling the Student Body in Academic Discourse*. Albany: State University of New York Press, 2004. Print.

—. "WAC as Critical Pedagogy: The Third Stage?" *JAC*, vol. 16, no. 3, 1996, pp. 389–405.

Mao, LuMing. "Thinking Beyond Aristotle: the Turn to How in Comparative Rhetoric." *PMLA*, vol. 129, no. 3, 2014, pp. 448–55.

McRuer, Robert. *Crip Theory: Cultural Signs of Queerness and Disability*. New York UP, 2006.

Powell, Pegeen Reichert. "Critical Discourse Analysis and Composition Studies: A Study of Presidential Discourse and Campus Discord." *College Composition and Communication*, vol. 55, no. 3, 2004: 439–68.

Price, Margaret. *Mad at School: Rhetorics of Mental Disability and Academic Life*. U of Michigan P, 2011.

Royster, Jacqueline J. *Traces of a Stream: Literacy and Social Change Among African American Women*. U of Pittsburgh P, 2000.

Review of *Working with Faculty Writers*

MARY HEDENGREN

Anne Ellen Galler and Michele Eodice, Eds. *Working with Faculty Writers*. Utah State UP, 2013.

In WAC studies, working with faculty and graduate writers is an exciting new frontier. Faculty writers work under difficult circumstances: the stakes of writing are high, as is the temptation for procrastination, and writing resources are often informal or underdeveloped. Whether initiatives to support faculty writers originate in writing centers or centers for faculty development, the novelty of such programs has the potential to define this new field of faculty writing support. In *Working with Faculty Writers* (*WWFW*), Anne Ellen Geller and Michele Eodice compile diverse voices to set the groundwork of this new field.

The diversity of contributors is one of the strengths of the book. More than forty authors contribute more-or-less evenly, representing WAC programs, writing centers, and faculty centers for teaching and learning—as well as disciplinary participants from veterinary science (Virginia Fajt), mathematics (Jill Zarestky), and ecology (Manuel Colunga-Garia). Readers familiar with composition will find some very well-known names among the contributors, such as Chris Anson and Bob Boice, but there are also perspectives from within the disciplines, from graduate students, and from adjunct faculty. The broad base of contributors emphasizes the book's primary claim: institutions of higher learning need to create writing communities that cut across disciplines, ranks, and seniority. *WWFW* argues pervasively and persuasively that creating such a community is well worth a university's investment of resources.

Geller and Eodice, along with their contributors, have created a foundational text for creating faculty writing programs, one that will be drawn upon by more and more institutions seeking to expand into this area. The contributors to *WWFW* recognize that to define a new field is risky, and scholars in the field need to dispel some prevalent academic writing myths while being careful to side-step the creation of new ones.

If there is one myth that haunts academic writing the most, it is the neo-romantic view of solitary, self-contained writing. While writing studies scholars, especially those of us in writing centers, have long recognized the need for community-supported writing, there persists in academia—as Lori Salem and Jennifer Follet mention in their chapter, "The Idea of a Faculty Writing Center"—"the romantic image of a writer who works alone in a garret creating his masterpiece" (70). The same teachers who encourage group projects and visits to the writing center for their students may find themselves alone in an office, not knowing where to get feedback or even just a conversation about their writing. Instead, as Trixie G. Smith et al. point out in a chapter titled "Developing a Heuristic for Multidisciplinary Faculty Writing Groups," they may feel like "isolated writer[s], alone in the academic tower" (182). *WWFW* proposes a different model for academic production. In practically every chapter, as in Lori Salem and Jennifer Follett's "The Idea of a Faculty Writing Center," the contributors assert that "the university and individual faculty members can and should productively collaborate on writing projects" (65).

The forms that these collaborations take are in some ways as diverse as the programs and facilitators sponsoring them. They can take place in a variety of settings and with a range of costs and interventions. Brian Baldi, Mary Dean Sorcinelli, and Jung H. Yun, in their chapter "The Scholarly Writing Continuum," present a sliding scale from very low-structure, low-commitment and low-contact offerings like providing faculty with "a room of their own" away from colleagues and office distractions, all the way to intensive multi-week workshops and writing coaches (43–46). Within *WWFW*, there are so many descriptions of "how we do it here" that almost any institution will find ways to strengthen their community of writers, regardless of institute size or faculty buy-in. There are many ways to provide support, showing faculty writers they are not left alone to founder through their writing projects.

The second myth that new faculty writing programs must work to dispel is that only tenure track faculty need to be engaged in writing. Letizia Guglielmo and Lynée Gaillet relate how, with resources and support, contingent faculty can form on-campus communities, contribute to their fields and share their experiences, especially of teaching, with a wider audience through scholarly production. Elena Mari-Adkins Garcia, Seunghee Eum, and Lorna Watt similarly find that graduate students who are given university-sponsored places to get and give feedback on writing are more likely to establish professional confidence, work in multidisciplinary modes and finish their dissertations: "We know that coursework is not where students get stuck," they dryly acknowledge (274–75).

The third myth claims that the only writing the university supports are those projects that lead immediately to academic publication. In fact, university-supported programs don't have to just include writing, but academic production in general. Violet Dutcher relates how among the abundant fruits of her university's scholarly writing retreat was a 36" by 48" oil painting created by a member of the art department (150). Providing a space to focus, discuss academic production aims, and give meaningful feedback can result in a variety of projects across the disciplines. Community, improved teaching, and creativity can also be outcomes of university-sponsored retreats and workshops, but maybe one of the greatest outcomes is for faculty to develop new identities.

Despite the importance of dispelling the myth of writing as a solitary practice engaged in only by tenure-track faculty who are exclusively seeking academic publication, the authors of this groundbreaking collection are in the difficult position of not creating new myths. The contributors want to stress the importance of writing skills, good habits, and strong communities, but these practices also tend to create a lot of writing, a lot of good writing, and a lot of publications. Good practices lead to good product, but university writing support should focus primarily on the process, on empowering writers. The temptation for many of the authors in this collection is to focus on the outcomes of working with faculty: crudely put, the increase in publication.

This is a good thing. Faculty members want to get published. University administrations want faculty members to get published. More publications mean more faculty achieve tenure and rank-promotion, and publications raise the profile not only of individual academics, but the university as a whole. Of course, they also increase the pool of relevant research being done in their respective disciplines. But, more cynically, publications are often seen as the coin of the realm in academia. Faculty members and administrators both want to increase publications. The stakes are high for everyone.

Surely with such high stakes, university buy-in to faculty writing support would be high and wouldn't it be easy for WPAs to argue that such programs result in more publications, which everyone wants? Yes, but. Salem and Follett are among the few contributors who explicitly recognize the hazards of focusing on the productivity of writing practices. They point out that if faculty writing support is seen as a product-driven, remedial service, then the same biases that have dogged undergraduate writing centers will extend to these new programs (63–64). Far better, they argue, to model student writing centers' insistence on creating "a place where writing can be transparently discussed and regularly practiced" (66) instead of focusing solely on publication. The subtext in Salem and Follett's article is the thirty-year-old rallying cry of writing center practice: "Better writers, not better [or more] writing!"

Ideally, faculty writers should feel as though writing is a sort of fulfillment of who they are, reflective of habits of thinking and working that are deeply intrinsic to their identities as writers, not something contingent on a single piece's success. It is just this identity that is highlighted by William P. Banks and Kerri B. Flinchbaugh's chapter "Experiencing Ourselves as Writers," where they point out that although most faculty members write often for their professional identities, they may still have a hard time recognizing themselves as *writers*. Ideally, writing programs would posit writing as much a part of each participant's identity as teaching and research. Such a change in identity requires far more than simply helping someone over the hurdles of tenure review.

The basis of faculty writing programs—with all respect to our colleagues' own content and generic expertise—is educational. Student writing services must reiterate to students and administration that our goals are not to create good papers or good grades, and, similarly, faculty writing services will have to fight against the assumption that the right workshop or writing group will guarantee publications. We can't make that promise to faculty members and we can't make that promise to the administrations that fund us.

Still, it's hard to ignore the economic realities. Tara Gray, A. Jane Birch, and Laura Madson in their chapter "How Teaching Centers Can Support Faculty as Writers" describe the institutional advantages when receiving "excellent reports [. . .] from college deans and department chairs" about the benefits of such programs (103). And I was very satisfied to see the results of Jessie L. Moore, Peter Felton, and Michael Strickland's faculty writing residency outcomes: more than half of participants complete their writing goals and ninety-five percent of those who finish the residency go on to publish their projects (135–37). That's fantastic news, not to be downplayed, but when the authors encourage directors to focus exclusively on productivity, there are latent dangers. Focusing on the number of products completed or published rather than creating sustained writing identities might create an unfair burden on the administrators of such writing programs to help every writer achieve publication, when such decisions are beyond the facilitator's ability. Just as writing centers can't promise an *A* to every student who walks in our doors, neither can faculty writing programs promise publications; both student and faculty services, however, can be attentive to best practices for creating sustained writing practices and identities.

Faculty writing support is still a relatively new concept, and *WWFW* represents the opening of a door that will, no doubt, lead down paths of new research for faculty writing programs. The volume will doubtless be cited in future publications as the field develops. Until that time, the practices described in *WWFW* demonstrate how versatile the new field can be. The wide variety of methods and spaces of intervention are enlightening not only for WPAs who would want to start their own faculty writing support program, but also for theorists in writing studies and writing in the disciplines.

Right now the research is mostly in the "This is how we do it here" phase, the same phase that early freshmen composition research went through in the fifties and sixties, where each isolated program reached out for each other, coalescing around best practices, building a base for future research. This book marks the beginning of what will no doubt be a fruitful field of inquiry for writing scholars who turn the microscope inward and wonder, How do we write the way we do in academia?

Contributors

Christopher Basgier is Assistant Professor of English at University of North Dakota, where he also serves as Academic Director of Composition and collaborates with the WAC program. His research uses rhetorical genre theory to investigate the intricacies of curriculum and pedagogy in composition, WAC, and general education, and he studies genres in digital environments as well. His work has appeared in *Computers and Composition* and *Across the Disciplines*, and he presents regularly at the Conference on College Composition and Communication and Conference of the Council of Writing Program Administrators.

Sue Doe is Associate Professor of English at Colorado State University. She does research in three distinct areas—academic labor and the faculty career, writing across the curriculum, and student-veteran transition in the post-9/11 era. Coauthor of the faculty development book *Concepts and Choices: Meeting the Challenges in Higher Education*, she has published articles in *College English* and *WPA: Writing Program Administration* as well as in several book-length collections. Her recent collection on student-veterans in the Composition classroom, *Generation Vet: Composition, Veterans, and the Post-911 University*, co-authored with Professor Lisa Langstraat, was published by Utah State University Press (an imprint of the University Press of Colorado) in 2014.

Dr. Jason E. Dowd is currently a postdoctoral associate in the Department of Biology at Duke University, where he is involved in interdisciplinary science education research with Dr. Julie Reynolds. He is interested in understanding how scientific writing may shed light on both students' scientific reasoning and differences in epistemic beliefs across disciplines. Dr. Dowd earned his AB in physics at Washington University in St. Louis and his PhD in the Department of Physics at Harvard University, where his research focused on the interpretation of assessments of student learning in the introductory physics classroom and laboratory.

Daniel Kenzie is a doctoral candidate at Purdue University, where he teaches healthcare writing and technical writing and serves as content coordinator for the Purdue Online Writing Lab (OWL). His current research traces the circulation of definitions of traumatic brain injury through scientific research, public discourse, and individual experience.

Jessica Gehrtz is a graduate student at Colorado State University pursuing a PhD in Mathematics with an emphasis in math education. Her research interests include undergraduate mathematics education and graduate teaching assistant training. More specifically, she examines the implementation of evidence-based practices in the calculus classroom and relationships between graduate teaching assistants pedagogical content knowledge, teaching, and professional development.

Travis Grandy is a doctoral candidate at the University of Massachusetts Amherst where he serves as Assistant Director of Writing Across the Curriculum for the University Writing Center. His research focuses on writing program administration, discourse, and ideology, and his current work examines WAC administration as situated practice within the framework of institutional ethnography. He has presented his work at the Conference on College Composition and Communication, and Computers and Writing, and has also written for GradHacker on Inside Higher Ed.

Mary Hedengren studies how writers inhabit new roles, from new freshmen to new graduate students to members of new disciplines. Her work has appeared in *Present Tense*, *New Writing,* and *Harlot*. She received her PhD in rhetoric at the University of Texas, Austin in 2015 and currently teaches at the University of Houston--Clear Lake.

Brian Hendrickson is a PhD candidate in Rhetoric and Composition and the Writing GA for the Anderson School of Management at the University of New Mexico. His research explores integrative, engaging, and inclusive approaches to teaching and assessing writing in composition, technical communication, and across and beyond the curriculum. Brian's dissertation involves a three-year study of rhetorical engagement in an engineering student organization constructing wells in an indigenous territory in Bolivia. His work has appeared or is forthcoming in Across the Disciplines and Journal of Business and Technical Communication.

Dimitrios Kokkinos received his PhD in Electrical Engineering from The City University of New York. He worked in the industry for 25 years and holds several US patents in fiber optics and communications. He joined Queensborough Community College in 2009 and is currently Associate Professor in Physics. His current interests are in helping students understand the concepts of physics, develop and improve their technical writing skills, and apply them in undergraduate research projects.

NamJong Moh is an associate professor at Queensborough Community College where he teaches mathematics. His research interests are analytic number theory and WAC.

Genevieve García de Müeller is an assistant professor at the University of Texas Rio Grande Valley. Her work focuses on civil rights rhetoric and multilingual composition. She is the founder and chair of the CWPA People of Color Caucus and her work "Digital DREAMS: The Rhetorical Power of Online Resources for DREAM Act Activists" appeared in the collection Linguistically Diverse Immigrant and Resident Writers.

Mary E. Pilgrim is an Assistant Professor in the Department of Mathmatics at Colorado State University. She teaches courses in Mathematics and Mathematics Education. Her research area is in undergraduate mathematics education. Her specific focus is in two primary areas: evidence-based pedagogical interventions in the calculus classroom (e.g., problem-based learning, oral assessments, write-to-learn, etc.) and self-regulated learning theory. She is Co-Director of the Calculus Center at Colorado State University and is part of the regular staff of the Park City Mathematics Institute Teacher Leadership Program.

Julie A. Reynolds is an Associate Professor of the Practice in the Biology Department and the Program in Education at Duke University. She holds a BA in government and public policy analysis from Pomona College, a MS in ecology from the University of California at Davis, and a PhD in integrative biology from the University of California at Berkeley. In 2002, she was one of the first scientists hired to teach in the award-winning Thompson Writing Program at Duke University. Her current research program focuses on pedagogies that promote science literacy among undergraduates, with a particular interest in retention of students from underrepresented populations

Carol Rutz has directed the Carleton Writing Program since 1997. As an early WAC institution, Carleton's program features faculty development and writing assessment as well as a curriculum rich in writing opportunities for students. Her research interests include response to student writing, writing assessment, and assessment of faculty development. With others, she is a co-author of *Faculty Development and Student Learning: Assessing the Connections* (Indiana UP, 2016).

Fernando Sánchez is Assistant Professor of English in Professional Writing at the University of St. Thomas in Saint Paul, Minnesota. He studies technical communication networks and processes within urban design professions and organizations. Additionally, he has taught courses in professional writing research, healthcare communication, and business and technical writing. His research has appeared in *The Journal of Technical Writing and Communication, Computers and Composition, Composition Studies, WPA: Writing Program Administration,* and *Trans-Scripts*. His book chapter (coauthored with Stacy Nall) in Alice Myatt and Lyneé Gaillet's *Writing Programs, Collaborations, and Partnerships: Working Across Boundaries* (Palgrave, 2017) provides an overview of the history of the ANSC/WAC Partnership at Purdue.

Kostas Stroumbakis is an assistant professor at Queensborough Community College where he teaches mathematics. He's interested in helping students achieve higher in mathematics through communication and conceptual understanding.

Sandra L. Tarabochia is Assistant Professor of English at the University of Oklahoma where she teaches courses in composition, rhetoric, and literacy. Findings from her research on teaching and learning writing across disciplinary contexts appear in *WPA: Writing Program Administration* and *Across the Disciplines*. She is finalizing a book about cross-disciplinary communication among faculty in WAC/WID contexts for the NCTE series Studies in Writing and Rhetoric. Recent research investigates the development of early career faculty writers.

Robert J. Thompson Jr. is Professor Emeritus of Psychology and Neuroscience at Duke University where he served as Vice Provost for Undergraduate Education and Dean of Trinity College of Arts and Sciences. His research interests address how biological and psychosocial processes act together in human development; coping with chronic childhood illness; and teaching, learning, and assessment in undergraduate education. His recent book, "Beyond Reason and Tolerance: The Purpose and Practice of Higher Education," was published by Oxford University Press in 2014. He has a BA from LaSalle College and a PhD in Clinical Psychology from the University of North Dakota.

How to Subscribe

The WAC Journal is published annually in print by Parlor Press and Clemson University. Digital copies of the journal are simultaneously published at The WAC Clearinghouse in PDF format for free download. Print subscriptions support the ongoing publication of the journal and make it possible to offer digital copies as open access. Subscription rates: One year: $25; Three years: $65; Five years: $95. You can subscribe to *The WAC Journal* and pay securely by credit card or PayPal at the Parlor Press website: http://www.parlorpress.com/wacjournal. Or you can send your name, email address, and mailing address along with a check (payable to Parlor Press) to

> Parlor Press
> 3015 Brackenberry Drive
> Anderson SC 29621
> Email: sales@parlorpress.com

Pricing

One year: $25 | Three years: $65 | Five years: $95

Publish in The WAC Journal

The editorial board of The WAC Journal seeks WAC-related articles from across the country. Our national review board welcomes inquiries, proposals, and 3,000 to 6,000 word articles on WAC-related topics, including the following:

- WAC Techniques and Applications
- WAC Program Strategies
- WAC and WID
- WAC and Writing Centers
- Interviews and Reviews

Proposals and articles outside these categories will also be considered. Any discipline-standard documentation style (MLA, APA, etc.) is acceptable, but please follow such guidelines carefully. Submissions are managed initially via Submittable (https://parlorpress.submittable.com/submit) and then via email. For general inquiries, contact Lea Anna Cardwell, the managing editor, via email (wacjournal@parlorpress.com). The WAC Journal is an open-access, blind, peer-viewed journal published annually by Clemson University, Parlor Press, and the WAC Clearinghouse. It is available in print through Parlor Press and online in open-access format at the WAC Clearinghouse.

Congratulations to These Award Winners & WPA Scholars!

The WPA Outcomes Statement—A Decade Later
Edited by Nicholas N. Behm, Gregory R. Glau, Deborah H. Holdstein, Duane Roen, and Edward M. White
Best Book Award, Council of Writing Program Adminstrators (July, 2015)

GenAdmin: Theorizing WPA Identities in the Twenty-First Century by Colin Charlton, Jonikka Charlton, Tarez Samra Graban, Kathleen J. Ryan, & Amy Ferdinandt Stolley
Best Book Award, Council of Writing Program Adminstrators (July, 2014)

Mics, Cameras, Symbolic Action: Audio-Visual Rhetoric for Writing Teachers by Bump Halbritter
Distinguished Book Award, *Computers and Composition* (May, 2014)

New Releases

Oral Communication in the Disciplines: A Resource for Teacher Development and Training by Deanna P. Dannels, Patricia R. Palmerton, & Amy L. Housley Gaffney

A Rhetoric for Writing Program Administrators, 2nd ed.
Edited by Rita Malenczyk

A Critical Look at Institutional Mission: A Guide for Writing Program Administrators
Edited by Joseph Janangelo

Play/Write: Digital Rhetoric, Writing, Games Digital Rhetoric, Writing, Games'
Edited by Douglas Eyman and Andréa D. Davis

www.parlorpress.com

www.ingramcontent.com/pod-product-compliance
Lightning Source LLC
Chambersburg PA
CBHW030242170426
43202CB00009B/592